THE
EVERYTHING

FLY-FISHING
BOOK

From casting to catching and everything
in between, the art and science of America's
most idyllic sport

by Jeff Zhorne

Adams Media Corporation
Holbrook, Massachusetts

An Everything Series Book.
The Everything Series is a trademark of Adams Media Corporation.

Published by Adams Media Corporation
260 Center Street, Holbrook, MA 02343

ISBN: 1-58062-148-1

Printed in the United States of America.

J I H G F E D C B

Library of Congress Cataloging-in-Publication Data
The everything fly-fishing book / by Jeff Zhorne.
p.   cm.
ISBN 1-58062-148-1
Includes index.
1. Fly fishing. I. Title.
SH456.Z48   1999
799.1'24—dc21   98-51816
CIP

This publication is designed to provide accurate and authoritative information with regard to the subject matter covered. It is sold with the understanding that the publisher is not engaged in rendering legal, accounting, or other professional advice. If legal advice or other expert assistance is required, the services of a competent professional person should be sought.
— From a *Declaration of Principles* jointly adopted by a Committee of the American Bar Association and a Committee of Publishers and Associations

Illustrations by Barry Littmann

This book is available at quantity discounts for bulk purchases.
For information, call 1-800-872-5627 (in Massachusetts, call 781-767-8100).

Visit our home page at http://www.adamsmedia.com

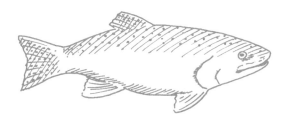

Contents

Chapter Four: Reading the Water / 53

Chapter Five: The Fly and the Life of an Insect / 69

Chapter Six: Casting and Landing / 109

Chapter Seven: Saltwater and Freshwater Trophies / 133

Introduction

My friends and family all had the same reaction to my writing a book on fly-fishing. "Whew! Fly-fishing is such an art. It's so difficult and expensive. How can you write *about* it—you have to *do* it." Well, they may be right, but drawing on every wordsmithing tool I know, I hope to make the complicated simpler—not simple, simpler—so you can wade into the watery world and catch fish.

What you'll find between these covers is for the uninitiated, not the grizzled thirty-year veterans of fly-fishing who tied their first fly knots at age ten. After you read my introduction, you'll realize I have no mystical methods for deceiving wily trout. Instead, I'm seeking to demystify this long-acclaimed sport. My feeling is that anyone can dip their toes into fly-fishing waters and experience the pleasure surrounding this great pastime. If you want to enjoy this sport, rediscover peace in nature, or experience good fortune on some of America's most breathtaking rivers and streams, this book is for you.

Maybe you were like me not long ago: interested but not experienced and not sure where to turn. Fly-fishing is an endless learning experience that can be daunting. Yet there is a beautiful simplicity to it that lies just beyond a few practiced basics like casting and matching reel, rod, line, hook, and fly sizes. What you'll find here is everything you need to learn about this style of fishing.

I have a hunch that most of you have fished with traditional spin casting equipment and are now peeping over the wall at fly-fishing. Many fly fishers come to the sport from bait and spinning reels. The perception that fly-fishing is an elite, exclusive pursuit is held by few actual fly fishers. Most welcome new anglers. Yet fly-fishing is still considered to be a daunting and expensive sport. It doesn't have to be.

The novice who wanders into the local fly shop may seem like a bull in a china shop. But everyone new to the sport starts out this way. I trace back my own entrance into the fly-fishing world to the

love of fishing in general, instilled in me as a youth growing up in
the East Texas piney woods. Large bass, plucky sunfish, and spiny
bluegill roamed the cow ponds nestled in forests crisscrossed by a
network of oil well roads. My brother and I spent hours during the
long summer days tossing nightcrawlers and grasshoppers with cane
poles. Turtles usually chewed off our stringered catches, but what
remained we soaked in salt water and fried. The delight of eating
fresh-caught fish has not waned to this day.

After settling into Los Angeles in my early twenties, I chose the
High Sierras as an annual destination. The five hours on Highway
395 was like time spent with an old friend. Netting glistening rainbows at 7,000 feet was pure magic. I had a brief run fly-fishing for
salmon on Oregon's North Umqua in the mid-'80s, but did not yet
take to the sport. And there was a reason for that.

I attribute the magic of fishing for trout on June Lake to an old
master who described a better way than the old Texas hit-and-miss
approach. He said to anchor my boat 30 to 40 feet from the reeds,
cast 20 feet from the shore in about 8 feet of water with a 2-foot,
2-pound leader and #18 treble hook jammed with floating cheese or
salmon eggs. Pretty mechanical. I thoroughly enjoyed it, though,
because bait casting in East Texas meant pretty much changing from
night crawlers to purple worms to grasshoppers to lures, then back
again. Trout fishing seemed like a formula for catching all fish, and it
was. The old-timer's recipe worked most of the time, as I came
home year after year with my limit. Today that view has changed.
Though fly-fishing is more of a challenge, its rewards exceed those
of bait fishing, and the concept of catching my limit has been
reversed to limiting my catch.

What happened during my first fly-fishing experience was that
my lack of casting ability quickly eroded my patience and enjoyment. As my fly-fishing friend so aptly insists, "Casting is the main
thing at first." If the novice can't learn even the basic cast, he or
she will quickly tire of fly-fishing and end up watching others from a
convenient rock. That happened to me.

So let me encourage you right now to spend the time and money on a lesson or two. You may know someone who fly-fishes, but are they a good teacher? A good fly fisherman does not necessarily make a good teacher. You start to pick up their bad habits, and spend years down the road trying to work out their kinks. Even the world's top golfing pros take lessons.

Fly shops offer guides and instructors. My first instructor was a Federation of Fly Fishing certified instructor who had me casting for nearly three hours in a duck pond until I learned to cast properly. Of course, I had to practice, practice, practice those good techniques. And you will, too.

FISHING LICENSE

SERIAL NO

CHAPTER 1

What to Expect

The quiet snip of scissors was enough to awaken me at 5:15 one morning as my friend and resident fly-fishing expert David Mulligan worked at a vise clamped to a table in the Inn at Soap Lake. In the barely lit room I could make out piles of feathers everywhere. Wings and feathers from game hens and pheasant, even fur from a rabbit. Dave hoped the maids wouldn't object to his odd assortments spread out on beds, table, chairs, even air conditioner.

I think fly tying is just in Dave's blood. Some fly fishermen get more pleasure from making flies than from catching fish. The wings, feathers, and fur are selected for making the valuable *hackle* (feathers or plumage of birds) that simulates wings on artificial fishing flies and allows the fly to float. The last three quarters of an inch on a feather tip provides the best hackle.

We had driven there the day before from Seattle. The scenery had changed ever so gradually—from Washington's rain-soaked coast east through Snoqualmie National Forest, and again through mountain passes along the Yakima and Cle Elum rivers, crossing the mighty Columbia to, now, the arid conditions in the center of the state, near Moses Lake. Our final destination was Rocky Ford, Washington, a spring creek lying just below a hatchery. Rocky Ford is an oasis of phenomenal natural springs bursting through the earth at precisely the temperature preferred by rainbow and brown trout.

With a hook clamped firmly in the vise—"Always buy the best vise you can"—Dave patiently wound fine dark thread around the hook shank and added the hackle. As he tied, the hackle began to stand upright on the hook. Before wrapping the final 4 inches of thread, he added dubbing fiber, which would simulate the insect body. At home he had gathered packages of dubbing (synthetic or natural fur) materials in colors ranging from yellow to olive and dumped them into a blender. What came out, he assured me, would most exactly "match the hatch" of emerging insects.

As he worked that still morning, a simple metal hook slowly took on an abdomen, thorax, legs, even a head (a hollow metal cone). The fly's appearance was truly lifelike, but how would it act

in the water? Would it imitate a real insect or nymph? Could it stand up to repeated casts, yanked off the water repeatedly, splashed down just as often, mauled by fish? That's why Dave was so focused.

Critical to fly-fishing is how flies are made. A quick way to test the quality of a dry fly is to hold it flat on an open palm (not clamped between thumb and forefinger) with the hook shank parallel to your palm. If the point of the hook touches your skin, the fly will float poorly and not simulate a real insect. This test also indicates whether the fly will hold together well. It's not an expensive fly rod that attracts fish but the fly you cast on the water. Another test is to drop the fly onto a hard counter top from several feet above. If the fly bounces, it indicates good hackle quality, usually a sign of a well-made fly.

Rising out of bed that crisp summer morning, I asked how many fly patterns Dave had ready. He had six scuds (freshwater shrimp), two damselflies, and a handful of leeches. Long before we hit the water that day, we readied our gear: a collapsible case for wet flies and a firm plastic case for dry patterns, two sizes of fly rods packed protectively in 5-foot tubes, foam-wrapped reels, fishing vests, pliers, sunglasses, sink and flotation liquids, extra braided leaders, several spools of tippet material with various break strengths, and fishing licenses.

After a quick breakfast of coffee and granola bars, we set off for Rocky Ford. Excitedly, we slowly made our way to the water's edge. The streams, cool and whispering, beckoned to us. A heron took flight, ascending ever so gracefully from a shoal. And then we saw them, some 26 inches long, black-spotted on top, pink and green flecks on the sides, and the constantly swishing black and silver tails. Rainbows streaked up and down the streamside as we approached. Occasional flashes of white underbelly caught the sun. It was magic.

Though anxious to wet our lines, we studied the fish for a while in their crystalline environment. The brook ran clear and cold and teemed with life. Scuds dove for cover in the thick weeds. Minnows scurried near the edge. Flecks of food and vegetation floated by. All the trout were facing forward, positioning themselves in various areas along the current.

Stocked with thousands of rainbow and brown trout, Rocky Ford is a haven for fly fishermen. Aerators in the hatchery above keep the fingerlings alive during cold winters. In the warmer months, Rocky Ford becomes a smorgasbord of food for the fish, with hatches of chironomids, leeches, scuds, and beautiful blue damselflies—all replicated by tricky fly tiers.

Back at our truck we assembled the sections of our rods, making sure the snake guides lined up properly, then attached the reel solidly to the reel seat. After threading braided loop connectors and joining tippets to braided leaders, we selected flies. I selected a

The Zen of Fly-Fishing

It's difficult to match what Jerry Dennis wrote in his book *River Home*: St. Martin's Press, 1998.

"Fishing makes us alert, pulls us out of our thoughts, and engages us in something bigger than ourselves. It's a restorative that cleanses us when we've become muddied and makes us healthy when we've become sickened. It's a brace against pessimism.

"Fishing, I should have explained, teaches us to perform small acts with care. It humbles us. It enriches our friendships. It cultivates reverence for wild things and beautiful places. It offers relief from overdue bills and endless chores and appalling world events. It makes us participants in nature instead of spectators, a crucial distinction because participants tend to become passionate and protective and spectators tend to become indifferent."

scud and Dave, a leech. We made certain to crush the hook barbs, leaving the bigger fish for other fly fishers. The joy of releasing fish unharmed back into their lair is expressed by fishing veteran Lee Wulff, one of America's most famous fly fishermen: "A trophy fish is too important to catch only once."

Once on the water, we pulled out the bright orange fishing line and started *false casting* (flicking the airborne line forward and back without lowering the fly) to shoot out the loose line. After we had about 20 feet of line flying through the air, we gently set the flies upstream, took up the slack and began *stripping* (pulling the line back in by hand) in the line. Through polarized lenses we patiently watched the trout appreciate their two new watery additions. Would they take what we had served up? Was it even lunchtime? We knew the best presentation is made just ahead and to one side of the trout so that the fly drifts into their field of binocular vision.

Throughout the day we moved up the length of stream, sometimes crossing over as the winds changed. The current slipped and braided as it moved through a variety of pools and weed-filled runs. Boulder-hopping, we threw flies into various eddies, branch overhangs, and rock areas. Dave and I tied and retied various flies, hoping to interest the trout. What are the trout gorging on today, we wondered? We watched damselflies hover above water and scuds scurry below. We served up various flies in an attempt to match the hatch.

Sometimes we would strip a dry fly back in subsurface, hoping to arouse some interest. At the head of a pool I made a *pile cast* (casting such that the line lands in a loose pile of coils) so there would be plenty of slack in the leader and the current could take the fly as it pleased. Occasionally the splash of a muskrat broke the steady lap-lap of the cool, clear water against the shoreline reeds.

Then it happened. A big one grabbed at a red damselfly. Exhilarated by my first catch of the day, I reminded myself out

loud to hold the rod tip up and keep the line taut. Dave produced the net while I zigged the fish right to left, then back again. He made a 180-degree turn several times, took the line and I let him do it. The hooked fish desperately sought help from the current. Repeatedly, I maneuvered it to shore, only to be met with further resistance. More than once the fish seemed to be dead, its whole body limp. Then it set off again. Finally, its energy exhausted, the rainbow capitulated headfirst into Dave's soft mesh net.

Dave held the stunned but uninjured fish for a long time while it regained its strength. We were careful to touch our finned friend as little as possible so as not to remove its protective mucus. Too many anglers are careless about how they handle caught fish. Internal organs are easily damaged if fish are not handled properly.

When I was first exposed to the world of fly-fishing, a buddy of mine said: "Fly-fishing is a way of life." One of our first trips was to an area where the limit was one fish and on barbless hooks. At that time, after years of fishing lakes with treble hooks and floating cheese, I thought the one-fish concept ludicrous. But my paradigm has shifted.

Fly fishers, for the most part, don't leave trash. They pick up after themselves, they pack everything out. Tackle and tools stay in vests, and jars of bait or hooks are pleasantly absent. Other anglers leave behind a trail of tackle victims. Countless birds, turtles, and other animals swallow fish hooks and become entangled in fishing lines, suffering debilitating injuries. Officials with the Virginia Marine Science Museum Stranding Team say fishing line is one of the top three threats to aquatic animals.

I think my paradigm shift came after I studied the great trout cruising the clear brooks and streams. They got to be large because responsible fishermen returned them to their natural habitat after enjoying the sport of catching them. Fly fishers care about the environment and the fish inhabiting it. The large German browns and cutthroats found in U.S. waters today are a rare breed, objects to be

appreciated, not hunted. I gave up my idea of fishing for food in favor of a greater, transcendent appreciation for the fish in their own milieu, at one with nature, carefully concealed among the waving weeds.

Perhaps the most satisfying part of fly-fishing are the breezes shimmering through the birch leaves, hearing streams gurgle, loons lament, the splash of a cormorant skittering across the water. Imbibe it all, for fishing is more than catching fish. Fly-fishing may be the only kind of fishing that can completely capture the soul and brain of intelligent people and imprison them for life. The buzz of locusts, puffy cumulus clouds overhead, and the thrill of rising, splashy trout are addictive.

Like so many things in life, serendipity seems to come when least expected. Frustration seems to kill good fishing fortune, so plan on picking a spot to enjoy, one that is calm and peaceful. The continuously changing environment will cause you to alter your on-the-stream strategy. But that's the most exciting part.

Successful fishing requires a connection to nature. It may be the buzz of insects, the swish of cattails in the breeze, a red-winged blackbird on a swaying limb. Maybe it's simply the tranquil gurgle of the brook that touches you deep inside. Whatever your spiritual connection to fishing, enjoy the moment and be patient. There is so much to see, to hear, to smell, and to feel near the water. As fishing prodigy Tom Meade writes: "Whether you catch a fish or not, the water will always give you a little of its strength, some of its energy and much of its peace."

You can be successful at fly angling if you're willing to spend the necessary (but not inordinate) time getting to know the subject. The more you learn about fly-fishing, the more you have to learn and the more you want to learn it. I agree with whoever said, "The greater the island of knowledge, the longer the coastline of mystery."

Fishing Views

". . . looking down into a lake, an ocean, or a river is like looking up into the night sky, that both water and sky are filled with mysteries, and when we stare deeply into them we connect with every man and woman who has ever sensed the tugging vitality of the universe. We become part of a larger community, united by mysteries so vast that they make our differences of opinion and philosophy seem very small.

"Anglers are people who want to get beneath the surface of things. . . . Fishing is simply a way to open our hearts to the world."

—*River Home*
by Jerry Dennis,
St. Martin's Press, 1998

FISHING   LICENSE

SERIAL NO

CHAPTER 2

Tackling Your Equipment Needs

I remember the first time I was ceremoniously handed a fly rod. "Welcome to the world of fly-fishing," my friend said. As I held the cherry-finished 8-foot, 6-inch graphite rod made by Sage, he said: "You're holding the finest rod in the world." We were indoors at the time and I waved the rod around for a few minutes. "Careful!" he warned, taking the rod and gingerly laying it down. "Let's save that for outside." It had three times as many guides as my old spin rods. I felt reverential.

Next came the reels carefully wrapped in styrofoam with Velcro closers. One had a 4-foot, 5-pound leader; the other a 6-foot, 10-pound leader. The various sizes would be used later for testing the water. Short rods are easier to maneuver near heavy brush, but you can cast farther with a longer rod.

A fly-fishing setup doesn't have to be expensive. A wise guide once told me: "A $150 outfit complete with fly rod, reel, line, the whole bit is certainly adequate. I certainly wouldn't buy gear at a discount house. If you wind up fishing a lot, your reel will start falling apart and the rod tip will come off. But people don't need to spend a lot of money, especially if they're going a couple times a year and are not interested in tying flies or entomology. Now if they're going more, then I'd consider investing some money."

In the following paragraphs is a bird's-eye, or better, fish-eye, view of some of the tackle and equipment you'll need. Some of the items are covered in greater detail in the rest of the book.

Your Hot Rod

First, let's start with fly rods. For whatever reason, the fly-fishing world doesn't refer to rods as "poles" or "sticks." Fly rods are made from one of three basic components: graphite, boron, and fiberglass, fiberglass being the least expensive. However, other materials like bamboo and glass make excellent rods. The beginner would be served well by a lightweight graphite rod because casting is simpler and more accurate and there is less fatigue. When it comes to purchasing a graphite rod (or any other), you get what you pay for. If fly-fishing is a sport you're going to stay with for the long haul, check out the $500 Sage rods. But if you're not sure, play it safe and purchase a $125–$200 rod.

Besides rod composition and quality, analyze the quality of the fittings, which are the rod (snake) guides, wrappings, reel seats, grips, tips and ferrules (sockets joining the rod together). You may want to ask for help in selecting the best-quality materials you can afford.

Another factor in selecting a rod is "action," which is described as fast, medium, or slow. The terms indicate how much a rod bends as you cast it. A fast-action rod is relatively stiff for much of its length and bends near the top. A medium- or moderate-action rod, which bends more, will compensate for many casting errors and generally is easier to fish with. Slow-action rods bend easily. They are accurate, but do not cast very far.

Shorter rods allow you more casting freedom, whereas longer rods lift more line off the water. An 8-foot rod may be the most ideal length for both beginner and expert. It depends on where you plan to fish. If it's wide open lake fishing, select a longer rod. Bushy, barely accessible areas require shorter rods.

If you're after pan-sized or small stream trout, an ultralight graphite rod may be just the ticket. These incredibly light fly rods take only 1-, 2-, or 3-weight lines. (There are even 0-weight rods!) These are not for heavy-duty saltwater or steelhead fishing, but for the angler who needs to noiselessly drop his fly right on the nose of a small spooky fish.

Most fly rods today are marked by the manufacturer to indicate the fly line best suited for the rod, and buyers should stick to these recommendations. The markings are just above the grip. Knowing the type and size of the fish you seek, and where to find it, will lead you to just the right rod for you, matched with exactly the right line.

Every rod has a different feel. When you shop for a rod, ask the clerk to load the rod with reel and line. If possible, make a few practice casts. Your rod should feel like an extension of your arm and will communicate to you the action of the line and strike of a fish. Many reputable retailers (Orvis, L.L. Bean, Hunter's Angling Supplies—all highly respected national mail-order firms) offer high-quality, entry-level packages where rod, reel, and line match quite nicely. They often represent a substantial savings over buying components separately, as well.

Finally, don't let your rod, reel, or fly line come into contact with sunscreen, insect repellent, or the bottom of your feet! Also, never pull on the tip of the rod. It may break off. Before stringing your fly line through the snake guides, loop it first. If the line slips, it won't slip all the way back to the reel.

The Reel Deal

Your reel is more than just a place for storing the line. It's important that the reel be lightweight yet solid, dependable enough for the greatest variety of fish sizes and strengths. The reel's package information should cite appropriate line sizes and the amount of backing it can spool.

Reels come in three types: automatic, multiplying, and single-action. An automatic fly reel has no handle or crank but a spring tension device. When a lever is pressed, the reel spool quickly respools the loose fly line. Multiplying reels have spools that turn at least two times for every turn of the handle. The line can be respooled quickly, but many fly fishermen believe that multiplying reels give too much advantage to the angler. Fishing tournaments often bar their use.

Today's most popular reels are single-action, which means the spool turns one revolution for every turn of the handle. Single actions have a large line capacity, and spools can be interchanged easily if lines get damaged. Sometimes you need to swap reels or reel spools to change from a floating to a sinking line. Most single-actions have reliable drag systems. The drag (usually on the side opposite the handle) is used to increase or reduce line tension. The drag mechanism, the most important part of your reel, works like a car's brakes. It reduces the speed of a spinning spool and puts pressure on a hooked fish trying to escape.

A particularly hard-fighting fish like the steelhead can cause an inferior reel to explode. That's why the more reliable reels are made of a single piece of aluminum or magnesium. Fly reels are punctured with holes to reduce weight and

Which Reel?

When deciding on a reel, select one to match the type of fishing you plan to do. A small reel may be fine for trout but not hold enough backing line to last more than a few seconds when hooked up to a powerful steelhead. A lower-priced reel may work as an entry piece of equipment or for occasional use. A moderate- or better-priced reel may be a wiser long-term investment.

EVERYTHING **FLY-FISHING BOOK**

to let the line dry while on the reel. Be careful to keep your reel free of dirt and sand.

Quality reels are critical, but they don't necessarily catch more fish. In fishing contests every year sport enthusiasts of all ages and both sexes fly in from various parts of the United States. Some have $600 rods and $500 reels, yet they often don't catch fish. A local fisherman, though, who knows the waters, where the fish hang out, and basic entomology—the science of insects—can grab a bamboo pole and win the tournament. Equipment may be 30 percent of fly-fishing while technique and knowledge make up the other 70 percent. Fish don't distinguish between expensive and inexpensive equipment.

If you are fishing for a specific type of fish, such as the powerful tarpon, you can't use cheap equipment. A tarpon can make such a huge jerk on the line that it actually can cause the reel to explode. The tarpon is powerful, strong, like a thoroughbred. If there were ever a fish with an attitude, the tarpon would be it. On the other hand, the bone fish is a long-distance sprinter that will take all your line and backing (spooled on the reel under the line) three or four times.

Many reels have what is called an exposed rim. This is an important feature. It allows you to apply drag directly to the spinning spool with the palm of your hand. Seasoned anglers say to insist on this feature when purchasing a reel.

On the Fly

Luring a fish into snagging a fly you either chose or created is one of the greatest satisfactions of fly-fishing. Herein lie much of the magic and mystery of the sport. Will the fly you have selected actually appeal to the fish? Are trout gorging themselves on top-floating damselflies, or are they hovering near the bottom in search of other food? What fly will you choose? Will it drift and move naturally in the water? For decades flies of many types and sizes have been created to mimic real insects. Some fishermen and women pride themselves more on their knowledge of entomology than their actual catch of fish—perhaps for good reason, especially if the fish aren't biting!

That doesn't mean you need to learn everything about insects, just enough so you can identify some basic ones like the caddisfly, mayfly, damselfly, and stonefly. Other fish fodder are caterpillars, grasshoppers, crickets, frogs, even small mice, which can accidentally fall into the water and become part of the fish's diet. Leeches, minnows, and crayfish are also delectable to fish. Artificial flies that mimic these creatures are called bugs, which are often made of cork or light wood. Bugs can be used effectively on northern pike, muskies, ladyfish, or tarpon. They are of various types: popping, sliding or skipping, floating-diving, or a hair bug type. Other types of flies are designed specifically for salmon, steelhead, or saltwater species.

Simply remembering that fish feed both on the surface and below the surface can keep many beginning anglers from getting discouraged. Often new recruits to the fly-fishing world are enamored of the concept of catching fish on top of the water. They may visit a stream or river and wait many hours for trout that don't rise to the surface. After a few more half-hearted casts with top-water flies, they eventually head for home downcast. The waters may have been very productive, however, because many species of fish—especially larger fish—spend 90 percent of their time feeding below the surface.

The way to ply these waters is to use a wet fly. Quality wet flies are made from soft materials like silk floss, fur, or chenille which absorb water readily and sink quickly. When the fly is pulled through the water with short jerks, the hackle and wings have a natural action. Flies are also tied to imitate nymphs, the immature stage in an insect's life. Fish constantly feed on immature insects swimming toward the surface before changing into winged insects. When the water is cold and no hatch is taking place, nymphs will yield substantially more fish than any other type of artificial fly because fish love nymphs, pupae, and larvae. Nymphs are dressed on heavy hooks with absorbent material so they sink quickly. Insects are discussed in Chapter 5, and flies, specifically, in Chapter 6.

A Fine Line

This brings us to perhaps the most distinctive difference between bait casting or spinning and fly-fishing. In traditional casting, the bait or lure pulls the line out. But with a fly rod, it's the other way around. The weight of the line pulls out the fly. That's why the line is so critical to fly-fishing. Standard fly line is about 90 feet long and comes in a variety of colors including fluorescent for easy visibility. Kids learning to fly-fish love the bright colors. Don't worry, brightly colored, highly visible fly lines don't spook the fish and enable you to keep track of your line at all times.

Backing attaches between the fly line and the reel. It simply adds length to your 90 feet of line without adding bulk and excessive cost. It allows the fish to make a long run while you play him. If you were to make a 60-foot cast to a northern pike, you would definitely need more than 30 feet of extra line to play the fish. If you ever stalk the mighty tarpon and land one, he can easily take all of your line, the backing, and then some!

Backing is made out of braided Dacron and is similar in diameter to regular monofilament. It usually comes in 20- or 30-pound test, 20 being most common for freshwater, 30 for saltwater. The amount of backing you choose depends upon the fighting characteristics of the fish. For a fish that does not make long runs, 50 yards should be fine. A hundred yards is the most common amount of backing used. For fish that are known to make very long runs, you may choose to have 200 yards or more.

One other reason to use backing on your reel is to increase the diameter of the spool where the fly line is wound. This helps prevent tangles, which can be caused by the line being wound into small circles. The increased diameter also helps you retrieve more line with every revolution of the reel.

Fly lines range from 1 to 15 weight (4, 5, or 6 are generally ideal). A 1-weight line would be used for the most delicate and fine trout fishing on tiny streams with dainty trout, while an 8-weight would be used to cast big bass flies. A 15-weight would be used on marlin, big tuna, and other such game fish.

If you choose a 4-weight *line*, you'll want a 4-weight *rod*. Rod weights match line weights. If you're casting a delicate trout fly with a bulky bass line, the splash caused by the heavy line slapping the water would certainly spook the trout. Fly rods should be selected according to the line you select. A rod labeled "5-weight" performs best with a 5-weight line.

Tuned angling skills make it possible to catch very big fish on comparatively light fly-fishing tackle. In the Florida Keys, for instance, you will be after bonefish, barracuda, tarpon, permit, cobia, and dolphin, among many other species. You will need a 10- to 13-weight rod and line for average tarpon and bigger barracuda, but a 6- to 9-weight will suffice for others, generally speaking. If you intend to pursue a bluegill in farm ponds or small trout in tight streams, use a wispy 1- to 4-weight. Inshore fly-fishing for spotted sea trout, red drum, striped bass, and bluefish needs about a 7- to 9-weight. Northern pike and muskie insist on 8- to 10-weight rods and lines.

Matching rod and line weights gives you a balanced fly-fishing system and the ability to cast the fly where you want it to go. All your casting power derives from the relationship of line to rod. The majority of today's fly lines come tapered— that is, they are thinner on the ends, making for easier casting, smooth delivery, and delicate presentation of the fly on the water.

Fly lines also differ in their density. There are floating lines which are meant to always stay on top of the water's surface. There are sinking lines which are meant to stay below the surface. And there are lines that fall in between the two. Your first one probably should be a floating line. They are the most common, the most versatile, and the easiest to learn with.

When it comes to fly lines, buoyancy is critical. If you've properly studied the water and how the fish are feeding, you'll know whether to use a floating or a sinking line. In simplest terms, if you're using a dry fly, you'll need a floating line. Wet flies, nymphs, poppers, and streamers (which imitate baitfish) can be fished with a floating, sinking, or sinking-tip line. All

Fly Lines: Short and Simple

Scientific Anglers invented the floating lines we know, and there were only two choices. Today, a whirling assortment of "special" fly lines can be overwhelming to the novice—one for cutthroat, a special sinking tip for cutthroat, a special fast-sinking tip for cutthroat, and an ultra line for cutthroat . . . all in a rainbow of colors.

Don't feel bad if you're confused. Line proliferation confuses everyone. Starting out, for moderate casts to trout, a weight-forward line for dry fly presentation is all you need. If you also want to heave nymphs, it will do that, too.

species of fish feed below the surface most of the time, so sinking lines are critical. And almost every species spends some time feeding on the surface, requiring a floating line to catch them.

Sinking lines are made to descend at various rates. Sink rates are measured in inches per second (ips), listed on the fly line box. Let's say you're fishing an 8-weight line in about 4 feet of water and the sink rate of your line is 4 inches per second (4 ips). Your line will sink at the rate of one foot every 3 seconds, and in roughly 12 seconds it should be where you want it. The greater the sink rate, the faster you can get your fly to the fish, and you'll spend more time at their feeding level instead of sinking slowly over their heads. A super fast-sinking line will get down faster, but it also will snag your flies on the bottom. That's why manufacturers make lines with different sink rates.

If the fish are feeding deep, you have to cast deep to reach them. If rivers and streams are high and turbulent, you'll also have to fish deep. In these instances, sinking lines work best. Some anglers tell of using a full-length, high-density sinking line attached with a floating bass bug. The line sinks, taking the corky bug with it, but the bug's buoyancy kept it off the bottom and at the tops of reeds. Gently stripping in the line will draw any nearby bass's attention.

The downside of high-density sinking lines is that they are difficult to use. They take some of the fun out of fly-fishing because it's hard to lift sinking lines out of the water. Some sinking lines have to be retrieved almost up to the rod tip before they can be picked up for the back cast. Some lines float most of their length but have sinking forward sections of 10, 20, or even 30 feet. These lines, which are easier to use than full-length sinkers, are called sinking-tip lines. This front end sinks your fly while the rest of the line floats. In many situations sinking tip lines offer the best of best worlds. You get the depth you need, but because the sinking portion of the line is so short, it can be picked up for another cast almost as easily as a floating line. The floating portion of the line also lets you "mend" the line in flowing water. Mending (discussed in Chapter 6) is

abruptly raising the rod so the line flips upstream, letting the fly retain a natural drift.

Another type of line is called the *shooting head*, or *shooting taper* line. Usually shorter than a regular fly line, a heavier head makes up the forward section of tapered line. Distance casting becomes much easier, but since a shooting head is so heavy, it is virtually impossible to present a fly delicately on the water. Lighter lines let you delicately present the fly to the fish so they don't get spooked (more on this later). Also, monofilament line runs so quickly through the snake guides that shooting taper line has a tendency to tangle.

Many successful anglers use a line that is weighted in the forward section (weight-forward line), while the rest of the line is mostly a light, small-diameter running line that slides easily through the rod guides. These weight-forward lines make long casts easier and you'll probably find it most versatile in the widest variety of fishing situations.

In fly-fishing, as in any other type of fishing, you get what you pay for when it comes to fly lines. When you pay $7 for a fly line, you get about $7 worth of performance. On the other hand, when you pay substantially more for a line made by reputable, proven manufacturers like Scientific Anglers, Fenwick, Orvis, L.L. Bean, and Wulff, you get a line you know you can trust, one that will perform as it was meant to perform. Don't ever skimp on a fly line.

As your fly-fishing interests and expertise grow, you'll want to seek out variations in taper, have on hand both floating and sinking lines on different reels, maybe even try a shooting head line for longer casts. Fly lines are expensive, so it's important to get the right ones and to take care of them properly so they last more than one or two seasons. Direct sunshine and harsh chemicals like gasoline and oil will wear down your line. Be careful that your line doesn't get pinched, and wipe it down occasionally with line dressing.

A Special Leader

Mulligans' also produces a fluorocarbon furled leader that sinks for use with wet flies. These leaders are available from C&D Professional Services in Lacey, Washington. Call 360-459-1395 for information on this revolutionary leader or to order products. Their web site is www.MulligansFinest.com.

Neater Leaders and Tips on Tippets

A critical component of your fly-fishing system is the leader, which is often composed of tapered or knotted together sections of braided monofilament line. The longer the leader, the farther away the fly will be from the heavy, bulky fly line. This means a long leader is less likely to spook the fish. Some anglers use leaders one and a half times longer than their rods—6-foot rod, for example, with a 9-foot leader; a 9-foot rod with a 13-foot leader.

In recent years fly fishermen have been able to take advantage of a technology that has created a tapered leader—heavy enough to be cast, yet light enough on the end to deliver the fly delicately to the water. A tapered leader is drawn through a machine to make it thick on the butt end and thin on the forward end, where the tippet ties on. The tippet is made of very thin monofilament so the fish don't notice it. (There is ongoing debate as to what exactly a fish sees.)

As you change flies and tie on new ones, you'll discover your tippet getting shorter and shorter if you don't use loop knots (see knot tying, Chapter 9). So be sure to carry extra tippet material. If you know you're using the right fly, but the fish don't strike, you may want to use thinner tippet material—especially in what fly fishermen call "gin-clear" water.

Leaders can be anywhere from 2 to 12 feet long. Shorter leaders are easier to cast, but in clear water you may need a longer leader so you don't spook the fish. Crystalline water usually requires longer leaders, smaller flies, and finer tippets. Generally, use a longer leader for dry flies, a shorter one for subsurface fishing. There are many fishermen who must always have the longest, strongest, thinnest leader—thin enough to fool any fish, strong enough to hold any fish.

Mulligans' Finest Furled Leader, relatively new on the scene, boasts a nearly neutral density that floats in calm water and slowly sinks with wet flies. Because this knotless leader stretches more than 15 percent of its length, it helps absorb the shock of a striking fish. Centuries ago British fly fishers twisted strands of horsehair together to create "furled" leaders. David Mulligan has revived the technique but uses modern materials to make lightweight tapered leaders that are furled. Mulligans' Finest Furled Leader comes in 4-, 6-, and 9-foot lengths, and in strengths of 5, 10, 15, 20, and 30 pounds.

A vital component of the leader is the *tippet*, or final strand. The tippet, a single piece of monofilament attached to the end of the leader and tied to your fly, is measured with the X system. As a general rule, match tippet size to the size of the fly you plan to cast and the size of the fish you hope to land. The lighter or finer the tippet, the less visible it is to the fish. Be careful, though; a tippet that's too light won't cast out your fly properly or be stiff enough to support it.

Length? Eighteen inches is adequate for most fishing situations. Other times a 4-foot tippet would work better, especially if fishing small dry flies in "gin-clear" water. A longer tippet would allow the fly to drift more naturally.

Fishing line companies describe tippet thickness in X numbers from 0X to 8X. The higher the X number, the thinner the tippet and the smaller the fly it will cast. For example, tippets measuring 6X, 7X, and 8X are used on the smallest flies. Tippets measuring 2X, 1X, and 0X are used for large bass bugs and some steelhead and saltwater flies. An established rule of thumb for selecting the appropriate tippet size is to divide the size of your fly by three. For example, for a #18 fly a 6X tippet is ideal. Dividing a #8 fly by three, the closest tippet size is 3X.

Beginners usually fish somewhere in the 3X to 5X range. The heaviest tippets are 1X and 2X.

Leader Basics

Crucial to fly-fishing is the leader, the connection between the fly line and the fly. Depending on design, it can either help or hinder a fly fisher.

Length, diameter, and stiffness of material influence how a leader will perform. Each depends on the other two for total leader performance, and each should be considered carefully so that the leader will perform as you want it to.

Hook Size Is Important

The size of the hook refers to the gap between the point and the shank. The length of the shank is referred to as 1XL for one extra long, 2XL for two extra long, and so forth, assuming the hook is a regular length, between size 2 and size 28. The lower the number the larger the hook.

Hook sizes, from smallest to largest, are represented by even numbers (28, 26, 24,...4, 2) and then by both odd and even numbers (1/0, 2/0, 3/0...).

For general trout fishing you will probably use sizes 6 through 20 the most. For panfish, sizes 10 through 16 are most common; however, these are usually a little heavier and more wind resistant than trout flies. For bass use sizes 2/0 through 8. These flies are even heavier and more wind resistant than most.

You probably know much more about leader design than you think you do. For example, would a short piece of material or a long piece (of the same diameter and stiffness) transmit energy more completely to its end? The short piece would, of course. The same applies to diameter and stiffness of material. Smaller diameters and softer materials are less efficient at energy transfer than are larger diameters and stiffer materials.

With these ideas in mind, consider three leaders that perform in very different ways:

1. If I were fishing a tiny dry fly that needed to be dead-drifted on the surface (i.e., floating at the same speed as the current), I'd want a leader that gave me extra slack when cast and was easily moved about by currents that otherwise might affect the natural drift of my fly. Such a leader would need to be long, thin, and made from supple materials.
2. When it comes time to fish a larger nymph down deep, a different type of leader is called for. The leader needs to be long enough to get down efficiently, yet made from relatively thick and stiff materials to help energy transfer and abrasion resistance.
3. Casting and rapidly retrieving big, juicy streamers requires a leader that straightens very rapidly and offers immediate control of the fly. A short, large diameter design made with tough, stiff materials is the ticket.

Understanding leader material and having a practiced knowledge of reliable fishing knots are as important to the angler as knowing how to cast. The leader and knots are the most fragile link between you and your fish. Frayed leader material, tangles, wind knots, or a badly tied knot can release your trophy prematurely. The leader and knots must be checked constantly while you are fishing. Problem areas should be repaired as soon as they are noticed.

A properly designed fly leader enables the angler to deliver the fly with precision. The leader should provide a strong, nearly invisible link between the fly line and the fly—in fact, fly lines and the leaders attached to them are truly the most important items of tackle. The line puts the fly where the fish are feeding.

A fly leader that's been correctly designed will actually transfer energy from the fly line to the fly in a manner that is predictably helpful to the fly fisherman. The basic design of the leader is this: a large-diameter butt section, a gradually tapering mid-section, and a terminal tippet that is fine yet strong.

Accepted Principles of Leader Design

The butt of the leader attaches directly to the fly line and must be of a diameter similar to the end of the fly line so it can smoothly transfer energy from the fly line to the rest of the leader. The graduated mid-section transfers the energy from the butt section to the leader's tippet. The butt and mid-section are designed as a delivery system for the tippet and fly. The tippet is the leader's single most important component. The tippet size and type are determined by the fish and fishing conditions.

Understanding knot construction and application is critical to any fishing situation. Only with a knowledge of knots can the angler manage his or her own gear. If you understand fly-fishing knots you can construct your own leaders. Without a knowledge of knots you can't. (See basic knots in Chapter 9.)

... and Accessories

Besides a selection of flies, your rod and reel, and a leader and tippet, you'll need accessories. A *sleeveless fishing vest* sports a maze of pockets and pouches to hold essentials: scissors, nippers, glasses, plastic envelopes holding various leaders, dry and wet fly patterns, fly floatant, and fly sinkant. No vest would be complete, however, without its share of mud, chocolate, and insect repellent. The back of the vest has a hook for

How Much Will This Cost?

Less than $1,000 including attending a fly-fishing school. After you complete the school, use your new knowledge to buy your tackle, flies, and accessories from a fly-fishing specialty shop. Here you'll get higher-quality equipment as well as valuable advice from experienced fly-fishing staff who can guide you to exactly what you need to get started. Build relationships at a specialty store so you can get your questions answered as you progress in this wonderful sport.

No matter how good the equipment, if the technique is not good, the equipment won't help much. Fly-fishing is similar to golf in the sense that, to become a good caster, there are techniques that must be learned. It is much easier, at first, if you have someone showing you. That's not to say you cannot learn from tapes and books, but it speeds up the process. You can also attend a fly-fishing school. There are probably several in your area. Check with local fly shops, Federation of Fly Fishing or Trout Unlimited clubs, or fly-fishing magazines.

carrying your net. All to keep your hands free for holding your rod and stripping the line.

The Original Bug Shirt

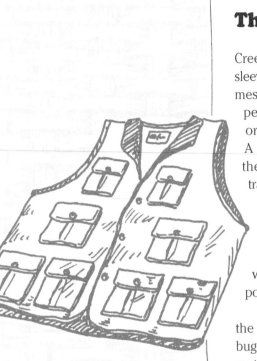

Featuring lightweight fabric, the Original Bug Shirt from Trout Creek, Ontario, is densely woven so bugs can't bite through. Mesh sleeves and sides allow cooling breezes in but keep bugs out. A face mesh provides excellent visibility and keeps out tiny biters. The zippered hood can be easily thrown back and fits over a baseball cap or hard hat. Wrist closures seal the sleeves against insect intrusion. A drawstring waist with bow cord lock provides a positive seal at the waist. The entire shirt folds into its own zippered pocket and travels easily on a belt clip. When buying clothing remember: Flying insects are attracted to dark colors.

Bug pants also provide effective protection. Zip-off legs quickly convert pants into shorts, when protection isn't needed. Other features are a zippered fly, elastic in back of waist, belt loops, reinforced knees, side seam and rear hip pockets, cargo pockets, and optional mesh legs.

Other items from the Bug Shirt Company are gaiters that protect the tasty ankle area yet allow you to wear your favorite pants, and a bug hood that provides protection for your face and neck. For information or products, call 800-998-9096.

Polarized Lenses

The first time you stand rod in hand on the bank of a stream, river, or lake can be exhilarating yet daunting. All that water and no points of reference. Where do you begin? Anglers are always anxious to get lines into the water and feel the excitement that comes with the first tightening of the line. However, instead of hurriedly tying on the first fly within reach and heaving away, experienced and inexperienced anglers alike would do well to look for signs of fish activities and subtleties in the watery environment. And I do mean *look*. For less than $20 you can pick up a pair of polarized sunglasses with which to watch the activities of trout and other fish in

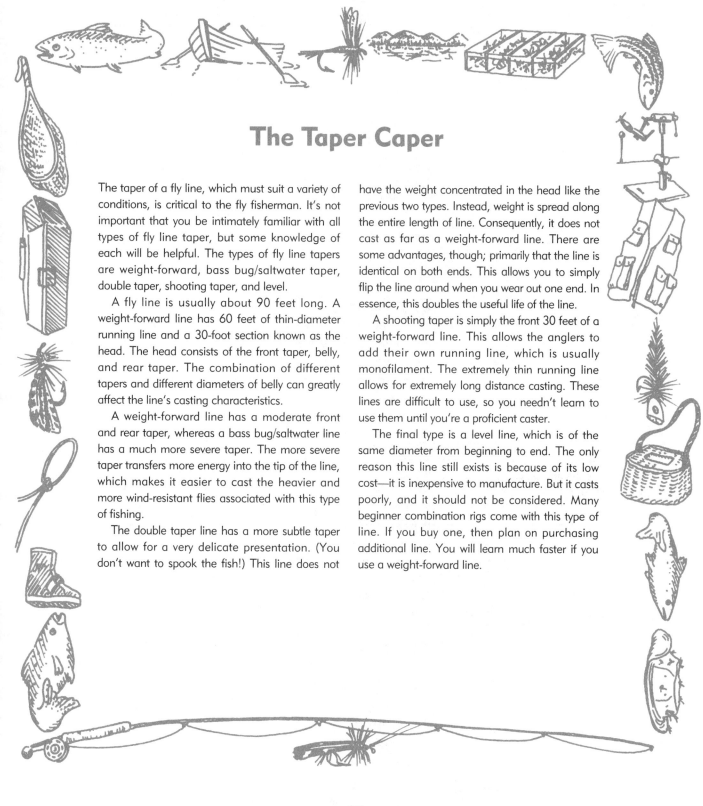

The Taper Caper

The taper of a fly line, which must suit a variety of conditions, is critical to the fly fisherman. It's not important that you be intimately familiar with all types of fly line taper, but some knowledge of each will be helpful. The types of fly line tapers are weight-forward, bass bug/saltwater taper, double taper, shooting taper, and level.

A fly line is usually about 90 feet long. A weight-forward line has 60 feet of thin-diameter running line and a 30-foot section known as the head. The head consists of the front taper, belly, and rear taper. The combination of different tapers and different diameters of belly can greatly affect the line's casting characteristics.

A weight-forward line has a moderate front and rear taper, whereas a bass bug/saltwater line has a much more severe taper. The more severe taper transfers more energy into the tip of the line, which makes it easier to cast the heavier and more wind-resistant flies associated with this type of fishing.

The double taper line has a more subtle taper to allow for a very delicate presentation. (You don't want to spook the fish!) This line does not

have the weight concentrated in the head like the previous two types. Instead, weight is spread along the entire length of line. Consequently, it does not cast as far as a weight-forward line. There are some advantages, though; primarily that the line is identical on both ends. This allows you to simply flip the line around when you wear out one end. In essence, this doubles the useful life of the line.

A shooting taper is simply the front 30 feet of a weight-forward line. This allows the anglers to add their own running line, which is usually monofilament. The extremely thin running line allows for extremely long distance casting. These lines are difficult to use, so you needn't learn to use them until you're a proficient caster.

The final type is a level line, which is of the same diameter from beginning to end. The only reason this line still exists is because of its low cost—it is inexpensive to manufacture. But it casts poorly, and it should not be considered. Many beginner combination rigs come with this type of line. If you buy one, then plan on purchasing additional line. You will learn much faster if you use a weight-forward line.

How to Read the Fly Line Box

You can tell the specifics of weight, taper, and function by reading the outside of the fly line box. The label lists, always in the same order, the type of taper, the line weight, and the function.

Taper/Line Sizes:

- Level - L
- Double Taper - DT
- Weight Forward - WF
- Sink-tip - F/S
- Shooting Taper - ST
- Floating - F
- Sinking - S
- Intermediate (sinking) - I

For instance, a double taper, 5-weight, floating line would be encoded on the fly box as DT-5-F, while a weight-forward, 8-weight, full sinking line would read WF-8-S.

the streams and rivers. Polarized lenses are a must if you want to know how and where the trout are feeding.

It helps to see the quarry, something impossible in most lakes. Streams are the ideal place to study trout, to see if they are feeding, to see what food alleys they are using, and to assess their size. Then it's just a matter of selecting the most palatable dry or wet fly, whether a damselfly, leech, or scud.

If your prey is trout, are they rising for surface insects or conserving energy at the stream bottom as food drifts by? Watch closely to detect which artificial fly would work best to arouse the interest of the game fish you seek.

Fly Boxes

Dozens of fly boxes are available in a variety of sizes, the majority made of plastic or aluminum. Dry flies are fragile. You need to protect their hackle from being crushed. So choose boxes with separate compartments and with clips or foam to keep your flies upright.

You might start out with a combination box, then graduate to two boxes—one for dry flies and one for wet flies or nymphs. Before closing the lid, be sure your dry flies are just that—dry—before stowing them away. One way is to expose them to direct sunlight for a while. Make sure *all* of your flies are dry—be they dry flies, wet flies, nymphs, or streamers—before stowing them away. Wet hooks rust, whether they are the foundation for a dry fly or any other type of fly. You might also suggest drying out the entire box if it (or you) fall into the water and the box is submerged. Water will get in and ruin your flies—be they dry flies, wet flies, or nymphs—if they aren't dried soon after being dunked.

Fly Floatant and Fly Sinkant

This liquid comes in spray or silicone paste and is invaluable when your fly is not floating properly. I suggest buying silicone because it can double as a floatant for your floating fly line as well as dry flies.

About Rods

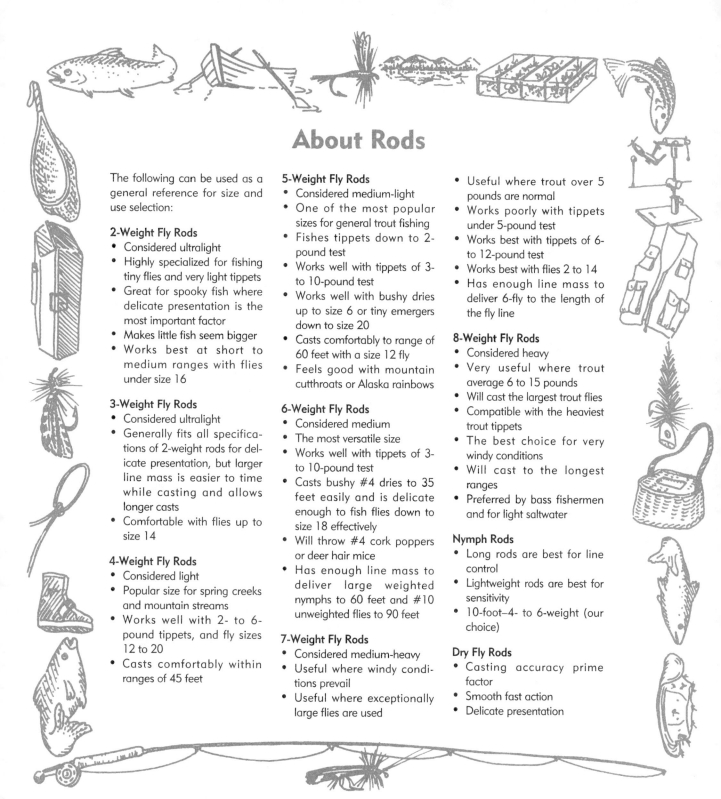

The following can be used as a general reference for size and use selection:

2-Weight Fly Rods
- Considered ultralight
- Highly specialized for fishing tiny flies and very light tippets
- Great for spooky fish where delicate presentation is the most important factor
- Makes little fish seem bigger
- Works best at short to medium ranges with flies under size 16

3-Weight Fly Rods
- Considered ultralight
- Generally fits all specifications of 2-weight rods for delicate presentation, but larger line mass is easier to time while casting and allows longer casts
- Comfortable with flies up to size 14

4-Weight Fly Rods
- Considered light
- Popular size for spring creeks and mountain streams
- Works well with 2- to 6-pound tippets, and fly sizes 12 to 20
- Casts comfortably within ranges of 45 feet

5-Weight Fly Rods
- Considered medium-light
- One of the most popular sizes for general trout fishing
- Fishes tippets down to 2-pound test
- Works well with tippets of 3- to 10-pound test
- Works well with bushy dries up to size 6 or tiny emergers down to size 20
- Casts comfortably to range of 60 feet with a size 12 fly
- Feels good with mountain cutthroats or Alaska rainbows

6-Weight Fly Rods
- Considered medium
- The most versatile size
- Works well with tippets of 3- to 10-pound test
- Casts bushy #4 dries to 35 feet easily and is delicate enough to fish flies down to size 18 effectively
- Will throw #4 cork poppers or deer hair mice
- Has enough line mass to deliver large weighted nymphs to 60 feet and #10 unweighted flies to 90 feet

7-Weight Fly Rods
- Considered medium-heavy
- Useful where windy conditions prevail
- Useful where exceptionally large flies are used

- Useful where trout over 5 pounds are normal
- Works poorly with tippets under 5-pound test
- Works best with tippets of 6- to 12-pound test
- Works best with flies 2 to 14
- Has enough line mass to deliver 6-fly to the length of the fly line

8-Weight Fly Rods
- Considered heavy
- Very useful where trout average 6 to 15 pounds
- Will cast the largest trout flies
- Compatible with the heaviest trout tippets
- The best choice for very windy conditions
- Will cast to the longest ranges
- Preferred by bass fishermen and for light saltwater

Nymph Rods
- Long rods are best for line control
- Lightweight rods are best for sensitivity
- 10-foot–4- to 6-weight (our choice)

Dry Fly Rods
- Casting accuracy prime factor
- Smooth fast action
- Delicate presentation

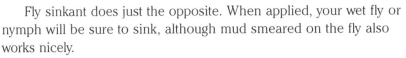

Fly sinkant does just the opposite. When applied, your wet fly or nymph will be sure to sink, although mud smeared on the fly also works nicely.

Other accessories include:

Strike indicator ("bobber" in bait fishing) to signal biting fish
Thermometer for measuring water temperature
Rain jacket
Nippers or needlenose pliers to cut line or remove barbs
     from hooks
 Hemostats to remove hooks from fish
    Safety pins
     First-aid kits
     Landing net of soft mesh
Insect net to collect samples of insects to match the hatch
Creel or cooler if you plan to keep fish
Boots and waders
Wading staff
Brimmed hat
Vest-pocket light for night fishing

Outfitting the Fly-Fishing Woman

Thinking about taking up fly-fishing? You've picked a great time. Gone are the days of oversized rubber boots, borrowed flannel shirts, and one-size-fits-almost-all tackle vests. No longer will you hear streamside groans of "What is she doing here?"

Women are now flocking to the fly-fishing arena. The advent of graphite rods cut the weight of a typical outfit in half, and since then fly-fishing has left the realm of aficionado and begun to cater to the masses. It's no longer necessary to practice for frustrating weeks on end in order to throw a decent loop 60 feet. With proper lessons, a novice angler can be effectively working a river in a matter of days.

Today there is a wide variety of equipment specifically tailored to women. From re-fitted waders to small-grip rods, fly-fishing is a sport where you no longer have to compensate for being female. Being petite and finer muscled doesn't mean you can't cast as far or fish as well as men; it just means you need to approach equipment from a different perspective.

"I never use anything heavier than a 6-weight unless I absolutely have to," explains Joan Wulff, world-class caster and internationally recognized angler. This brings up an excellent point about rods. For the female gender, the lighter the rod, the better. Men's stronger wrists and larger hands allow them to control larger, heavier rods for longer periods of time. Women once had to learn to compensate for this, but they no longer have to.

A cast of 50 feet, plenty of distance for most angling situations, can be achieved with finesse and good timing. Rod weight has little to do with casting accuracy, and brute strength has nothing to do with being able to snap a tight loop or shoot a line. The key to casting is proper technique and tackle. Choose your gear carefully, and you'll be fishing with the best of them.

Fly Rods

Two significant physical differences between men and women are hand size and wrist strength. These distinctions affect every relationship you have with a rod. Salesmen or well-intentioned husbands may try to push a rod they personally prefer. Don't listen to a word they say. What's right for the gander is oftentimes very unwieldy for the goose.

Women should look for softer-action rods utilizing older-generation graphite design. These place less stress on wrists and forearms, allowing the female angler to make repetitive casts over longer periods without discomfort. Newer-generation rods are high-speed casting tools. They require stouter wrists and forearms to cast for any length of time. Listen to your body, not the hype.

Do not underestimate the grip size when purchasing a rod. The grip plays a key role in casting. A poorly balanced rod creates tension on the wrist and hand, often forcing overcompensation on the cast-forward motion. A forceful splash when line hits the water is hardly tempting to any trout. In order to avoid bad habits before they start, purchase a rod with a grip that conforms to your hand size. If

Important Warning

It is dangerous to wear waders in fast-moving water. Your waders can fill with water and the swift-moving current can then sweep you into deeper water.

you find yourself straining to hold a rod, don't buy it. If you are having trouble finding a rod with an appropriate grip, have the grip modified to fit your hand. Many rod manufacturers and fly shops customize grips to suit individual preferences.

When Winston enlisted the help of Joan Wulff as technical adviser, they developed a collection of rods designed with the female angler in mind. Designed with soft-action graphite and smaller grips with thumb depressions, the "Joan Wulff Favorites" are rods that far exceed the standards of any so-called women's rod.

Accessories

Waders are a "must-have" for any serious fly fisher, yet only a few years ago the only waders that fit women were those made for boys. This is no longer the case. Simms' figure-flattering women's neoprene stockingfoots run about $200. Orvis also makes women's stockingfoot neoprenes ($175) and women's bootfoot neoprene waders ($250). For the more thrift-minded, Cabela's also offers women's stockingfoot neoprene waders (about $60). L.L. Bean also offers quality gear for women tested by women.

Felt-soled wading boots are also necessary. Simms ($80), Orvis ($75), and Cabela's ($50) have boots in women's sizes. When matching waders with boots, make sure the boot is large enough for a roomy fit. Ill-sized boots force wader stockingfeet to fold over inside, creating painful blisters.

Vest designs have also undergone major changes. From attractive floral-trimmed patterns to muted colors that step away from the typical tan, fly-fishing vests are now designed to fit a woman's body.

Gender-neutral fly-tackle packs can be a superb alternative to vests. Preferred by some professionals, they are available in a variety of colors and styles. Slung across your shoulder, packs prevent the stress of over-heavy vests. Check out your favorite fly shop and see what they have to offer in women's styles. If it's your first visit, or you haven't been in in a while, you'll be pleasantly surprised.

A Poem on Fly Fishing

From *The Compleat Angler*, published in 1676
by Izaak Walton

This day dame Nature seem'd in love
The lusty sap began to move;
Fresh juice did stir th' embracing vines.
And birds had drawn their valentines.

The jealous trout, that low did lie
Rose at a well-dissembled fly
There stood my Friend, with patient skill,
Attending of his trembling quill.

Already were the eves possess
With the swift pilgrim's daubed nest;
The groves already did rejoice
In Philomel's triumphing voice:

The showers were short, the weather mild,
The morning fresh, the evening smil'd.
Joan takes her neat-rubb'd pail, and now,
She trips to milk the sand-red cow;

Where, for some sturdy foot-ball swain,
Joan strokes a syllabub or twain.
The fields and gardens were beset
With tulips, crocus, violet;

And now, though late, the modest rose
Did more than half a blush disclose.
Thus all looks gay, and full of cheer,
To welcome the new-livery'd year.

—Sir Henry Wotton

FISHING LICENSE

CHAPTER 3

What Are You Fishing For?

When starting out, consider the species of fish you expect to spend the most time chasing. You have probably already decided what kind of fish you'd most like to catch, at least to start. Maybe it's trout in clear flowing streams, bass in local ponds and lakes, or bonefish or tarpon on saltwater flats. If you live in the Northwest, you may have your heart set on tangling with salmon or the powerful steelhead. Knowing which species you want to pursue will help you determine what flies and gear to select.

Nothing is out of range to the fly fisherman except for, perhaps, species such as the black marlin, which lives in extremely deep water and cannot be reached by standard fly-fishing methods. Some species seem especially suited to the fly angler—most notably, the trouts and the American grayling. Both rise readily to flies. Or bass. Nothing takes fly rod popping bugs faster than largemouths and smallmouths. Northern pike, muskie, and tarpon will take large streamer flies before any other lure.

Where you live and the fish in your local waters largely determine what you fish for. But here are only a few of the many species that are ideal for fly-fishing—waiting and willing to hit your flies.

Atlantic Salmon

The king of fly rod fish, the Atlantic salmon has devoted followers in North America and Europe. Unlike Pacific salmon, Atlantic salmon can spawn more than once. At sea, the fish stores enough energy to return to its native stream, climb waterfalls, and spawn without having to eat. This species of salmon strikes a variety of dry and wet flies. When hooked, this baby will jump several feet above the water in a majestic, watery display of power.

Landlocked Salmon

This inland version of the Atlantic salmon also strikes tiny insect imitations. When winter ice melts in northern New England, anglers celebrate the arrival of spring by trolling flies for landlocked salmon. In the Western states, the kokanee salmon is the dwarf, landlocked version of the sockeye. Hatcheries have introduced the kokanee to waters in several Eastern states, where the fish strike trolled streamers.

Pacific Salmon

Five species of Pacific salmon thrive on our continent and all are exciting to catch on a fly rod. Sockeye, pink, and chum salmon are great game fish, but Chinook and coho salmon are fly-fishing favorites. The Chinook or king salmon is the largest, topping more than 100 pounds. The coho or silver is a spectacular leaper when hooked. Chinook and coho strike colorful streamers resembling herring. When they enter their spawning streams, Pacific salmon stop eating but still strike flies and other lures out of curiosity. These salmon spawn once, then die.

Bass

As often as largemouth, smallmouth, and spotted bass ambush and devour bass bugs, they can be finicky strikers. In streams, smallmouths and spotted bass are especially selective during large-insect hatches. Artificial flies need to match exactly the size, color, and behavior of natural insects called "match the hatch." Largemouth bass attack almost anything that invades their territory, including snakes, lizards, mice, birds, and frogs. Mostly, largemouths eat crawfish, minnows, and other small fish. Fished on or near the surface, bass bugs (poppers, divers, and sliders) offer much excitement because you can see the raw violence of a predator striking prey.

Largemouths can grow to 30 inches and weigh more than 20 pounds. The spiny-rayed fish do best in warmer water of about 80 degrees, and in weedy lakes and backwaters of rivers. They prefer clean water with bottoms of mud, sand, and aquatic vegetation. They are often found beneath undercut banks during daylight hours. At dawn and dusk they move into open water to feed but return to cover during the day.

Smallmouths, on the other hand, inhabit lakes with current and cool, clear streams at least 35 feet across with bottoms of rocks, gravel, or sand. Smallmouths do not travel long distances. In lakes they are found around rocky reefs and gravel bars. Smallmouths are considered an excellent game fish. They stage spectacular aerial shows when hooked and fight better than largemouth bass.

Bluefish

From Florida to Maine, bluefish slash at flies resembling fish trying to escape. They use their sharp teeth and powerful jaws to chop their prey into bits. When feeding, a school of bluefish can make the water look like it's boiling with the blood of baitfish. Bluefish are attracted to saltwater streamers and poppers simulating silver-and-white baitfish. Attach them with wire or a braided material that can withstand the bluefish's teeth.

Bonefish

These devils are ravenous bottom feeders inhabiting shallow salt-water flats, where wading fly fishers cast to fish they can see. Much of the time bonefish—as they sweep over a flat to feed in water only 1 to 2 feet deep—reveal their dorsal fins and the top half of their caudal fins. Like shrimp, they live in turtle grass near the bottom of shallow water.

An inshore species, they seldom frequent water more than 10 to 12 feet deep. Bonefish weighing more than 20 pounds have been caught on bait in deep water, but they are much smaller on the flats. But even small fish can tear line off the reel, while larger bone-fish make a full spool of line disappear in seconds. American fly fishers release most of the bonefish they catch.

Catfish

Bottom dwellers, these babies are generally caught on bait, but they will strike artificial flies that simu-late baitfish. In some parts of Pennsylvania, catfish will rise to the surface to feed on abundant fly hatches at night.

Char

Brook trout and lake trout are actually chars, closely related to trout but with a different mouth structure. The other two North American varieties of char are the Dolly Varden and the arctic char. These beautiful fish have light spots on dark skin, whereas trout have

dark spots on light skin. Char readily take flies simulating baitfish, shrimp, and insects.

Grayling

These strong fighters with long, continuous fins on their backs rise to artificial flies. Though the American grayling is known to strike an unusual fly with its small mouth, the fish often shies from a heavy leader. American grayling group together in schools in lakes and streams in Canada, Alaska, Michigan, and some Western states.

Mackerel

Boasting deeply forked tails, narrowed where they join the body, the iridescent, streamlined mackerel are superb, swift swimmers that travel in schools. Feeding on herring and squid, they also strike shiny streamers retrieved quickly. These fish are exciting catches for the fly angler.

Muskellunge

The largest member of the pike family, the "muskie" is a long, thin fish with spineless dorsal fins, large anal fins, and long, narrow jaws with formidable teeth. It eats fish, frogs, snakes, even water fowl, and can grow to 70 pounds. The fly you cast must look like a large meal, and you should retrieve it quickly, working it all the way to your rod tip, where the fish may strike.

Perch

Related to sunfish and sea bass, white and yellow perch usually offer only a sluggish fight but a delicious dinner. Colors range from brassy green to golden yellow above with lighter bellies. Yellow perch are easily recognizable by the distinctive six to eight broad, dark vertical bars on their sides. Yellow perch also have a dark area near the posterior base of the shiny dorsal fin. They grow to 14 inches and can weigh as much as 2 pounds.

On ponds, perch take a variety of flies including small streamers and nymphs fished slowly. During a major insect hatch, the fish will feed on the surface. Sea-run white perch hit flies resembling grass shrimp and baitfish.

Pike

This ferocious predator of arctic waters, with powerful jaws in its toothy duckbill mouth, is a suitable adversary for the fly fisher. A pike can grow to more than 50 pounds, but 8- to 10-pound fish are more common. In the spring, a pike (like the bass) charges at long flies that simulate another fish invading its territory.

Shad

The largest member of the herring family, the shad is found from Florida to New England. They boast spectacular leaping ability and bright flanks. Each spring shad migrate from the salt water to their native streams, where they strike brightly colored flies drifted on stream bottoms. Though bony, American shad are delicious.

Steelhead

Natives of North America's West Coast, steelhead resemble giant rainbow trout. They are like salmon in that they are born in freshwater streams, migrate to sea, then return to spawn. Unlike Pacific salmon, steelhead do not die after spawning. They take a variety of wet flies, many of which look like salmon patterns, and even dry flies. Like Pacific salmon, steelhead have been transplanted to the Great Lakes, where they thrive and provide exceptional fishing action.

Striped Bass

Sporting game fish, stripers are most abundant along the East Coast. They are often called rockfish because they hug rocky shorelines and reefs. Fly fishers cast baitfish imitations to stripers, but the fish also take poppers, worm simulations, and floating bugs that look like miniature crabs. Because striped bass commonly feed at night, the best time to catch them on a

Three Basic Needs of Fish

Fish have some fundamental needs: (1) *protection* or shelter from predators such as the heron, cormorant, eagle, hawk, or other bird of prey; (2) a *food source* ranging from mice to insect larvae; and (3) *water quality*, oxygen levels, aeration, and temperature.

fly is just after sunset and before dawn. Striped bass are found on all three American coasts.

Sunfish

Spiny-finned, freshwater fish with flattened bodies, sunfish are the most colorful and include bluegill, bream, and pumpkinseed. They strike a variety of flies including most nymphs, dry flies, small streamers, and poppers. Because sunfish have small mouths, flies should have hooks smaller than #8. Besides offering anglers much action, sunfish provide good fishing practice. Besides, they taste delicious fried.

Tarpon

This fly line devourer can weigh more than 200 pounds and is strong enough to tow a boat for miles. Tarpon range from Cape Hatteras to Brazil. Just hooking one of these giants is a dream of many experienced anglers. Landing a tail-walking silver king on a fly is a bonus. "Smaller" tarpon in the 20-pound range hit drab streamers as well as brightly colored feathers.

Big tarpon haunts include the Gulf Coast, Caribbean, and Mexico's Yucatan Peninsula. Most anglers agree that of all the game fish in salt water, these are the toughest of the jack family. Among its many species are the amberjack and jack crevalle.

Walleye

Sometimes erroneously called "walleyed pike," walleye are actually the largest member of the perch family. In summer, walleye feed in shallow water at night and move to deeper waters during the day. Spawning occurs in early spring in cooler water, and they return to the same spawning area year after year. They feed throughout the year and can be caught through the ice in winter. Walleye can be difficult to catch until you learn to locate them in a particular body of water.

Whitefish

While purists may disdain this fish because they usually take any fly you throw at them, that very quality makes them fun to catch.

Mountain whitefish in Western streams offer action throughout the winter, taking various small flies.

Let's Talk Trout

Mexican golden, paiute, Dolly Varden, apache, Snake River Firespot cutthroat—more than twenty-four kinds of trout and char swim in American waters. All of them strike flies that imitate a wide variety of natural foods. Fly fishers love trout because they usually live in beautiful areas far from teeming crowds. More has been written about trout than any other game fish. Here is a sampling of trout.

Brook Trout

Common names: brookie, speckled trout, speckled char, sea trout, mountain trout

Description

Blue halos surround small red spots on the side of the body. Wormlike markings (vermiculation) on the back and dorsal fin are lacking in other salmonids. The caudal (tail) fin is slightly forked and edges of the lower fins have white margins. Size: length to 21 inches, weight to 14½ pounds.

Life Facts

This non-native char is most commonly found in mountain lakes and streams. Brookies prefer cool, clear headwater pounds and spring-fed streams. They also thrive in lakes with cool water and highly dissolved oxygen levels near bottom, usually best in water temperatures less then 68 degrees Fahrenheit. Water temperatures as high as 77.5 degrees F will kill brook trout in a few hours. In fresh water, brook trout do not migrate far. They are most active in the morning and late afternoon. At night they can be found under banks, boulders, logs, and other shelters. Brook trout spawn in the fall from August to December. They are almost the easiest of all trout to catch.

Brown Trout

Common names: German trout, German brown trout, brownie

Description

The body color is generally olive to yellowish-brown on the back, lighter on the belly, with dark spots surrounded by pale halos on the sides of the body. The orange adipose fin helps distinguish the fry from other species. Size: length to 27 inches, weight to 22 pounds. Saltwater browns can top 40 pounds.

Life Facts

Native to northern Europe, browns were introduced onto the U.S. waters in 1900. Browns can thrive and survive in warm waters (65–75 degrees F), lower oxygen levels, and more turbid waters than other species of trout. They feed at night and early morning and tend to stay in deep pools of streams or under banks during the day. They grow fast and big, with males growing faster than females in general. Spawning occurs from October through December. Spring and seepage waters are necessary for trout eggs to survive winter water temperatures. Browns are considered to be the most difficult trout to catch.

Cutthroat Trout

Common names: sea-run cutthroat, harvest trout

Description

The common name comes from the red or orange slash marks on each side of the lower jaw. These marks, along with dark spots on the back, sides, and fins, are often missing on the fish in salt water or fresh from the sea. Body color is generally dark olive on the back, highly variable on the sides, silver in salt water or fresh from the sea. Size: length to 20 inches, weight to 5 pounds.

Life Facts

The coastal cutthroat is one of three cutthroat races, or sub-species, found in Washington. Cutthroat trout can be found in virtually all of our large and small unspoiled coastal streams, especially in the Rocky Mountain West. Sea-run forms are present within the inter-tidal zones (between the low and high tide marks) in most of our marine areas. They are late winter–early spring spawners,

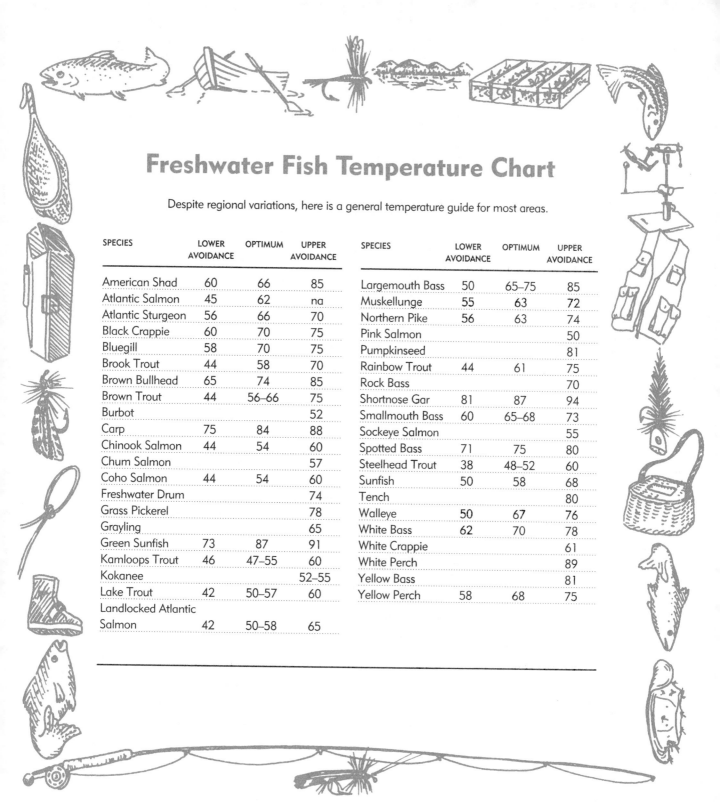

Freshwater Fish Temperature Chart

Despite regional variations, here is a general temperature guide for most areas.

SPECIES	LOWER AVOIDANCE	OPTIMUM	UPPER AVOIDANCE	SPECIES	LOWER AVOIDANCE	OPTIMUM	UPPER AVOIDANCE
American Shad	60	66	85	Largemouth Bass	50	65–75	85
Atlantic Salmon	45	62	na	Muskellunge	55	63	72
Atlantic Sturgeon	56	66	70	Northern Pike	56	63	74
Black Crappie	60	70	75	Pink Salmon			50
Bluegill	58	70	75	Pumpkinseed			81
Brook Trout	44	58	70	Rainbow Trout	44	61	75
Brown Bullhead	65	74	85	Rock Bass			70
Brown Trout	44	56–66	75	Shortnose Gar	81	87	94
Burbot			52	Smallmouth Bass	60	65–68	73
Carp	75	84	88	Sockeye Salmon			55
Chinook Salmon	44	54	60	Spotted Bass	71	75	80
Chum Salmon			57	Steelhead Trout	38	48–52	60
Coho Salmon	44	54	60	Sunfish	50	58	68
Freshwater Drum			74	Tench			80
Grass Pickerel			78	Walleye	50	67	76
Grayling			65	White Bass	62	70	78
Green Sunfish	73	87	91	White Crappie			61
Kamloops Trout	46	47–55	60	White Perch			89
Kokanee		52–55		Yellow Bass			81
Lake Trout	42	50–57	60	Yellow Perch	58	68	75
Landlocked Atlantic Salmon	42	50–58	65				

although sea-run typically ascend rivers from late summer through fall. Puget Sound cutthroat tend to move into streams later than Juan de Fuca Strait and ocean cutthroat. Most salt water–caught cutthroat are taken within the inter-tidal zone.

Lake Trout

Common names: mackinaw, laker, salmon trout, gray trout, landlocked salmon, togue

Description

The body is dark olive to gray-green above, blue-gray to greenish-bronze below, covered with light (whitish), irregular spots. Leading edges of pectoral, pelvic, and anal fins are reddish-orange with a narrow whitish margin, and the caudal fin (tail) is deeply forked. Size: length to 50 inches, weight to 120 pounds.

Life Facts

Lake trout prefer water temperatures of around 50 degrees, although they will venture into warmer water on occasion. Lake trout are solitary and do not school or congregate except during spawning season. Spawning occurs in fall from mid-October to early December. Lake trout do not build beds but simply scatter eggs among the rocks. Males do not defend territories, unlike males of other species of trout and salmon. Although they inhabit deep waters (60–300 feet), they can be easily caught.

Rainbow Trout

Common names: steelhead, rainbow, bow, redsides

Description

Rainbows are generally metallic-blue above, shading to silvery-white on the belly. Small black spots on the back side, dorsal and caudal fins are more prominent in resident freshwater populations than in sea-run rainbow (steelhead). Freshwater rainbows also exhibit a distinctive red band on the sides that is not seen on fish fresh from the sea (but steelhead assume this coloration after some time in fresh water). The absence of orange-red slash marks on the underside of the jaw and lack of teeth near the base of the tongue

are good ways to distinguish rainbows from cutthroat, although cutthroat fresh from salt water often do not show slash marks. Size: length to 42 inches, weight to 42 pounds.

Life Facts

Rainbows prefer cool water, less than 70 degrees, with plenty of oxygen. If surface water temperature rises above 70 degrees, they will retreat to deeper and cooler water if enough oxygen is present. Steelhead spend one to three years in fresh water before going to the ocean for two to three more years (very rarely four years) before returning to spawn.

Dreaming of Salmon? Try Your Backyard

Growing up in East Texas, I dreamed of hooking huge Chinook salmon and trout in the Pacific Northwest. But I had to be content with sunfish, bluegill, catfish, crappie, and the occasional bass. There were no trout, no grayling, no salmon. I had to satisfy my fishing desires with bank fishing under a straw hat.

Fly-fishing brought to mind glorious images of wading a clear stream where colorful, spotted brookies broke the surface for floating mayflies. Oh, to be among the privileged trout and salmon fly-fishing elite!

If you live in an area that's too warm for brook trout, don't despair! In all likelihood, streams and rivers near your home are abundant. Perhaps cool and warm water fill creeks, rivers, ponds, and lakes all loaded with wild game fish. You may want to take another look at spots that may have been your favorites in the past.

With just a few tackle and fly modifications, you can catch an amazing variety of fish on flies. In East Texas alone, there are largemouth bass, smallmouth bass, spotted bass, white bass, bluegill, and at least eight or ten species of sunfish.

Farm ponds are everywhere and have a definite place in the world of fishing. Grumping bullfrogs, blue herons, and a

John Gierach's View on Fat Trout

This famed sportsman says every fisherman wants to catch big trout. "It seems to me there are two ways to get big trout. One is to spend thousands of dollars to fly into some remote wilderness camp and, once there, do what the guide tells you to do. The other is to fish for big trout close to home. It's an article of faith among anglers that there's always a trout in the water you're fishing that's bigger than the biggest one you have caught so far. As articles of faith go, that's truer than most."

variety of ducks and geese that descend here seem only slightly annoyed by the fisherman's presence.

If you miss a strike or lose a bluegill in the farm pond, you'll find it much less important than losing a bonefish, tarpon, muskie, or salmon. The quiet, almost lawn-chair fishing is available in most anyone's backyard, if you take time to look.

Bluegill is a beautiful fish, and the setting is one that only nature can provide. From the quiet lapping of waters against the shoreline to the hapless hopper that an ever-hungry bluegill smacks from the surface, you may find the fishing less intense and the rewards smaller in size, but enjoyment cannot be measured in such a way.

But that's just the beginning. Also waiting to be caught on your flies are drum, sauger, channel catfish, carp, chub, gar, bowfin, freshwater herring, shad, and bullfrogs! What fun! All these species have their own special qualities.

So do yourself a favor this season: Try your flies in your "home" waters. Chances are, you'll find more elbow room, have more success, and perhaps even more fun fly-fishing. You'll definitely be able to get more fishing in!

Study Shows What People Fish For and Where

Bass and trout fishing are the focus of two reports developed by the U.S. Fish and Wildlife Service. "Black Bass Fishing in the U.S." and "Trout Fishing in the U.S." include information on demographic characteristics of bass and trout anglers as well as participation levels and how they compare with other freshwater fishing statistics.

The new reports highlight information specifically related to bass and trout fishing. This information is compared to the number of anglers who participated in any type of freshwater fishing; how many days they spent angling; and their age, gender, and education and income levels. The reports also include breakdowns of anglers by geographic region and population density. All data in the bass and trout reports represent freshwater anglers sixteen and older in the United States.

Black bass (including largemouth, smallmouth, and spotted bass) appealed to more anglers than any other fish the survey covered. Of the 30 million freshwater anglers in the United States, 12.9 million, or 43 percent, fished for bass. Overall patterns show bass anglers tend to be male, have above average incomes, and live in southern and urban areas.

More than 9 million, or 30 percent, of freshwater anglers fished for trout. Patterns for trout anglers show they also tend to be male, have above average incomes, and most often live in the western or northeastern regions of the country.

Eighty percent of bass anglers and 77 percent of trout anglers were male. For freshwater fishing overall, 8.4 million women fished, representing 27 percent of all anglers.

Anglers fished for bass on more than 158 million days for an average of 12 days, while trout anglers fished on more than 81 million days for an average of 9 days. This means bass were sought on 37 percent of all freshwater fishing days and trout on 19 percent.

Bass fishing was most popular in Florida, Maryland, Oklahoma, Rhode Island, Massachusetts, and Delaware. In the South, bass fishing is pursued most often in Alabama, Arkansas, Louisiana, North

4 9

Carolina, and Texas. Trout fishing was most favored in Colorado, Idaho, Montana, Utah, and Wyoming.

Bass and trout anglers' participation rates increased with their education levels. Anglers with up to eleven years of education participated in bass fishing at a rate of 37 percent; those with twelve years of education, 43 percent; those with one to three years of college education, 45 percent; and those with four or more years of college, 45 percent. For trout fishing, anglers with up to eleven years of education participated at a rate of 23 percent; those with twelve years of education, 23 percent; those with one to three years of college education, 34 percent; and those with at least four years of college, 35 percent.

Overall, freshwater anglers had higher annual incomes than the national average of about $30,000. Fifty-four percent of bass anglers and 55 percent of trout anglers came from households with incomes above the national average.

The participation rate of freshwater anglers in bass fishing was highest for the $25,000 to $29,900 income bracket (46 percent), while the highest participation rate for trout fishing was in the $75,000 or more income category (39 percent).

People in rural areas participated in freshwater fishing almost twice as much as urban residents. However, bass fishing was about the same for all population density categories, which included rural, small city or town, or big city or urban area. The popularity of trout fishing, as judged by participation rates, was similar for rural and small-city residents but much greater among urban dwellers.

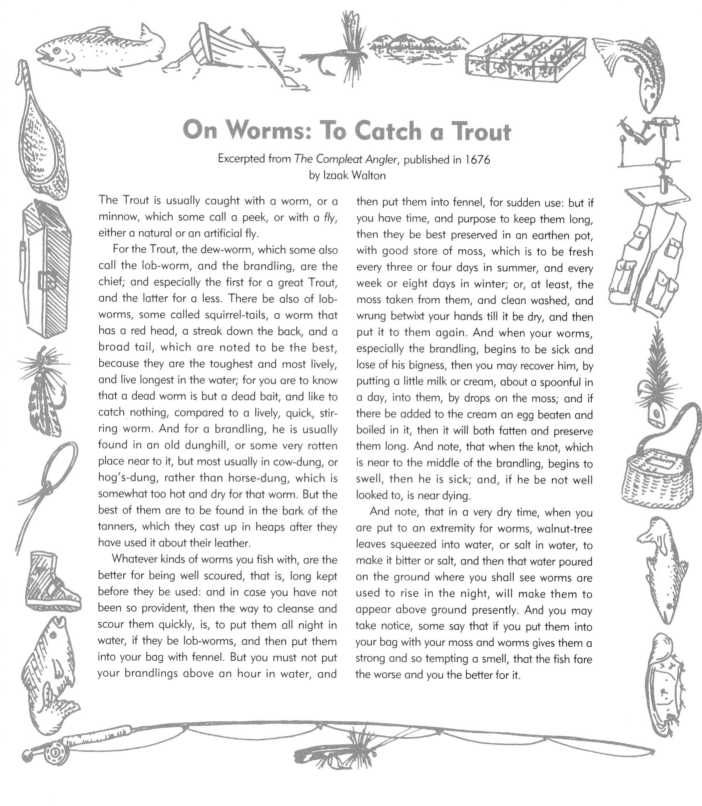

On Worms: To Catch a Trout

Excerpted from *The Compleat Angler*, published in 1676
by Izaak Walton

The Trout is usually caught with a worm, or a minnow, which some call a peek, or with a *fly*, either a natural or an artificial fly.

For the Trout, the dew-worm, which some also call the lob-worm, and the brandling, are the chief; and especially the first for a great Trout, and the latter for a less. There be also of lob-worms, some called squirrel-tails, a worm that has a red head, a streak down the back, and a broad tail, which are noted to be the best, because they are the toughest and most lively, and live longest in the water; for you are to know that a dead worm is but a dead bait, and like to catch nothing, compared to a lively, quick, stirring worm. And for a brandling, he is usually found in an old dunghill, or some very rotten place near to it, but most usually in cow-dung, or hog's-dung, rather than horse-dung, which is somewhat too hot and dry for that worm. But the best of them are to be found in the bark of the tanners, which they cast up in heaps after they have used it about their leather.

Whatever kinds of worms you fish with, are the better for being well scoured, that is, long kept before they be used: and in case you have not been so provident, then the way to cleanse and scour them quickly, is, to put them all night in water, if they be lob-worms, and then put them into your bag with fennel. But you must not put your brandlings above an hour in water, and then put them into fennel, for sudden use: but if you have time, and purpose to keep them long, then they be best preserved in an earthen pot, with good store of moss, which is to be fresh every three or four days in summer, and every week or eight days in winter; or, at least, the moss taken from them, and clean washed, and wrung betwixt your hands till it be dry, and then put it to them again. And when your worms, especially the brandling, begins to be sick and lose of his bigness, then you may recover him, by putting a little milk or cream, about a spoonful in a day, into them, by drops on the moss; and if there be added to the cream an egg beaten and boiled in it, then it will both fatten and preserve them long. And note, that when the knot, which is near to the middle of the brandling, begins to swell, then he is sick; and, if he be not well looked to, is near dying.

And note, that in a very dry time, when you are put to an extremity for worms, walnut-tree leaves squeezed into water, or salt in water, to make it bitter or salt, and then that water poured on the ground where you shall see worms are used to rise in the night, will make them to appear above ground presently. And you may take notice, some say that if you put them into your bag with your moss and worms gives them a strong and so tempting a smell, that the fish fare the worse and you the better for it.

FISHING LICENSE

CHAPTER 4

Reading the Water

Have you ever thought that fish use the water for everything? If they're not hiding behind boulders, they're darting out into the current to grab a tasty bug or worm before it floats by. Most of the time, though, they are looking for a "lie," or position, that combines safety and protection from predators and a steady stream of food. These "food alleys" are often found on the lee side of boulders and at crosscurrents. Here the fish can expend minimum effort for maximum gain.

Knowing where the fish are feeding comes from learning basic skills in reading the water. Rivers and streams have different depths, rocks both submerged and protruding, overhanging brush, weed beds, logs, debris, even temperature changes. These all provide clues about where fish are likely to be. Consistently successful anglers remain flexible from cast to cast in determining what flies to cast as well as where the fish are taking them.

In fast-moving currents (riffles), rocks help break up the current's flow. The oxygen-rich turbulence around rocks provides ample food. Fish hang out both in front of large rocks as the current veers around them and behind, where the water is still and food can accumulate. Around boulders and rocks it's more important that your flies are large enough and float well than that they exactly match real insects.

Areas between calm and faster water develop pronounced current edges, which anglers call seams. The faster water is also broken water—that is, the surface of the water is not smooth. That gives the fish a certain amount of protection from their enemies.

Salmonids (salmon and trout) prefer fast-water runs, so riffles are good places to fish. Others are:

- Eddies. These form in the bends of a river and around objects that break the current. Food becomes trapped, making eddies a good holding area for game fish.
- Eroded banks. These sites provide protection for fish.
- The mouth of a tributary. The junction of two currents creates a back eddy and pool.

Types of Trout Streams

There are three basic types of trout streams: freestone rivers, tailwater fisheries, and spring creeks. Freestone rivers are typified by free-running waterways, whereas tailwater fisheries are formed downstream from dams where cold water is released from underneath a large body of water. Spring creeks, like the one at Rocky Ford, Washington, are formed when one or more sources of underground springwater provide the main flow of water. The temperature of a freestone river and its tributaries fluctuates dramatically with the change of seasons. Spring creeks and tailwater fisheries have relatively stable water temperatures.

Each stream type has its own fish food patterns and topography, and may require specific presentation techniques. A "gin-clear" spring creek, for example, requires the angler to set the fly down as lightly as a feather so the fish don't get spooked. As you gain more experience, similarities and differences in water types and in fishing techniques become easier to recognize. Your local fly shop can offer invaluable advice when it comes to fishing the various types of streams in your area.

- Deep shaded pools. These provide sanctuaries during the day and good feeding at dusk.
- The base of minor rapids. Here fish find everything they need: an eddy, sufficient depth, lots of oxygen. It's a natural trap for food.
- Pools and deeper areas with slow-moving currents. Food collects here too. Cast to the edges rather than the center of the pool.

Overhanging brush and trees draw fish because grasshoppers and other terrestrials drop into the water after a stiff breeze or gust of wind. These provide tasty meals for the underwater denizens. Aquatic insects, after hatching, often take to nearby brush before mating over the water. The trout seem to know this and wait patiently for female insects to hover above the water, dip to the surface to deposit their eggs, then collapse. These dead insects cover the water's surface ready for the hungry mouths of waiting trout.

A typical river may have only three different types of insects hatching, but those three types may comprise as many as ten to fifteen different species each. Thankfully, an exact match isn't necessary. All you need do is look in the surrounding brush and along the shallows to see what's flying around. Look for the type of insect and color first. Other areas of interest to anglers are weed beds, especially those in spring creeks. Crustaceans and insects breed here, and fish find ample protection from predators.

Lies, or fish haunts, are deep water, undercut banks, and log jams. These provide relief from swift currents and shelter for fish, which seek out these areas when hooked. Deep water and broken surface water offer protection, and rocky bottoms reduce the force of the currents. Trout tend to hold at the upstream edges of pockets and watch for food drifting in the currents.

During an insect hatch, or at other times when large amounts of food are adrift, fish move into feeding lies. These are usually found in shallow water, the tail of a pool, and the shallows near the banks. If you're patient and the fish don't see you (especially in clear water), you'll likely be rewarded when the fish move to these areas for food.

The confluence of two currents is also host to food organisms, and provide excellent feeding areas for trout. Two streams joining into one create a confusion of upwelling, plunging, and crosscurrents that scatter jumbled food.

When fishing streams and rivers, try to cover all of the water. Carefully fish every likely spot. Cast your streamer downstream near rocks, logs, and undercut banks, places that hold trout. Cast your weighted nymphs upstream, letting them swing down with the current and bounce over the bottom. If that doesn't work, try fishing wet flies across- and downstream, perhaps with two or three patterns on the leader so the fish have a wider choice.

Lakes are not much different from pools. If there is no insect activity taking place on the surface, trout will usually stay out of sight in the deep, sheltering water. Flooded trees offer them shelter. Since lake water doesn't move that much, trout move around in search of food. This means you need to be attuned to the feeding lanes,

which can be close to shelter and anywhere shallow water steeply drops off to deep water.

Trout also linger near channels where streams enter or leave the lake, edges of gravel bars, drop-offs, deadfalls, dams, and islands. Don't pass up a chance to work a fly around weed beds, the food and oxygen manufacturing centers of the lake. Trout move in to the shoreline toward dusk, and on windy days, when food is blown near the shore. If not spooked, trout will work close in.

Warm-water species of fish such as bass, pike, and walleye have the same patterns as cold-water fish like trout. A distinct difference, however, is their diet. Walleyes and bass feed largely on minnows and crayfish and move to feeding lies when these prey organisms are most active—usually from late evening until just after dawn. Schools of panfish like bluegills and crappies follow similar patterns.

In lakes, warm-water species will cruise in search of food, wandering in and out of weed beds, over sunken weeds, along cliffs and flooded timber, and around islands and places where shallow water drops off into deeper water. Here food, oxygen, and protection are most readily available and most suited to the murky inhabitants.

Knowing how to read lakes and cast for fish in them can be daunting, especially if the lake is large and unfamiliar to you. Early in the season look for shallow areas in sheltered bays, where the sun can warm the water and draw aquatic insects. Mid-season, check out bays where a breeze rippling the surface first brings food, then fish. The breeze breaks up the surface of the water, and the fish feel secure. You have a good chance of finding fish where shoreline trees hang over a shoal, or area of shallow water, where a hatch is likely to take place. Even better—the trees provide shade that shelters the fish.

It's easier to read the bottoms of streams and rivers. Lakes are a little more difficult. When fishing a lake, especially in a boat, you might want to use a depth finder—not to find fish but to determine the slope and consistency of the lake bottom. You could work a nymph along a weed bed beside a ledge, or heave a streamer along the gradual slope of a rocky ledge at the end of a bay, where the wind concentrates food. In the middle of the day, work the deeper

parts of the water column. At dawn and at dusk, fish the more shallow levels and even the surface.

How Fish Think

Trout have three basic needs: protection, water quality, and food. Trout are most wary of attack from above, the striking hawk or osprey. They also watch out for dangers in front of and below them. Trout spend a lot of time cruising beneath overhanging brush and near midstream rocks, which confound predators seeking fishy morsels. Primary predators of trout are man and various birds—the heron, cormorant, eagle, and hawk. The heron pokes the water and stabs for fish. Otters are also a threat.

Oxygen levels and water temperature are critical to fish. If you're fishing for trout in the summer, use your thermometer to see if water temperatures are too high, thereby depleting oxygen levels. Trout generally prefer water temperatures between 45 and 70 degrees; 61 is optimal for rainbow trout. Bass like it warmer, between 65 and 82 degrees. As cold-blooded creatures, fish depend on the water around them to regulate their body temperature. When the water is very cold or very warm, fish tend to be inactive and don't eat much.

Fish will expend the least amount of energy to find food. When fish are not feeding on the surface, look for them in feeder streams or inlets that dump in food and cool water with lots of fresh oxygen. Fish often congregate to feed at the stream's mouth. Other areas where fish lurk are near rocks and submerged structures, drop-offs, shelves, shade, and weed beds.

Fly-fishing has its share of frustrations. After a while, watching a 16-inch rainbow flick in the water, you might begin to think he is taunting you. After repeated attempts to lure him, the trout seems to be mocking you as he "escorts" your nymph downstream, maintaining a healthy distance. The key is persistence. And you must present the wily trout with what he's looking for. During periods such as a hatch, when swarms of similar insects float atop the water, the trout lock in the shape

What Do Fish Hear?

Fish don't hear as humans do, but they do have a form of hearing. Their "lateral line," a highly developed system of nerves that runs the length of their bodies, allows them to feel as much as hear vibrations in the water. You can see this line running down the side of the trout. The line also arches forward over the eye and along the lower jaw. This "ear line" hears in nearly the same range as man's.

Sounds generated in the water travel five times the speed of sound waves in the air, so anglers need to be light-footed while wading or walking the stream beds. Be careful not to grind gravel beneath your feet or plough through water as you wade.

But you *can* talk with your buddies. Conversation does not travel from the air into the water.

and color of food organisms and may refuse all objects of other dimensions or color. This selectivity often requires that the angler match the hatch with an artificial fly.

After protection and water quality, fish think food. Trout, especially, need to constantly feed. Among the thick weeds growing on the edges of streams and rivers are tiny scrumptious creatures fish love—creatures such as freshwater shrimp (scuds), chironomids, and caddisflies. On the edges of water lurking trout can expend the least amount of effort for the greatest gain, lying in wait to pick off scuds darting out of the weed beds.

Other times fish stay behind rocks and wait for insects, disoriented by the current, to float downstream and spin around a rock. Deer and other animals crossing streams can stir up insects and send them shooting downstream. In lake beds trout cruise the feeding lanes. Trout have personalities. Most don't move around much in streams, but some cruise up and down the waterways in search of food, especially around rocks.

Bass, on the other hand, are opportunistic and ambush their prey. For instance, if a bass sees a mouse on a limb, it will get into position and wait until the perfect opportunity to strike. Bass are often called the shark of fresh water.

What do you do on a stream or river that doesn't seem to have fish? First, remember how fish think. They tend to be (1) close to the bank for cover and food, (2) near the edges of currents—food flows in and out of fast- and slow-moving water and the trout rush to intercept the food, (3) in flat areas where it's easy to take in food on the top while largely remaining near the bottom for safety, and (4) in areas with natural cover.

Signs of Fish

If the fish are surfacing, they will "rise" and leave rings in the water where they have surfaced. Rings or bulges indicate a feeding fish. Of course, if you are fishing in rapids, or if the fish are feeding on subsurface insects, this isn't going to help.

Game fish such as bass make pronounced swirls on the water. Trout are more subtle. Fish will leap out of the water to catch

Musings from John Muir

Everything is flowing—going somewhere—animals and so-called lifeless rocks as well as water. Thus the snow flows fast or slow in grand beauty-making glaciers and avalanches; the air in majestic floods carrying minerals, plant leaves, seeds, spores, with streams of music and fragrance; water streams carrying rocks. . . . While the stars go streaming through space pulsed on and on forever like blood . . . in Nature's warm heart.

Another glorious Sierra day in which one seems to be dissolved and absorbed and sent pulsing onward we know not where. Life seems neither long nor short, and we take no more heed to save time or make haste than do the trees and stars. This is true freedom, a good practical sort of immortality.

When in making our way through a forest we hear the loud boom of a waterfall, we know that the stream is descending a precipice. If a heavy rumble and roar, then we know it is passing over a craggy incline. But not only are the existence and size of these larger characters of its channel proclaimed, but all the others.

Some portions of its channel will appear smooth, others rough, here a slope, there a vertical wall, here a sandy meadow, there a lake-bowl, and the young river speaks and sings all the smaller characters of the smooth slope and downy hush of meadow as faithfully as it sings the great precipices and rapid inclines, so that anyone who has learned the language of running water will see its character in the dark.

insects flying above the surface. If insects lie on the water's surface tension, trout may "porpoise"—that is, expose their back and dorsal fins. *Swirling* in the water is caused by fish feeding below the surface; *dimpling* occurs when trout feed on dead or inactive insects on the water surface.

Here are a few other indicators of what to look for:

Sipping—sipping occurs when the fish are feeding on the surface. They wait in the current until they sight a passing insect. After zeroing in on the target, a trout will drift back under the insect to feed. Feeding in this manner leaves a trademark ring on the surface. After the trout has risen, it will most often return to where it was waiting and hover there until another meal is spotted.

Keep this in mind when casting for a fish that has just surfaced: casting at the location of the rings is probably going to be well behind the fish. The trout could have been drifting for 10 to 15 feet before it surfaced, so cast well ahead of the rise in order to present the fly where the fish can see it. Use a dry fly or a floating nymph to target the surface film. In faster water, trout will remain nearly stationary in the current (and not drift along under their food before taking it), tipping themselves upward ever so briefly to grab floating

insects off the surface as they whiz by. Mother nature will conserve energy whenever possible.

Jumping trout—the full body of a trout leaping from the surface may indicate that it is feeding on emerging insects. As an insect is emerging, the trout attacks as it nears the surface. It could also be after a low-flying insect that is depositing eggs in the water. Use wet patterns such as nymphs, larvae, and pupes. Dry flies can be skimmed along the surface.

Feeding off the bottom—if you can spot fish tails on the surface, it probably means they are bottom feeding, and nymphs and wet flies are the way to go. However, porpoising trout can also feed just beneath the surface.

Through your polarized sunglasses, walk up and down the stream or across a bridge or log to see if fish are hiding around midstream rocks, on the edges, or under low-lying branches. Lift up the rocks to see what kinds of prey live on the bottom. Pick out a handful of subsurface plant life, lay it on the ground and go through it. What's living there can provide clues to what types of wet flies or nymphs to use. If you see lots of freshwater shrimp, tie on a scud.

The various ways that trout rise to the water's surface indicate how selective they are in their feeding activities. Study their rise patterns so you will know how they feed.

Partial rise—you see the trout come part way up to look at the fly but then go back down. The trout never gets close enough to strike at the fly. Essentially, it comes to get a better look, then quickly refuses.

Simple rise—the normal rise where you see the trout come up to take the fly. If he misses, it was probably a late refusal. The trout is facing upstream when he takes the fly.

Compound rise—the trout comes up to the fly but does not take it. He floats with the fly downstream before either taking or refusing it. After taking the fly he can still swim forward back to his lie.

Complex rise—the trout comes up to the fly and floats downstream with it as in a compound rise. His body is turned vertically underneath the fly as he inspects it. He continues to inspect the fly so he is turned downstream before he decides whether to take the fly or not. If he takes the fly, he takes it facing downstream. After the take or refusal, the trout must turn around before he can swim back to his lie.

Where the Lunkers Lie

People who catch more fish are those who know how to read the water. Large game fish, or lunkers, want cover, shade or low light, and good food availability. So look for deep-plunge pools in the shade of a cliff or a stand of trees under which a big trout can seek refuge. Cover can be almost anything: a fallen tree, a logjam, deep water, deep shade, cloudy skies, or broken water. Centuries ago, fly fishermen prayed for enough wind to disturb the water surface and to conceal themselves from the trout.

No trout wants to work too hard, so he'll want a fast current carrying food next to a slower current that he can rest in. Bankside currents are usually slower than those out in the middle of a stream, and the current is slower along the bottom than at the surface.

One way to find fish is to look for the most difficult places to fish, something like a deep, shady slot overhung with alders way over on the far side of a ripping fast current. Lots of fishermen pass up spots that are too hard to get to or where the cast is too difficult; consequently, that water is lightly fished and is more likely to hold a nice trout.

Fish rising for insect life on the surface betray their exact location. This makes the fisherman's job considerably easier. Each cast can be placed right in the feeding zone. The peak feeding activity of any hatch period rarely lasts long. The key is to use this precious time wisely. Pay close attention to the head and tail of pools and shallow to medium runs. These areas can be fished more quickly and efficiently than deeper water. Pay particular attention to the head of a pool you know holds fish. During a hatch, trout seem to stack up just below the riffle as it tumbles into a pool. You will probably not see many rises in this broken water, but the fish will attack if a wet fly or nymph rushes by.

Stop, Look, and Think in Spring

One mistake anglers make in besieging spring waters is to quickly inflate their float tubes and shove off without reading the environment. With more anglers competing for space on trout waters, western stillwaters continue to gain in popularity. Many of those who hit the water, though, don't really know how to fish them effectively. Stillwaters are not always easy, and tactics used by experts can benefit both the more competent and the novice fly fisher.

Especially in the West, countless stillwaters provide tremendous trout fishing. Spring is when most of these waters are at their very best. Many seem to "come to life" by the beginning of March and are in full swing by April. After the long winter dormancy, areas below lakes and streams spring to life. Aquatic plants once again start to grow in the shallows and insect life germinates. As their metabolism increases in the spring, trout begin consuming just about any food item that comes their way.

Surroundings offer clues that can give you valuable insights into what fish are foraging for. Being keen to these clues, having an eye for detail, can mean the difference between catching fish or simply admiring nature. Check the shoreline vegetation for insect life. Simply looking around you can reveal plenty. Are there insects in the air? What do you see in the water? Are there scuds, nymphs, or leeches visible? And if there are, what size and color are they? These are things that will give you a definite advantage once you enter the water.

If bugs are not flying, an insect hatch may have just concluded. You might need to try subsurface fishing. That's why it's helpful to have two reels on hand—one with floating line, the other with sinking line. You might get by with only one line and catch plenty of fish if conditions are just right. But this is rarely the case.

What Makes an Angler?

It is diligence, and observation, and practice, and an ambition to be the best in the art, that must do it. I once heard one say, "I envy not him that eats better meat than I do; nor him that is richer, or that wears better clothes than I do: I envy nobody but him, and him only, that catches more fish than I do". And such a man is like to prove an angler; and this noble emulation I wish to all young anglers.

—Izaak Walton

Next, study the lake or stream. Are there cliffs or rock ledges entering the water? Do you observe submerged weed beds? How about cattails or reeds? Are there color changes in the water indicating shallow or deep sections? Is the shoreline uniform, or are there coves and points? These physical observations can help you decide where to start your prospecting and, combined with your observations of insect life, can give you a good idea of what fly to start with. In other words, if at all possible, make your plan of attack while you're still onshore.

When you enter the water, don't stop observing. Springtime hatches or feeding frenzies can start at a moment's notice. It's all too easy to keep fishing one of your favorite flies with anticipation, even if it's drawing a blank. If fish are rising all around you, they are feeding on something. If your fly isn't working, make it your mission to find out what is.

Trout are not deep thinkers. They can be found and caught if you keep a few points in mind. Water temperature, availability of food, oxygen, and weather—though ever changing—are a few factors that influence where you can find trout in a lake. Where the trout were "last week," and what they were hitting, might be completely different from what's going on this week. What trout prefer can change from one day, even one hour, to the next.

It's critical that you stay observant and that you adapt if you want to be good at this game. Remember, at least 90 percent of the trout's feeding time occurs under the surface. It only stands to reason, then, that if you emulate subsurface aquatic food items your success rate will be much higher than if you used only adult, top-water patterns.

With the growing popularity of still-waters, some say that fishing isn't as good as it used to be. Perhaps we as anglers just have to try harder. You can give yourself an edge over the shore angler if you use some kind of floating device: boat or float tube.

Many anglers make the mistake of continuing to fish the same water with whatever fly they are using and don't take the time to change lines, flies, leaders, or presentation. It's enjoyable to use a favorite fly, sometimes even long after trout have clearly shunned it. But a willingness to consider the environment and change tactics—to adapt—will result in catching fish. Sometimes you need only downsize your tippet to avoid spooking the fish or to give your fly a more natural drift. Other times you may need to fish only in the early morning or late evening. Sometimes night fishing is the answer.

In a world with ever increasing population, and an ever increasing demand on our nation's fisheries, more people are turning to the stillwaters for one reason or another, often because their favorite stream is getting too crowded. Some of the more popular stillwaters are now facing crowding as well as other problems. All of the man-made problems can be rectified with common courtesy and common sense. The West is covered with stillwaters. If we take care of them, they will be around for our angling enjoyment, hopefully, forever.

FISHING LICENSE

CHAPTER 5

The Fly and the Life of an Insect

You don't need to be a junior entomologist to become a good fly fisherman, but you do need to understand the life cycles of a few aquatic foods. Dragonfly nymphs, damselfly nymphs, midges, leeches, scuds, snails, and mayflies are major food items. Your flies need to match all stages of their lives, especially the under-water stages, since those are the ones that trout eat most often.

You should know not only what these food items look like, but when and where the trout are likely to encounter them, and just how these foods move in the water. Mimicking the natural move-ments is sometimes as important as choosing the right imitation to begin with. Finding the right fly for the right day is one of the first and most important tasks of a fly fisher. And it all begins with insights into the staple of a fish's diet: insects.

There's a deep-down sense of satisfaction in knowing a wild fish finds a fly you've selected (or tied yourself) appealing—so much so that he actually thinks it's real food. All kinds of flies have been cre-ated to imitate the shape and color of a myriad of insect life. No small feat, considering that entomologists estimate that more than 700,000 species of insect life have been identified and named! Fortunately, all we need to do, especially beginners, is to choose generic representations that we need most of the time.

Virtually every type of freshwater environment—whether a churning river, crystalline lake, or small pond—holds some type of aquatic insect that spends a large portion of its life in the water and lays eggs on the water or in it. For example, the mayfly is to trout what raw meat is to a tiger or eucalyptus leaves to a koala. Someone once said, if it weren't for mayflies, fly-fishing as we know it would probably not exist. References to artificial flies that imitate mayflies date back to 1496, a full five centuries ago.

Mayflies are an important link in the freshwater food chain. Present in running water as well as lakes and ponds, they are one of the most common orders of aquatic insects. Biologists estimate there may be nearly 700 species of mayflies present in North America, ranging in size from a few millimeters to almost 2 inches in length.

Beginning fly fishers often find it helpful to understand various stages in the precarious lives of insects. In the following sections we take a closer look at the insects that fish find most delectable.

Mayfly

Mayflies are born on the bottoms of streams and in stillwaters. After hatching from an egg, a mayfly spends about a year under the water as a nymph. During that year the nymph continually molts, shedding its armorlike skin for the next stage. To match an artificial fly to this stage of nymph, check under rocks to see what kinds of nymphs inhabit the water. Colors range from olive to brown.

After a year below water, mayfly nymphs rise to the surface to shed their armor, dry their new wings, and fly away. Emerging mayflies often struggle to break through the water's surface film, or tension. Trout tune in to this struggle and often attack the emerging hatch in a feeding frenzy. At the moment of emergence, mayflies are very vulnerable, and fish feed aggressively both on the nymphs as they make their way to the surface or shoreline and on the winged adult insects waiting on the surface for their wings to dry sufficiently for them to fly away.

When a mayfly emerges from the water, it unfurls its gray wings and floats on top of the water until the wings dry. This is called the *dun* stage. As soon as the wings dry, the mayfly flies to nearby trees, where its body changes again. Within hours, the dun has transformed into a spinner. On glassy wings, spinners have one purpose: mating. Females hover above the water, dip to its surface to deposit their eggs, then collapse. Dead spinners fill the water's surface film and drift downstream to the waiting trout.

Watch the natural environment to see what types of insects are prevalent and also how they move under or on the surface of the water. Use your imitations to match their size and color as well as movements. You will not see a live mayfly, for instance, creating ripples or drag on the water. Be sure your imitation doesn't either.

Dry fly imitation
of adult mayfly

Nymphs
- three fringed tails, all the same size • two long antennae • large gills on the abdomen • mottled tan, olive or pale green also light to dark gray

Dun (adult):
- a dull cast to their colors of almost black to mottled gray • their upright, opaque wings are darkly speckled • prominent eyes • two or three elongated tails

Spinner (reproductive stage):
- a glossy almost black to mottled gray in color • translucent wings, likened to those of a sailboat, are held upright as they cannot fold them over their backs • slender abdomen

Nymphs:
- medium brown to light tan in color

  Dun (adults): brown body, solid white wings.

Spinner (reproductive):
- often have a creamy brown-white body. Translucent wings. More slender body.

Eggs: female spinners dip the tips of their abdomens on the water surface or just below it to release the eggs which gradually sink to the bottom where the larvae hatch.

Larvae: after several molts, the larvae or aquatic nymphs swim to the surface where they hatch into the adult (dun).

Dun: prime time for emergence seems to be between late morning and mid-afternoon. The hatch may take from a few days to several weeks depending on the length of day, angle of sunlight, and water temperature. As the nymphs rise they swim for 2 to 4 inches, then pause before continuing.

Spinner: After a span of up to forty-eight hours, the dun will molt its outer skin and the spinner will emerge to begin the

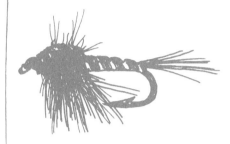

Imitation of mayfly nymph

cycle again, swarming and mating in flight then depositing eggs on the water's surface—after which they die. A few days after the mating the males will also die.

Food and Habitat

Nymphs feed on organic and vegetable matter that has settled on the lake bottom. They also feed on algae, diatoms, and sometimes small insect larvae. The duns and spinners do not feed.

Nymphs can survive in a wide variety of habitats—from alpine lakes up to 13,000 feet in elevation to lowland stillwaters. The most important requirement is an abundance of food—organic and vegetable matter that has settled on the lake bottom. They also feed on algae, diatoms, and sometimes small insect larvae. The mats of vegetation, rocky or woody debris, also serve as cover. Habitat will be shallow or shoreline areas not usually found in over 22 feet of water. Water should be relatively clear.

Fishing Techniques

There are a variety of signs to look for:

- Fish often target immature nymphs who leave their cover of dense vegetation. When it appears there is no action on the surface, it may indicate that the fish are concentrating their efforts below the surface. When the emerging nymphs are closer to the surface the fish will show bulging rises, often with part of their back showing—floating lines are effective here.
- If you see both the head and tail of the fish "sharking" through the water, there is a good chance they are feeding on nymphs that are lying on the surface waiting to emerge as duns. Splashes will occur as the fish chase newly emerged duns rising from the surface. Lazy bulging rise forms indicate they are scooping up the exhausted and dead spinners floating on the surface. After their egg-laying is over, a "dead drift" with a floating line and spinner pattern often yields results.

- A light breeze and overcast skies often herald a good mayfly hatch. Dry lines with long leaders or slow sinking lines are best for the emerging nymphs. Dead drift a nymph on a floating line. Start by casting at 45 degrees to the current, and then letting the fly drift naturally downstream. As the fly nears the end of its drift, tension on the line created by the current will start to swing the fly toward the surface—just like the real thing.

Recommended fly patterns:
- For larvae (nymph): Tiny Terror, Little Green, Copper Creek, Western Brown, Halfback
- For dun: Tom Thumb, Mayfly Dun, Blue Dun, Green Mayfly
- For spinner: Mayfly Spinner

Other fly patterns are Royal Wulff, Green Drake Wulff, Duns, Spinners, Cahills, March Browns, and small Hexagenias. Don't forget about nymphs. Emerging flies can cause a feeding frenzy on or slightly below the surface film. Try some floating nymphs to utilize this specific area.

Caddisfly (Sedge)

Common Names: caddis, caddisfly, sedge, shadfly, periwinkle, alderflies

Small mothlike insects, caddisflies flaunt their trademark folded V-shape wings. Larvae are wormlike with six legs near the front and often build small cases for protection. After about a year, they pupate. There they remain for several weeks until ready to emerge to the surface. Once on the surface they molt and fly off as adults.

Fly patterns include various colors and hair type including elk and deer. Stimulators and parachute relatives work well. A good "meaty"-looking fly will work well in most caddis hatches. For nymph fishing try Beadheads and elk-hair nymphs. Depending on where you're fishing, different larva and pupa patterns work well. The smaller pupae might be harder to see in turbulent waters.

#1 larva

Sedges are the aquatic cousins to butterflies and moths. Indeed, the adult sedge looks much like a moth except that it doesn't have the scaly wings or the siphon tube of the moth. Many names, such as hellgrammite, are erroneously applied to the sedge.

Life Cycle

Caddis go through the egg, larva, pupa, and adult stages. Adult mating usually occurs on the ground or among shoreline vegetation. After fertilization the female skims over the lake surface depositing eggs. The eggs, often bright green and usually laid in strands, sink to the bottom and hatch into larvae. The young larvae then form their cocoonlike casings. The larva grows within its casing, which is remade or enlarged about five times before the larva pupates.

#2 pupa

About three weeks prior to emergence, the larva seals the entrance to the casing and pupates within. When developed, the pupa breaks the seal, crawls out, swims to the surface, and hatches into an adult. Pupal skins can be seen floating on the surface. Adults live from two weeks to two months. Most caddis hatches have one or two generations per year but some of the larger species take two years to complete a generation.

Larvae: In their larval stage the sedges are wrapped in their cocoonlike casings and are not normally found in the feeding samples of trout in our interior lakes. However, trout in streams and rivers seem to feed on the larvae more frequently as they become dislodged from the bottom and drift with the current. For the lake fly fisher, the sedge larvae are of little importance for imitating with flies.

Pupae: As the caddis pupa leaves the casing and swims to the surface it is one of the main food sources of the trout. Yet many fly fishers don't tie caddis pupa patterns, and the patterns tied often don't look much like a caddis pupa. About one quarter of the flies in my fly box are caddis pupa patterns of different sizes and colors. I believe that many fly patterns are often taken by the trout thinking it to be a caddis pupa.

When caddis first become available is the best time to fish the pupa patterns. Often, at this time of year, the larva has pupated and the pupa has crawled out of the casing but isn't quite ready to hatch. It will crawl around the lake

#3 adult

bottom as it waits for exactly the right hatching conditions. They are easy prey at this time and the trout will actively seek them out. To a lesser extent the same thing is happening throughout the remainder of the sedge season. When the pupae swim to the surface for hatching they are also easy prey and readily eaten by the trout.

Adults: Adults are usually taken while they are hatching and letting their wings dry, or when they return to the lake for laying eggs. How you present your fly in each of these circumstances is totally different. When the caddis is hatching, just let your dry fly sit on the surface and wait. Let it drift with the wind but don't retrieve it. When the sedge is laying eggs you will see it skimming over the water's surface. When you see this skimming or traveling of caddis is when you want to retrieve the dry fly at about the same speed as the actual caddis. In both these cases the dry fly will work better if there is a breeze or slight wind—as opposed to perfectly calm wind conditions.

Hatches: The first caddis hatches of the year vary with elevation; start watching for them about the last week in May. The numbers and frequency increase until about the last week in June or the first week in July and then steadily decrease for the remainder of the season. Hatches often occur in the late afternoon and evening and many are after dark.

Appearance

Larvae are grublike and hide within their protective casings, made by binding together small rocks, twigs, leaves, or other material. The materials and design determine the species of sedge. Within the casing the larva pupates. When developed, the pupa looks much like the adult but with underdeveloped wings. It has longish legs and antennae and a well-developed abdomen. The abdomen usually has eight segments and a row of gills along the sides. On many species the abdomen is wider at the posterior than near the thorax. With the smallish thorax, this gives the pupa a somewhat pyramidal shape. Adults are much like the pupa but with fully developed wings. The wings give the adult an even more pyramidal shape than the pupa. Some adults have wings that are transparent.

Size and Color

The adults of larger species will grow to about 30 mm (1¼ inches) in length, while some of the smaller relatives will not exceed 6 or 7 mm (¼ inch). On most of the interior lakes they average 12 to 18 mm (½ to ¾ inch). Pupae are much the same body size as adults.

The larva has a dark head with an abdomen generally cream-colored to light green within the casing. The pupa is commonly a dirty or khaki green to a very bright green. Various shades of brown are not uncommon. Adults generally have a greenish body with a mottled grayish color to the wings (like many moths). Some species have semitransparent wings, often tan to reddish-brown.

Movement

Larvae slowly crawl along the lake bottom carrying their portable casing. After the caddis pupates, the pupa crawls out of its casing and may immediately swim to the surface or spend some time on the lake bottom depending on its readiness for adulthood. At the surface the pupa breaks the water surface tension and is stationary for a couple of minutes while the adult breaks opens the pupal shell and hatches and dries its wings prior to taking flight. After mating, the adult female is back on the lake and skimming over the water surface while she lays her eggs. She is not flying but is actually running on the water surface tension.

Habitat

Caddisflies are able to withstand a wide variety of water conditions. However, they seem to prefer shallow, cool, well-oxygenated waters. A few sedges are predacious but most obtain food from algae, diatoms, plants, and animal materials that have settled to the lake bottom. These foods are more abundant and available around weed beds than a muddy or sandy bottom. Caddis are easy prey for the rainbow trout and their populations are among the first to decrease as trout populations increase. Trout readily feed on the adult and pupal stages as well as the larva.

Importance to Fly-Fishing

Daytime feeding samples show that 8 percent (varies by region) of the trout's daytime feed is on caddis. For fish feeding in the evening or at night, feeding samples rise to 19 percent of total food intake; therefore sedges are considered the second most important evening or nighttime food source. Only shrimp are more frequently consumed in the evening hours. Caddis are one of the last aquatic bugs to start hatching in the spring and one of the first to disappear in the fall. This means that during the time they are available to the trout they are one of the primary foods. Indeed, from the last week in June until about mid-July they are often the main food source of the trout.

Stonefly

Nymphs: 5–50 mm. in body length, two long antennae, eyes widely separated, gills usually found on the throat and the base of the legs and abdomen, three pairs of crablike legs with terminal tarsi with two tarsal claws, two separate pairs of wing pads, two long tails (cerci), over 460 species known to inhabit North America. Color is varied, however shades of yellow, orange, green, brown, and black are the most common. Quite often stoneflies are two toned.

#1 nymph

Eggs hatch into a nymph stage which, depending on the species, can last up to three years requiring up to twenty-five molts to develop completely. Stoneflies do not go through a pupae stage; therefore, their metamorphosis is considered incomplete.

Adults: Adult stoneflies look much the same as the nymphs except that their wings are folded flat over the back, often extended 10 to 20 percent past the tip of the abdomen, and they have two short tails (cerci).

Nymphs will crawl out of the stream onto a stone, tree branch, or log and remain there long enough to dry and split the nymphal case. The adults emerge from the exoskeleton, looking very much like nymphs with wings added, and then fly or

#2 adult

climb into nearby trees. Following their emergence, the adults mate (males attract the females by drumming their abdomens on a tree branch). Then the females start the life cycle over again by depositing their eggs back into the stream. Depending on the species, stonefly adults may live for several weeks.

Life Cycle

Eggs: Most female stoneflies skim the surface of the stream, dipping their abdomens in the water and releasing their eggs. Others crawl to the bottom of the stream and then release their eggs on submerged objects. Stoneflies are very clumsy fliers. During the egg-releasing procedure they cause quite a fluttering and splashing on the water surface. This immediately attracts the attention of hungry fish, especially steelhead.

Food and Habitat

Nymphs will feed on organic and vegetable matter found in the stream substrate. Some species are carnivorous, feeding on mayfly nymphs and other insect larvae.

Stonefly nymphs require well-oxygenated water so are found in rivers and streams among the rocks and bottom debris. A few species can be found in the rocky shoals of cold lakes.

Fishing Techniques

Nymphs are available to fish year round, are very poor swimmers, and prefer to crawl among the rocks on the river bottom using their clawed crablike legs. Quite often they lose their footing and drift helplessly down current, thereby at the mercy of fish. Fish often target nymphs as they attempt to crawl out of the water during emergence. In either case fishermen must imitate this action by keeping the fly near the bottom; this can be achieved by casting upstream or up and across and letting the fly sink and tumble with the current along the stream bottom. Adult female stoneflies, highly prized by fish, clumsily make contact with the water to deposit their eggs. This is an extremely important time for the dry fly fisherman. Imitating the fluttering, splashing movement of a female stonefly on the water surface often provokes a violent response from trout or steelhead.

Chironomid

Scientific name: Class—Insecta, Order—Diptera, Family—Chironomidae (over 2000 species) Common Names: bloodworm, midge, gnat

Chironomids are small, two-winged flies in the adult stage and are closely related to mosquitoes and chaoborus (phantom midge or glassworm). However, chironomids do not bite like mosquitoes. Because they are similar, I include the chaoborus in this discussion.

Life Cycle

Adults swarm and mate in flight. Most lay eggs singularly or in strings while skimming over the water's surface. Some species lay eggs directly on vegetation or bottom substrates. The eggs hatch into larvae and form mud tubes from bottom material and mucus. A few species, such as the bloodworm and glassworm, have free-swimming larvae. The larvae grow and develop into the pupal stage. When fully developed, the pupae wiggle their way to the lake surface. It often takes several minutes for the pupa to get through the surface tension of the water before it can hatch. The process of breaking open the pupal skin, the adult crawling out, drying its wings, and flying away is usually accomplished in less than a minute. Once hatched, the adults may live from a few hours to a couple of months before mating and dying.

Larvae: In their larval stage, only the free-swimming larvae (bloodworm and glassworm) are normally found in the feeding samples of the rainbow trout. Most other larvae stay in their mud tubes on the lake bottom and so there is no point in imitating them with flies. The transparent glassworm is almost impossible to imitate. Bloodworms, however, which are up to 3 percent of the trout's diet, should not be ignored. Retrieve the bloodworms much the same as you would a chironomid pupa and in the same types of water.

Pupae: To the fly fisher, the pupal stage is the most important point of chironomid development. Pupae leaving the bottom of the lake and traveling to the surface to hatch are most vulnerable to predation by trout. Even the largest trout, which actively feed on these pupae, are successfully fished throughout the year. Chironomid pupae should be fished on a dry line and the flies should be weighted. The retrieve should be very, very slow, even still. Vary your leader length to achieve the desired depth for the fly. Pupae can be found at most any depth in the lake, but the trout will feed on these more actively on the shoals and drop-offs. The color and size of the fly seem to be more important than whether the flies have ribbing or gills. Flies with or without the gills and/or ribbing seem to work equally well. Here is a hint that most fly fishers haven't yet picked up on when tying flies to imitate the chironomid pupa: make the bend and point of the hook appear as the tapering abdomen and tail part of the pupa rather than something the pupa is attached to. It will look like the pupa is in the curled position for wiggling to the surface. This is one of the few flies on which you can completely camouflage the hook.

Adults: Chironomid adults (or when chironomid are emerging into adults) are taken throughout the year by the rainbow trout. Most any of the very small dry flies will do as an imitation. Although taken by the trout, the adult chironomid is often more actively taken by the smaller fish than the larger fish. When presenting the adult, try to get an S shape in your leader (or even an arc) and retrieve with a long, slow, steady pull to imitate an adult skimming the surface laying eggs. Letting the fly just sit on the surface also works. For an emerging chironomid, try tying an unweighted pupa, but where the gills would normally be tied, insert a clump of deer hair (or other lighter-colored floating material) of about two-thirds the pupa length.

Hatches: Various species of chironomid hatch whenever there is water free of ice. Seasonal peaks occur from the third week in May to the second week in June and then steadily decline into the fall months. However, very large hatches of individual species can occur at most any time of the year. Chironomid larvae on the lake bottom will sometimes exceed 50,000 individuals per square meter and thus form major hatches. If you are fishing in a major hatch, use a fly that is slightly larger than the actual size of the pupa. For the fly

fisher, minor hatches often result in more fish than a major hatch. Hatches usually occur during the daylight hours but various species will hatch at night.

Appearance

The larvae have segmented bodies, are wormlike, and look much like a long skinny grub or maggot. This appearance gradually changes as they develop into pupae. The pupae develop an eye-spot and wing casing and most notably have feathery white gills near the head. The head and wing casing are usually one quarter to one third of the body length and the abdomen has seven or eight body segments. The adult looks like a mosquito with feathery antennae.

Size and Color

Pupae are up to 20 mm long (¾ inch) but average about 8 to 15 mm (¼ to ½ inch).

Pupae are usually black, brown, reddish-brown, or green but often come in a variety of other colors. Larvae tend to be cream colored or may have a greenish tinge. The bloodworm is a type of free-swimming chironomid larvae that stores oxygen in its blood and is thus blood red in color. The glassworm is a free-swimming larva of the chaoborus family is virtually transparent.

Movement

Free-swimming larvae, like the bloodworm, do just that. They crawl, float, or swim around the lake, but generally they tend to hide under rocks or rotting logs and remain fairly immobile. Most larvae build and stay inside a mud tube on the lake bottom and don't move very far from that. When the larvae develop into pupae they leave their mud tubes or hiding places, fill air sacks within their skin for buoyancy, and slowly wiggle their way to the surface to hatch. Often during this process they are stationary, suspended between lake bottom and surface. As adults, chironomids fly over the water surface laying eggs and sometimes land on the water surface.

Smart Fish

Trout-fishing legend Gary LaFontaine: "Food is the stimulus and the response is the rise. They get locked into a target and they want it to look exactly like that insect and anything that doesn't is ignored. That is not intelligence, it is simply rote repetition."

The View from Down Under

Curious about what trout do underwater, fly-fishing legend Gary LaFontaine donned scuba gear in the early 1970s and observed trout feeding on caddis pupae newly hatched from burrows in the mud. He quickly discovered that most published ideas about the behavior of the emerging caddis and fish were wrong. He found that, despite claims to the contrary, trout almost never strike the emerging pupae as they rise from the bottom to the surface. Instead, trout feed on pupae when they drift along the bottom after emerging from the cocoon and when the pupae are in the surface film.

After his experiments, LaFontaine designed new flies that proved far more effective, especially flies that captured the most unique feature of the caddis: air bubbles. His flies are still in use today. More details of his study can be found in his 1981 book *Caddisflies*.

Habitat

As long as they can get a food supply, chironomid larvae will live in almost any type of water. Clear or polluted with bottoms that are muddy, rocky, weedy, or sandy doesn't seem to matter. Their food source is generally most abundant on or near shoals, and this is where their numbers peak. The preferred food seems to be blue-green algae. Chironomid adults and pupae don't feed.

Importance to Fly-Fishing

After freshwater shrimp, chironomids are the next most important food source for the monster Kamloops trout. Throughout the fly-fishing season, daytime feeding samples show that in some areas 27 percent of the trout's daytime feeding consists of chironomid. This drops for those fish feeding in the evening or at night. Chironomid are much more significant as a daytime food source.

Recommended fly patterns:

- For larvae: Bloodworm, Bent Bloodworm
- For pupae: Little Black Chironomid, Red Butt, Tunkwanamid, Moosemane, Red Chironomid, PKCK, Hatheume, Emerging Chironomid
- For adults: Lady McConell, H.C.H., Humpy, Mosquito

Leech

Appearance and Life Cycle

Colors run from black and brown to maroon, solid or mottled. Average size is up to 50 mm, but some reach up to 150 mm when fully extended. The body is flattened and segmented like an earthworm.

Reproduction is on an individual basis; all leeches are capable of producing egg masses, which they attach to an object under the water's surface.

Food and Habitat

Leeches are scavengers that feed on decaying or dead organic matter. They also hunt insect larvae, snails, and shrimp.

Leeches like to live in shallow areas with a good covering of vegetation or woody debris which provides both food and cover. They are also found in dark lakes with abundant cover of lily pads.

Movement

Leeches have sucking discs on each end of the body that enable them to "inch" along an object or the lake bottom. They swim with an undulating up and down motion.

Fishing Techniques

Fish seem to find leeches more appealing in spring and again in mid to late summer. Fish close to the bottom in shallow waters, retrieving with continuous hand twists or long slow strips. You can use trolling to imitate the leeches swimming, as they cause considerable movement with their undulating motion; boat speed and direction should be varied. The evening is often a good time as it is thought that leeches do most of their traveling and food search at night. Fish prefer the young small leeches up to 1½ inches. In deeper waters use a sinking line and a weighted fly; retrieve using a pull, rest, sink movement.

Recommended fly patterns: Little Fort Leech, Upside Down Leech, Blood Leech, Weighted Marabou, Black Woolly Bugger, Olive Woolly Bugger, Maroon Woolly Bugger

Other Food Sources

Terrestrial insects are another source of food for fish. Their life cycles are completed on dry ground, and so they become prey to game fish only when they fall into the water or when wind gusts blow them into the current. The most common terrestrials are grasshoppers, crickets, caterpillars, ants, grubs, and larvae of other insects. When selecting flies to match terrestrials, anglers most often copy grasshoppers, crickets, and ants.

Terrestrial

Other creatures also find themselves on the fish menu; the most common are minnows, small fish, frogs, crayfish, freshwater shrimp, and even mice. Streamers are artificial imitations of these creatures.

HatchCards

Get a better understanding of entomology and insect hatches. Moose Creek Company, with the help of many fine guides and biologists, has compiled insect hatch data for more than sixty rivers and lakes, including the Bighorn, Green, and San Juan, and regional areas such as Southern Idaho, Yellowstone National Park, and central, southwestern, and northwestern Montana.

HatchCards are compact enough to carry inside your fly vest and are made of durable waterproof vinyl. HatchCards describe the major and minor insects throughout the season for the specified river or region. Sizes, hatch dates, and daily timing and hatch locations, as well as color and behavioral descriptions of the adult, nymph/pupal, and spinner/egg-laying stages are included. They are handy to refer to onstream or when preparing for your next trip. HatchCards are available for the Midwest, Northeast, Rocky Mountains, Southeast, and West. New HatchCards cover California, Oregon, Washington, Utah, Wyoming, Colorado, Minnesota, Wisconsin, Michigan, Pennsylvania, and New York, so check with your fly-fishing dealer for availability or call 800-535-6633.

Yellowstone National Park HatchBook

If a person could just have these waters to himself. Who'd need to fish anywhere else? Gorgeous mountain scenery and beautiful brightly colored cutthroats. Learn the insects and hatches of the Firehole River, Gallatin River, Gardner River, Gibbon River, Lamar River, Madison River, Slough Creek, Soda Butte Creek, Yellowstone River, Grebe Lake, Trout Lake, and Yellowstone Lake.

Northwest Montana HatchBook

Don't forget to enjoy the view when you're fishing and make sure you visit and hike throughout Glacier National Park. In this book

learn about entomology, fly-fishing techniques, and knots, while also learning the insect hatches of the Big Blackfoot River, the Bitterroot River, the Clark Fork of the Columbia River, the Kootenai River, the Missouri River, Rock Creek, and the Smith River.

Southwest Montana HatchBook

Beautiful valley and mountain scenery and rolling rivers with big trout. Learn about entomology, fly-fishing techniques, and knots, while also learning the insect hatches of the Beaverhead River, the Big Hole River, the Gallatin River (below Yellowstone National Park), the Jefferson River, the Madison River (below Quake Lake), the Ruby River, Hebgen Lake, and Cliff and Wade Lakes.

Central Montana HatchBook

Challenge yourself on Livingston's Spring Creeks, float the trout-rich Bighorn, or disappear on the Boulder or Shields. Learn about entomology, fly-fishing techniques, and knots, while also learning the insect hatches of Armstrong's Spring Creek, the Bighorn River, the Boulder River, Depuy's Spring Creek, Nelson's Spring Creek, the Shields River, and the Yellowstone River (below Gardiner).

Southern Idaho HatchBook

You owe yourself a day on one or all of these rivers. Life's a pain sometimes, and you'll have a better focus on things if you explore any of these trout-rich southern Idaho rivers. Learn about entomology, fly-fishing techniques, and knots, while also learning the insect hatches of the Big Lost River, the Big Wood River, the Henry's Fork of the Snake River, Silver Creek, the South Fork of the Boise River, and the South Fork of the Snake River.

If you have difficulty finding HatchCards, order them directly from Moose Creek. Include $1.75 for handling for five or fewer HatchCards or $3.95 for all other orders. Allow four to six

The Deadly Emergers

An emerger pattern is fished to imitate an aquatic insect emerging on the surface as it transforms from a nymph or pupa into a winged adult. This process of surface emergence is typically referred to as *the hatch*.

When it is time to emerge, most caddis and mayfly species simply float or propel themselves to the surface, where they hatch into winged adults. Other nymphs, such as larger stonefly species, crawl out of the water where they metamorphose on land. For these insects, there is no aquatic emergence so fly fishers have no need to tie emerger patterns.

However, most other winged aquatic insects spend anywhere from a couple of seconds to a few minutes on or near the water's surface struggling to free themselves of the nymphal shuck. Meanwhile, the emerger is floating with the current and may drift over dozens, sometimes hundreds, of fish feeding on the vulnerable insects in the surface film.

This hatching process, unique for each insect species and particular river or lake, takes place during the same general time period each year but can be altered by a variety of conditions including water temperature and weather. Fishing with emergers can be done using either dry fly or nymphing techniques.

weeks for delivery. Send check or money order to Moose Creek Co., Box 309, Lakeville, MN 55044.

The Magic Behind the Fly

Fishing the Owens River in Northern California reveals much about artificial flies. In downtown Bishop, fishing guide Gary Gunsolley, owner of Brock's Fly Fishing Shop, together with his wife, Pat, have transformed Brock's from a sporting goods store to a fly shop. The first time I walked in, Pat greeted me heartily then quickly returned to tying up purple marabou and chenille for a perching trip on Crowley Lake. She seemed to especially enjoy painting dazzle eyes on her fly.

I overheard Gary helping a couple of people new to the sport. "I'd try a #18 or 20 caddis fly. They're small emergers, olive and black," he said. "At midday try the Adams or Blue Dun parachutes, and they've been hitting on caddis dries at dusk." The folks who strolled through the doors of Gary's fly shop were smart. They could have tried the hit-and-miss method of fishing any of the literally hundreds of color variations between olive and brown. But they simply strode inside the fly shop and asked, "What have the fish been hitting on lately?"

Gary and I hopped into his old Toyota pickup and, with temperatures hovering near the century mark, headed for the Lower Owens. As we turned off the highway onto dirt, his "Let's see where the holes are" did not refer to fishing holes. We bottomed out the truck a few times but eventually landed streamside in one piece.

He pointed to a nearby sign specifying the wild trout stream that permits artificial barbless hooks only. "They think we're all snobs," he said, referring to bait fishermen. "We're supposed to be elite, the top guns of the fishing world. Probably 2 percent of fly fishermen have those attitudes. I'd say 99 percent of fly fishermen came from bait—throwing out for crappie, bass, and perch."

The snow-draped and towering Mt. Tom looking on, Gary and I angled up and down the east bank of the river. The current was brisk and varied. Clad in waders, Gary slowly eased between the cattails into an entry point, seine in hand.

While I surveyed the very large holes and deep pockets that hide the trophy browns here, he returned with his catch. In a clear, round Petri dish wriggled a cross-section of the Lower Owens. Larvae snuggled in sticklike cases, stoneworms wriggled close to one another to mate, even a small 20-sized chironomid trolled the edges of the bowl. Gary gently squeezed one end of the sticklike case and out popped a caddis larva. If you ever have a chance to look at the stomach contents of a trout, notice how many cases they ingest just to get at the tasty caddis.

We knew the three-tailed mayfly nymph circling the bowl would one day have a tough time eluding trout on its ascent to the surface, but if it made it successfully it would fly away gracefully. At the top of the current, emergent mayflies wait for their wings to dry, then fly off for one purpose: to reproduce. The mayfly nymph in the plastic bowl was easily identified by its two or three tails and bulging single wing case behind its head. This contrasts to the stonefly, which has two tails as well as two wing cases.

Adult mayflies are easy to identify by their single set of wings and long hairlike tails (usually three, but two tails are not that uncommon). These flies, once hatched from their eggs, live in the nymph stage for about a year until fully grown. They then rise to the surface and molt into the winged fly or dun. At this stage they are still not considered adult flies and will eventually molt a second time before entering the adult stage. Mayflies are the only aquatic insects to have this two-step molting process. Once an adult, the mayfly will die within a few days. Another easy way to spot these flies is to study their swarming behaviors. Mayflies swarm along shore and rise and fall in unison.

The chironomid Gary "caught" is actually midge larvae that live in mud or mucky stream and river bottoms. Because they're not bottom feeders, a trout would not ordinarily choose to take a chironomid. Knowing this can help you because you wouldn't cast a chironomid fly into midstream

An Outsider Looking In

Here's a guy standing in cold water up to his liver, throwing the world's most expensive clothesline at trees. A full two thirds of his time is spent untangling stuff—which he could be doing in the comfort of his own home with old shoelaces if he wanted. The whole business costs like sin and requires heavier clothing. Furthermore, it's conducted in the middle of black fly season. Cast and swat. Cast and swat. Fly-fishing may be a sport invented by insects with fly fishermen as the bait.

From P. J. O'Rourke, in "Age and Guile Beat Youth, Innocence and a Bad Haircut," *On the Pleasures of Fly Fishing: Collected Diatribes* (1995).

unless you knew the water had a muddy bottom. However, on the Owens, as Gary pointed out from years of experience, chironomids live in the reeds on the river's edge, which means you need to cast there.

This river is also home for the rockworm, free-living caddis larvae that don't build a case. Under a smooth midstream stone we saw caddis worms in clumps of sand. These clumps serve as their homes until they pupate. Evenings and mornings here see the trout fiercely strike emerging caddis, which are good swimmers but poor fliers.

Because all the small creatures we saw were in the nymph stage—so 85 percent of your fishing should be done subsurface—we "matched the hatch" by tying on small #18 caddis nymphs and casting away. One thing to remember about using small flies on small hooks: using large hooks eliminates small fish, but small hooks will catch anything. Gary told of taking a 5-pound brown on a #20 fly. "The size of the hook is irrelevant, really," he said. "Big bait, big fish? That's just a theory."

About 7 inches above the caddis nymph we tied on a B-split shot to take the fly down to the fish. Our rigs were completed by strike indicators, which, as a rule of thumb, should be located on the line about two to three times the average water depth. You cannot see a fish strike a nymph, so the strike indicator is essential.

Sometimes you can use a top-water fly to serve as a strike indicator.

Another rule is, every time a strike indicator goes under, strip in line with your line hand. Assume it's a fish. Which is exactly what I did on my sixth cast that day on the Lower Owens. After taking my nymph, the brown jumped a full 3 feet out of the water. It was spectacular. I was careful to keep my rod tip up, but he eventually bee-lined to the shoreline. Before I could zig him back to the middle of the stream, the wily fish used the full force of the current to unhook himself. "Hey, you got an LDR!" Gary quipped. Puzzled, I soon learned LDR was his acronym for long distance release.

Typical fly pattern

The Challenge

The challenge of fly-fishing is making fish strike dressed-up hooks that appear to be living creatures. These are called fly patterns. Perhaps the most famous fly pattern of all time is the Royal Coachman. This pattern calls for a tail of a golden pheasant wound around the hook.

Fly-fishing offers so many alternatives that the beginner would do well to use a general approach to selecting flies. More seasoned anglers prefer to match the hatch or use flashy attractors. But the novice can select from a basic arsenal of wet and dry flies so he or she can focus attention on casting and fly presentation. It's a simple yet effective approach to flying right.

Wet fly

Flies need not be pretty to catch fish. Nymphs whip up fast if you wax thread and spin on a mix of fur and flash materials. Shaggy types often take more fish. Dry flies assemble quickly if you use the tap of your hackle as a tail, strip off a bit of hackle, spin on a wax body, and complete the fly by winding on hackle. You can skip patterns, too. With colors from white through gray to black, and through tan to brown, as well as a few green types, you can get the job done in most areas most of the time.

Streamers, feathered trailer hooks on lures, and other oddments wrap up quickly, too. A basic fly-tying book and a few simple tools are all you need. Unfortunately, few can stop here. So we invest hundreds of dollars into super hackles, hooks in all sizes and types, and more exotic feathers and fur than you could find in the San Diego Zoo.

The first time I witnessed the miraculous art of fly making was in a hotel room in Washington, when my compatriot set up his fly vise on the bedside table, dumped out a peculiar collection of feathers and fur, and went into action. Thread, hackle, and scissors were flying faster than my eye could follow! In the end appeared buglike creations he called chironomids, serendipities, and scuds. They didn't look like much in my hand but were very lifelike in the water.

Dry fly

It's better to start with a wet fly, which can cover a greater area. As a wet fly drifts downstream, use your rod to slowly follow the fly the whole way through the drift. Work down and across the stream as you slowly take up (strip) the line. Also, start in calm or slow-moving water because it's more difficult to control the line in fast-moving (broken) water.

Every basic selection should include a classic, upright winged dry fly such as the Adams, caddisfly, or mayfly. But trout feed under the surface 80 to 90 percent of the time, gorging themselves on the preflight stages of insects called nymphs, larvae, and pupae. That's why you should also have in your fly arsenal subsurface flies that mimic these stages of insect development.

What size of fly? That depends on the type of water you're fishing. The higher the number used to size a fly, the smaller the fly. For larger rivers, use the larger sizes 2, 4, and 6; for streams try the smaller 8s, 10s, and 12s. Before your first cast, though, seek out local advice on what works best.

The real key is to be willing to change flies. Sometimes fly fishers become too enamored of the concept of fishing with dry flies. Of course, there's nothing like watching a monster trout ascend from the deep to take a fly from top-water. But if you want to catch fish, you'll need to know that at least 85 percent of a trout's diet is subsurface. As I said earlier, anglers must be willing to change fly patterns, distance of strike indicator, thickness of tippet (or amount of lead weight if you're getting snags). Simply keep changing until you get hooked! Flies that catch bass and saltwater fish are much larger than trout flies and require heavier lines and more powerful rods to cast them.

Another type of fly is the bass bug, composed of cork, deer hair, or other buoyant materials. Bass bugs simulate frogs, mice, and other creatures eaten by bass. In other cases, however, fish are attracted by crippled creatures, so erratic movements may signal a preying trout or bass to strike. A crippled minnow, for instance, is at the mercy of moving water, and predators watch for bait being tossed by the currents. Fish will never attack an insect that appears

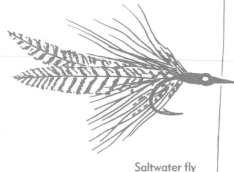

Saltwater fly

itself to be on the attack, so manipulate your fly so it seems to be escaping, not attacking.

What Makes Nymphs So Enticing?

Although more trout eat flies in the nymph stage than in their later phases, most fly rodders prefer the dry fly because of the excitement of watching a trout rise to the surface and take the fly. Can't blame 'em. But dry fly fishers could be much more productive fishing sub-surface. Much has been said about nymph fishing—entire books have been written on this one subject. Why? Because fish spend as much as 90 percent of their time feeding on this food of choice. It's always readily available.

Nymph fishing is one of the most productive ways to take fish. No other method offers the opportunity to take fish anytime or any place. Dry fly-fishing is simply too inconsistent and brief, even on the best of streams. That's why we need to go subsurface.

Nymphing is a technique that involves reading the water, presenting the fly, detecting strikes, and other nuances. Similar to the wet fly, the nymph is more specialized. Its purpose is to imi-tate an immature form of insect life creeping, crawling, or burrowing underwater in its transition from larval stage to mature adult. Many of these insects spend the greater part of their life cycle as subaquatic life forms, living in, on, under, and around the rubble and plant life at the bottom and banks of streams and lakes.

Nymph

Swimmers live in swift water with rock bottoms. These smooth-bodied creatures tout long, delicate legs and gill plates down their abdomens. Their fringed tails propel them through the water. Two well-known fly-tiers' nymphs are Blue-Winged Olives and Isonychia, both examples of swimmers.

Crawlers live in both still and moving water. They seek cover in vegetation, bottom gravel, and under rocks—places where they can crawl around because they're not great swimmers. Common flies that imitate crawling nymphs are called Hendrickson, Tricos, and Pale Morning Duns.

Clingers have short, compact bodies and prefer swift currents. They have gills that work like suction cups and they need to hang on to something. Trout love feeding on clingers that move to quieter water when they are ready to hatch. March Browns and Quill Gordons are two members of this group.

Finally, *burrowers* take up residence in the silt and mucky bottoms of rivers, lakes, and streams. They have long jaws and plumed gills used for extracting oxygen from the water. The Green Drake and Giant Michigan Mayfly are two examples of burrowers.

What Nymph Patterns Work Best?

Most anglers agree that the best patterns include at least one of three particular materials: pheasant tail, peacock herl, and the fur from a hare's mask. All three seem to exhibit a special, almost magical, appeal to the fish.

The male ringneck pheasant is a flashy bird decorated with a number of different feathers that are highly useful for fly tying. Most important are the long, elegant tail feathers—two long center feathers flanked by six shorter ones on each side. Ringneck center tail feathers average 18 to 22 inches long. The top side is medium to light brown with black bars while the underside is nearly black. The outer edges of the feather are a rich reddish-brown, and these are the fibers that create a nymph body that trout find irresistible.

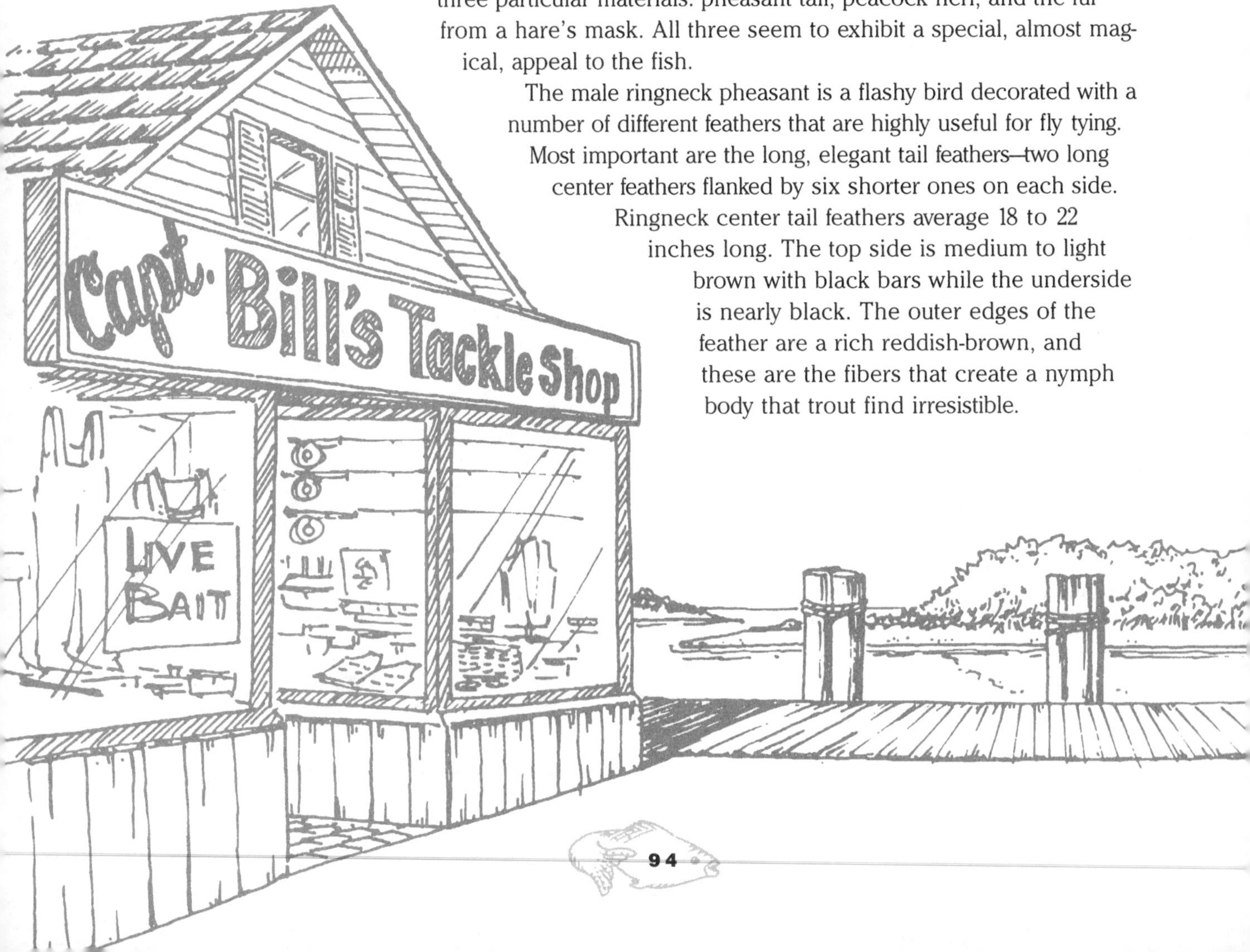

Capt. Bill's Tackle Shop

LIVE BAIT

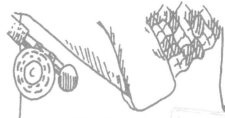

The characteristic rusty shade of ringneck pheasant tail closely matches the color of numerous species of small mayfly nymphs so prevalent in healthy trout streams. Look closely at pheasant tail fibers and you will notice they are slightly fuzzy. When wound around the hook, this fuzziness imitates the gills and other features of the naturals. This combination of color and texture might explain, in part, why the Pheasant Tail Nymph and its variations are so universally successful in American streams.

As showy as the cock pheasant may be, he is completely outdone by the next supplier of a magic material. The peacock is the epitome of ostentatiousness. His extravagant tail feathers are an adornment unmatched by any other creature in the world. Individual quills from the large, captivating "eye" at the top of each tail feather are used for the bodies of many popular dry fly patterns. But the most desirable parts of the feather for nymphs are the long strands of herl that grow out of either side of the main stem.

Strands of peacock herl average 5 to 8 inches long. Color is usually an iridescent, almost metallic, green. Sometimes the herl will exhibit a bronze or purplish cast, especially if the feather is exposed to direct sunlight for any length of time. Peacock herl reflects light unlike any other material, displaying subtle flecks of color in a most lifelike manner.

The third magical material is hardly as exotic as the previous two, but every bit as effective. Dubbing from the face and ears of the European hare has been used for fly bodies since the beginnings of fly tying. Hare's mask dubbing is generally a mixture of guard hairs and underfur blended together. The result is a coarse, grayish-tan dubbing with flecks of black and brown. Look at a pinch of it with a magnifying glass: it resembles dried grass clippings, but the fish seem to love it. Every angler, beginner or experienced, should have in his or her fly box nymphs with one of these three ingredients: pheasant tail, peacock herl, and hare's mask.

Tie One On!

Want to save money and increase your enjoyment of fly-fishing? Learn to tie your own flies! Anyone who fly-fishes can become skilled at tying flies. If you can tie your shoe strings you can tie flies.

Fly tying is relaxing, engrossing, and practical. But most rewarding is catching a fish on a fly you made yourself, be it the first one you tie or one you created that is like no other ever tied. Fly tying also frees you from the dependence on others for your flies.

Before you purchase a tying kit, seek instruction and materials from your local fly-fishing pro shop, tying friends, or area fly-fishing clubs, or purchase one or more good beginner-level fly tying videos. Lots are listed in Internet catalogs these days, or in fly-fishing mail-order catalogs.

Most fishing experts believe every fly fisherman or woman, boy or girl, should tie at least a few of their own flies. When it comes down to it, many fly fishers spend as much or more time each year tying flies and talking about tying as they do getting out and fly-fishing them!

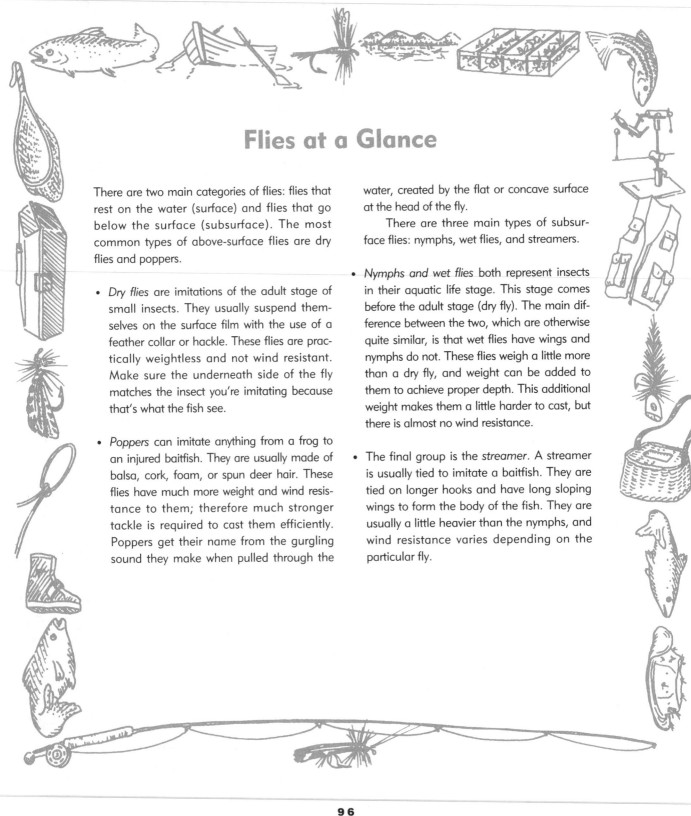

Flies at a Glance

There are two main categories of flies: flies that rest on the water (surface) and flies that go below the surface (subsurface). The most common types of above-surface flies are dry flies and poppers.

- *Dry flies* are imitations of the adult stage of small insects. They usually suspend themselves on the surface film with the use of a feather collar or hackle. These flies are practically weightless and not wind resistant. Make sure the underneath side of the fly matches the insect you're imitating because that's what the fish see.

- *Poppers* can imitate anything from a frog to an injured baitfish. They are usually made of balsa, cork, foam, or spun deer hair. These flies have much more weight and wind resistance to them; therefore much stronger tackle is required to cast them efficiently. Poppers get their name from the gurgling sound they make when pulled through the water, created by the flat or concave surface at the head of the fly.

There are three main types of subsurface flies: nymphs, wet flies, and streamers.

- *Nymphs and wet flies* both represent insects in their aquatic life stage. This stage comes before the adult stage (dry fly). The main difference between the two, which are otherwise quite similar, is that wet flies have wings and nymphs do not. These flies weigh a little more than a dry fly, and weight can be added to them to achieve proper depth. This additional weight makes them a little harder to cast, but there is almost no wind resistance.

- The final group is the *streamer*. A streamer is usually tied to imitate a baitfish. They are tied on longer hooks and have long sloping wings to form the body of the fish. They are usually a little heavier than the nymphs, and wind resistance varies depending on the particular fly.

On the Water

When setting out to go "nymphing," check your tackle. Fly lines for nymphing should be in the mid-range of 5-, 6-, or 7-weight. Use floating weight-forward (WF) or double-taper (DT) lines for moving water and sink-tip and full sinking lines for nymph fishing in lakes. Leaders for a floating line should be fine and long (from 9 to 12 feet), but short (2 to 4 feet) if you're using a sinking-tip line in order to keep the nymph at the right depth. If your leader is too long, your nymph will float, thus defeating the purpose of nymphing. If you wanted it to float, you'd have used a dry fly, right?

Next comes selecting the right type and size of nymph. There are a few ways to do this. A good rule of thumb is that the nymphs can be a few sizes larger than the appropriate dry fly. You can pull out some weeds on the edge of the stream or lake and see what's living there. Turn over a midstream rock and see what's zigging around the stream. Walk the bank and look for stonefly husks or caddisfly cases to get an insight into the type, color, and approximate size of nymphs present and which to duplicate from your fly box. Sizes 4, 6, and 8 flies imitate stonefly nymphs, while sizes 20 and 22 duplicate midges.

Another way of detecting watery inhabitants is to use a seine, which is available at fly shops or through mail order. Use it to strain floating or drifting bugs for observation. Cheesecloth or fine netting material works great for seining larvae in the water. Coffee filters work well, too, because they show the bugs against a white background. Put the critters you net into a small clear tray or petri dish. You may also find an identification book and magnifying glass useful.

Another way to sample a stream is to disturb the soil and pick up rocks to see what's living underneath. Don't worry about not being able to see if you are actually catching anything in the cloudy water. Let the mud settle for a few minutes to ensure you pick up the most amount of larvae that are present. It's smart, and much more rewarding, to sample the stream rather than just trudge through it, wondering what the fish feed on.

Sampling need not be limited to just the spring and summer months. Nymphs and flies hatch at various times of the year. You should have no trouble finding caddis larvae, mayfly nymphs, scuds, larvae, and pupae. Flies with soft hackle or scruffy bodies will suggest tails, gills, and legs of nymphs as they float or tumble in the current. Colors will include olive, tan, cream, light green, gray, brown, and darker tones.

When nymphs first emerge, they rise from their beds in the gravel and get caught in the flow. They bounce over riffles, spin in currents, and lodge in eddies and pools. They fill the water with a creeping, squirming, then suspended abundance that rises and falls with each beat of the river.

If the water temperature is below that favored by trout, for example, the fish won't feed actively. But sometimes they will take a slow-moving nymph drifted along the bottom. When trout are dimpling the surface or bulging the water and refusing all dry flies, they usually are catching nymphs just below the surface.

Sometimes a trout taking nymphs just below the surface will show its back, dorsal fin, and tail. If you see trout flashing underwater, sunlight reflecting silver from their sides, you know they are nymphing. Other times the feeding trout noses along the bottom, dislodging pebbles and sand, in a quest for nymphs.

Before casting, rub your nymph on a rock to remove your natural odor and to give the nymph a natural rough look. Work the edges of the current, and keep your rod tip up to take the nymph to the bottom quickly. As the nymph bounces on downstream, play out some line and extend the drift to a sunken log or a shaded area. As the nymph starts to swing, give it a lively swimming action by stripping line in short pulls and twitching the rod tip. Most nymphs are good swimmers so little jerks are called for.

Experienced anglers are loathe to give up working a particular fishing area. Instead, they work with painstaking exactness, sweeping every crevice, crack, and corner of the streambed until certain that the trout there have had a chance to grab the nymph. Bringing to the net a game fish hooked by your nymph is a truly high point in fly-fishing.

Popper

A Blast with Bass Bugs

Despite the name, and the fact that more Americans fish for bass than any other game fish, "bass bugs" are used for trout, northern pike, largemouth and smallmouth bass, crappie, and sunfish.

A large fish's powerful attack on a bass bug is one of the most thrilling events in fishing. But excitement is not the only reason for using these bulky flies; few lures are as effective when fish are taking terrestrials on the surface. Some anglers use bass bugs only when they spot fish feeding on the surface, but these flies can be productive anytime fish are found in shallow water.

Though they are dressed to imitate baitfish, large insects, frogs, and even mice, their appeal is in the noise and disturbance they create on the surface of the water. Because they are heavy and bulky, bass bugs are the most difficult to cast. Each error in casting form or timing is magnified when casting popping bugs, which make noise when dragged across the surface film.

Bass bugs are made of cork, balsa wood, cedar, Styrofoam, deer hair, or hollow plastic. Seasoned anglers say the best bugs are made of cork, not balsa. Balsa tends to break from around the hook and the hook turns more easily before you have a chance to land many fish. A few of the popular bass bugs are called Bullet Bug, Bluegill Bug, Powder Puff, Marm Minnow, and Standard Popper.

Fishing the bug is something learned through experience. The key is to make the bass bug look alive to the bass, popping it, playing it both fast and slow, making it wobble and waggle. Often, bass hit best when a bug is allowed to rest motionless for some time.

Tom McNally, former angling editor of *Field & Stream* magazine, notes: "Much of the time it's best for a bug to remain absolutely motionless just after striking the water. I wish to emphasize this because many fishermen just *think* their bugs

The Late Great Lee Wulff

Lee Wulff is the most significant American contributor to the sport of fly-fishing. His recognizable fly patterns are fished the world over, particularly the Royal Wulff, first designed in 1930. The foundation for this fly can be found in the potent Royal Coachman with its peacock herl and red silk body. Like many of the flies created by Wulff, the Royal Wulff can be fished for salmon in larger sizes. Lee Wulff lived from 1905 to 1991.

Fishing Two Flies at Once

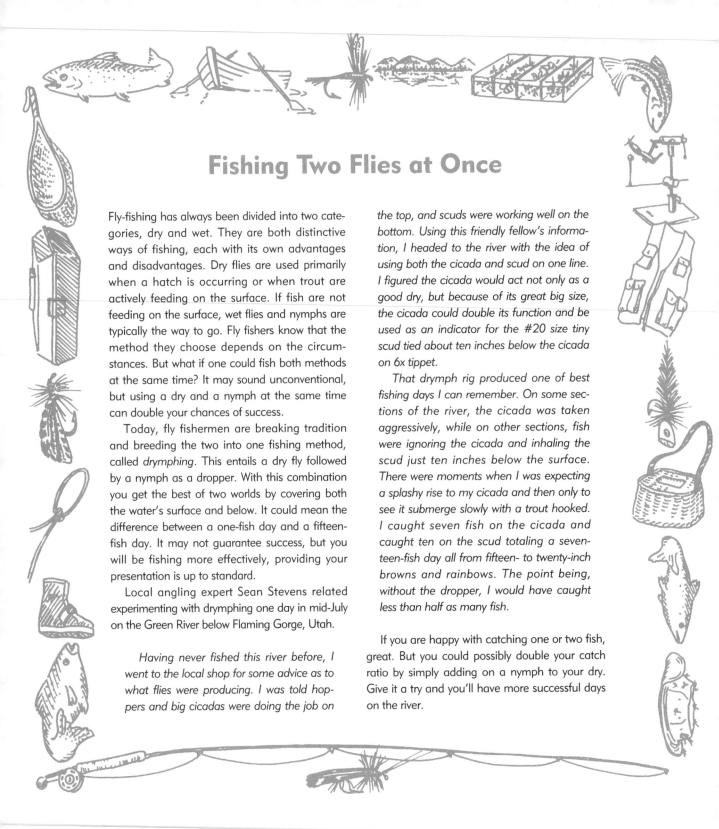

Fly-fishing has always been divided into two categories, dry and wet. They are both distinctive ways of fishing, each with its own advantages and disadvantages. Dry flies are used primarily when a hatch is occurring or when trout are actively feeding on the surface. If fish are not feeding on the surface, wet flies and nymphs are typically the way to go. Fly fishers know that the method they choose depends on the circumstances. But what if one could fish both methods at the same time? It may sound unconventional, but using a dry and a nymph at the same time can double your chances of success.

Today, fly fishermen are breaking tradition and breeding the two into one fishing method, called *drymphing*. This entails a dry fly followed by a nymph as a dropper. With this combination you get the best of two worlds by covering both the water's surface and below. It could mean the difference between a one-fish day and a fifteen-fish day. It may not guarantee success, but you will be fishing more effectively, providing your presentation is up to standard.

Local angling expert Sean Stevens related experimenting with drymphing one day in mid-July on the Green River below Flaming Gorge, Utah.

Having never fished this river before, I went to the local shop for some advice as to what flies were producing. I was told hoppers and big cicadas were doing the job on the top, and scuds were working well on the bottom. Using this friendly fellow's information, I headed to the river with the idea of using both the cicada and scud on one line. I figured the cicada would act not only as a good dry, but because of its great big size, the cicada could double its function and be used as an indicator for the #20 size tiny scud tied about ten inches below the cicada on 6x tippet.

That drymph rig produced one of best fishing days I can remember. On some sections of the river, the cicada was taken aggressively, while on other sections, fish were ignoring the cicada and inhaling the scud just ten inches below the surface. There were moments when I was expecting a splashy rise to my cicada and then only to see it submerge slowly with a trout hooked. I caught seven fish on the cicada and caught ten on the scud totaling a seventeen-fish day all from fifteen- to twenty-inch browns and rainbows. The point being, without the dropper, I would have caught less than half as many fish.

If you are happy with catching one or two fish, great. But you could possibly double your catch ratio by simply adding on a nymph to your dry. Give it a try and you'll have more successful days on the river.

are motionless. . . . I've observed that the average bug fisherman makes his cast and then unconsciously moves the rod tip up, causing the bug to slide a foot or so across the surface. Most times the bug should be dead-still after striking the water, and this can be accomplished only by continuing to lower the rod on completion of the cast."

Streamers Are a Scream

Minnows teem the streams in springtime and trout love 'em. Fly fishers use streamer patterns designed to imitate these small baitfish to draw a trout out from very heavy cover. Tied on to the streamer's hook are hackle feathers or animal hair that simulate a swimming fish that attracts the attention of finned passers-by.

Day in and day out, streamers will take the biggest trout. Big trout want a big mouthful. Streamers are easiest to see in heavy, turbid water, and they need to be fished slowly, tantalizingly and repeatedly in the same place. In streams where minnows are abundant, the streamer should be your first selection, especially if you don't observe any surface activity.

A favorite streamer on western streams is the Muddler Minnow, which you have to work in the water to simulate a fast-swimming minnow, a loafing minnow, or an injured minnow. Visualize what the streamer is doing and attempt to imitate one of these types. If a streamer is left to simply drift, it becomes nothing more than a glob of feathers and fur drifting downstream. It becomes a little stick, a colorful leaf, or flotsam—something not to be eaten.

Streamer

Cast across-stream and work the streamer slightly downstream near, perhaps, a rock or submerged log. Try to present these flies as delicately as you can. Avoid the tendency to cast too far in big rivers. The shorter the line, the better you can work the fly and the more trout you will hook. Cast in the near water first, then move out. Keep your rod tip low so you maintain complete control over the line, leader, and fly and can react quickly to a strike.

California's Famed Owens Valley

The Owens Valley, which skirts the John Muir Wilderness, is nestled among the sage, savannah, a variety of habitat grasses, chaparral, ponderosa pine, black oak woodland, mixed conifer, red fir, riparian, Jeffrey pine, and bitter brush.

This is the land famed naturalist John Muir grew to love. Inyo County, specifically, is a land of extremes ranging from the harshness of Death Valley to the majestic splendor of the Sierra Nevadas. About 112 miles long by 132 miles wide, the area is bordered by the Nevada State line in the east and the Sierra-Nevada mountains in the west. This remarkable area boasts both America's highest and lowest points: Mount Whitney at 14,495 feet and Death Valley's Badwater at 280 feet below sea level. It also contains the Palisade Glacier, the southernmost active glacier in the continental United States.

Three streams there have earned official designation as wild trout streams, where the fish are left to reproduce naturally. Take a walk along the San Joaquin or Hot Creek and you will see a slew of fishermen trying to hook these wily creatures. Or head into the high country and try your luck in the lakes, many stocked by the Forest Service.

The climate varies with the elevation, offering cold snowy winters and cool summers at higher elevations, and rainy winters and mild summers in the foothills. Summers are dry. Snowy winters in the northern Sierras are crucial to California's water supply, which depends heavily upon spring snowmelt to feed the reservoirs of the State Water Project and a portion of the federal Central Valley Project. The projects supply about two thirds of California's water for drinking, irrigation, and industrial use.

The Owens River is the main artery for water deliveries south to the storage reservoirs that belong to the City of Los Angeles Department of Water and Power. Storage capacity and water needs for Southern California dictate the amount of flow through the Owens banks. Although this may sound a bit glum, giving way to impressions of a canal-type environment, it is not. Locals may resent

Southern California's water needs but largely appreciate how the area has not been commercialized.

Above the Owens Valley River to the east is the 2-million-acre Inyo National forest, which extends 165 miles along the California and Nevada border between Los Angeles and Reno. On the eastern slope of the Sierra-Nevada Mountains, the forest is unique in California. It is composed of pristine lakes, fragile meadows, winding streams, and rugged peaks. There are 2,200 family campsites, and fishing attract thousands of visitors. More than 500 lakes and 100 miles of stream provide habitat for golden, brook, German brown, and the iridescent rainbow trout.

Fishing the Lower Owens

The Lower Owens is called a tailwater fishery because it flows from a dam, but it acts like a spring creek because it abounds with insect population and has good hatch activity year-round, especially caddis. On the Owens there are a certain amount of flow fluctuations. These are due at times to spring-runoff dam releases and power generation at Pleasant Valley Reservoir. During high periods the fish leave their bank-side cover and move into mid-river current lines and seams to feed, which is not the case when flows are low and water shallow.

The actual trout population of the Owens is not really known, although guide Gary Gunsolley claims there are 6,000 fish per mile, or about one fish per foot. He cites the Department of Fish and Game, which takes a stream census every second season. Whatever the exact population, the wild trout section has always had very good numbers of 11- to 14-inch fish with many more in the 15- to 19-inch class per mile. This water also has a healthy population of fish in the 19-inch plus category, and it is these fish that present the ultimate challenge on the Owens. And you can tell a wild trout: it's healthier, and has bright-red gill plates. Rainbows have vibrant pink stripes down their sides. Gary says hatchery rainbows look more like aluminum cans.

Since the water is not "gin-clear," anglers need to blind-cast to rising trout. Brown trout are spooky, and with a quick flip of their tails can dive deep for hours at a time. These wary fish like small offerings presented with a drag-free drift. It's not so much the type of fly as the presentation you make with it.

There is always a hatch on the Owens. At any given time of year you might see caddis, mayflies, and several different types of stoneflies. As the bottom of the Owens is primarily gravel and sand, it is fairly easy to traverse, but it does not lend itself well to heavy wading. A better approach is to walk the banks in search of prime water and only enter the water to cross or gain better advantage in casting.

Lining the banks are tule reeds, willows, buck brush, salt cedar, and huge cottonwood trees, many of which were planted by the early valley settlers as protection from the ever present wind, the nemesis of many a fly caster. The weather in the Owens Valley is warm in summer, temperate in spring and fall, and not too cold in winter, but frequently windy in all seasons.

Seasoned veterans of the Owens River spend many hours in the same few hundred feet of water area. They don't make a couple of casts, then walk upstream, but pick each run apart. This type of intense fly-fishing may not be for everyone, but it's a wonderful experience for those who are willing to learn.

On-Stream Tactics

Streamer fishing on the Owens is also a thrill; one of the better patterns that is readily available is the venerable Muddler Minnow. For winter and early spring, it's hard to beat. Colors should include black, olives, and several shades of natural deer hair in sizes 8 through 14 and tied without lead weight.

Use a long leader and tippet to allow the fly to run very deep while still retaining drag-free control to slow down the presentation, preferably slower than the current you are fishing. Small spring-creek nymphs lend themselves well to this type of presentation all season long but are especially effective in the winter.

When dead-drifting small nymphs on light tippet, if you detect a take, all you need is a slight tensioning of the line to check and see if the fish is there. The violent hook set is improper and shows a lack of discipline and control. A little tension sometimes causes the fish to clamp down harder on the fly and turn away, which will result in a hook up; a little more tension and the fish will set the hook itself. Many anglers break off big fish by over-aggressive hook sets. This is very apparent in soft hackle fishing. The takes many times are visual, and by maintaining good contact with your fly (no slack), all that is required for a hook set is a slight pickup on the rod. Aggressive hook sets with this type of fishing will result in immediate break-offs and too much time spent tying on fresh flies. Just lift the rod, and check for positive contact. If there's none, continue fishing.

Even with tailwater rivers like the Owens, where water temperature is less of a problem than on many freestone waters, anglers sometimes become too intent on pursuing the elusive hatch and miss out on some great fishing that is always within reach. During slow periods, or when multiple hatches have gorged fish to the point where they will no longer take traditional offerings, try simple imitations of terrestrials like crustacea or an underwater streamer. A streamer is a kind of wet fly that is long and narrow, tied on long-shank hooks, and generally meant to imitate a live minnow or small baitfish.

Streamer collections are essential. Include Woolly Buggers, Byford's Zonkers, deer hair, Woolhead Sculpins, Muddlers, and Crystal Buggers. Sizes, which should cover the full range of bait fish, should start at size 6 and be tied as small as size 12. Be sure to include several color and shade variations for each pattern as you will want to be able to adapt to water color and light conditions.

Tackle needs for the Owens are simple. Rods of 9-foot length in medium action are perfect. Choose line weights from 4 to 6 to negotiate the wind and single-action reels filled to capacity with 20-pound dacron backing (150 yards is adequate). You might need to chase a trophy brown downriver in your waders, so you may get into your backing.

Wading gear should be adapted to the seasons. Neoprene for cold temperatures and hip boots or even shorts and wading shoes for the warm summer months. Shoes need to be equipped with felt soles for no-skid contact with the bottom. The one thing the angler should not be caught without on the Owens is a noncaustic insect repellent. Avon Skin-So-Soft is ideal because it is effective as well as gentle on your skin.

Plan to spend some time during your stay in nonfishing pursuits. The valley is one photo opportunity after another. Side trips are worthwhile, such as the Tule Elk Preserve in Independence (south on Highway 395), or spend an afternoon photographing the many resident animals in the Owens corridor such as ringtail cat, beaver, mule deer, sage hen, and valley quail.

The area's crowning glories, however, are the magnificent Sierra-Nevada Mountains that appear to rise straight up from the valley floor to pierce the sky. The Owens Valley has incredible vistas and unbelievable contrasts. This is truly an outdoor paradise, one of California's treasures, and should be visited and appreciated by all.

On Minnows: To Catch a Trout

Excerpted from *The Compleat Angler*, published in 1676
by Izaak Walton

Now for the Minnow or Peek: he is not easily found and caught till March, or in April, for then he appears first in the river; nature having taught him to shelter and hide himself, in the winter, in ditches that be near to the river; and there both to hide, and keep himself warm, in the mud, or in the weeds, which rot not so soon as in a running river, in which place if he were in winter, the distempered floods that are usually in that season would suffer him to take no rest, but carry him headlong to mills and weirs, to his confusion. And of these Minnows: first, you are to know, that the biggest size is not the best; and next, that the middle size and the whitest are the best; and then you are to know, that your minnow must be so put on your hook, that it must turn round when 'tis drawn against the stream; and, that it may turn nimbly, you must put it on a big-sized hook, as I shall now direct you, which is thus:

Put your hook in at his mouth, and out at his gill; then, having drawn your hook two or three inches beyond or through his gill, put it again into his mouth, and the point and beard out at his tail; and then tie the hook and his tail about, very neatly, with a white thread, which will make it turn quick in the water; that done, pull back that part of your line which was slack when you did put your hook into the minnow the second time; I say, pull that part of your line back, so that it shall fasten the head, so that the body of the minnow shall be almost straight on your hook: this done, try how it will turn, by drawing it across the water or against a stream; and if it do not turn nimbly, then turn the tail a little to the right or left hand, and try again, till it turn quick; for if not, you are in danger to catch nothing: for know, that it is impossible that it should turn too quick. You may salt them, and by that means keep them ready and fit for use three or four days, or longer; and that, of salt, bay-salt is the best.

At some times, and in some waters, a minnow is not to be got; and therefore, let me tell you, I have, which I will show to you, an artificial minnow, that will catch a Trout as well as an artificial fly: and it was made by a handsome woman that had a fine hand, and a live minnow lying by her: the mould or body of the minnow was cloth, and wrought upon, or over it, thus, with a needle; the back of it with very sad French green silk, and paler green silk towards the belly, shadowed as perfectly as you can imagine, just as you see a minnow: the belly was wrought also with a needle, and it was, a part of it, white silk; and another part of it with silver thread: the tail and fins were of a quill, which was shaven thin: the eyes were of two little black beads: and the head was so shadowed, and all of it so curiously wrought, and so exactly dissembled, that it would beguile any sharp-sighted Trout in a swift stream.

FISHING LICENSE

CHAPTER 6

Casting and Landing

The art of the cast is simple but not always easy. The best way to learn is from a skillful fly fisher. If a friend got you interested in fly-fishing, perhaps he or she can help you with casting. The risk, however, is that you pick up their bad habits. Your friend may be an excellent caster but not an excellent teacher. Perhaps the best teacher is a fly-fishing school. In a short time you can go from rank novice to a respectable fly fisher. Another way to learn casting is to rent or buy instructional videotapes that you can view over and over again, for instance, *Fly Fishing Success with Joe Humphreys*.

Get your hands wet, so to speak, by practicing under the watchful eye of a seasoned fly fisherman. Believe me, it will accelerate the learning process as will fishing alongside someone familiar with the water and its resident population. Casting is important to learn correctly, then practice to build muscle memory. One thing about muscle memory: I've played basketball for the past thirty years. I've shot a lot of free throws. If I stand at the free throw line and close my eyes, I can still sink baskets. Why? Muscle memory.

First, with spinning tackle, the weight of the lure sends the line out. In fly casting, the weight is distributed all along the line so you're actually casting the *line*, not the *fly*. The best way to practice is to stand in the middle of an open space about 70 feet long. Lay the rod down, reel handle up, and, line in hand, walk out about 30 feet of line, leader attached.

Return to the rod and pick it up, being careful to keep the rod tip pointing down. Grasp the grip like you would shake someone's hand. Keep your thumb on top, pointing forward. Make sure the snake guides and reel are facing down.

Assuming you cast with your right hand, hold the line firmly in your left hand just as the line comes off the reel. Begin to lift the line off the ground, smoothly but gradually accelerating the line up. Clutching the line comfortably with your left hand, don't let any of the line slip through the guides as you bring the rod back. By the time the rod reaches the 11 o'clock position, the line will be coming toward you in the air. Bring the rod back no farther than 1 o'clock,

tense your forearm to lock the line, pause while the line straightens out behind you, then start your forward cast.

As in tennis, you don't want to break your wrist when you cast. Use your forearm and elbow, but remember the pivot point is really your shoulder. The entire cast is smooth but brisk. As you bring the line back, it takes on the shape of a candy cane loop as it first circles above your head and then behind you. When the line nearly straightens out, you're ready to begin your forward cast. Make sure the line doesn't fall any lower than the top of your head. This back cast prepares you for accelerating the line forward. Without a good back cast, a good forward cast is nearly impossible. This takes practice.

Casting has to do with line speed (how fast the line moves through the snake guides). Line speed has to do with technique, not strength. For the forward cast, accelerate the line forward smoothly and rapidly until your wrist reaches the 11 o'clock position, no farther. Then stop. You need to abruptly stop the movement of the rod forward. Do this by tensing your forearm at 11 o'clock, and the line should start to lay gently on the ground in front of you. Slowly let your rod lower forward until it is horizontal with the ground. Use the rod tip to follow the fly to the water. Don't drop the rod tip down too quickly.

Remember that your forward cast is like using a hammer to nail a picture to the wall. Cast backward like you're throwing nails over your shoulder. Others liken it to throwing a chunk of potato off the tines of a dinner fork. Whatever image works for you and is easier to remember is fine. Critical to good casting is abruptly stopping the movement of the line during the back cast when you reach 1 o'clock and during the forward cast when you reach 11 o'clock. When you stop the rod suddenly, energy is released into the fly line and it surges forward with the leader and fly. You don't have to heave the rod for a forward cast like bait rods. The release of energy through the fly rod builds line speed.

If the line doesn't straighten out or falls coil-like onto the ground, it may be because you're so used to bait casting. The first time I learned to cast, the line crashed into my face, but with time and practice (not on a lake or stream at first), I got the hang of it. If you've used a spinning reel for any length of time, you know that you don't have to jerk the line backward or forward because the weight of the lure does this for you. In fly casting, on the other hand, you need to use power to accelerate the line back to 1 o'clock. Stop. Then cast forward to 11 o'clock and stop. You don't want to whip the line because you'll lose your fly, but you do need some snap.

Note that the 11 and 1 o'clock positions are good to begin, but this concept is limiting and causes big loops. Wind and stiff breezes will have a field day with large loops, so you need to keep them small on the back and forward casts. A good rule of thumb is the

EVERYTHING **FLY-FISHING BOOK**

longer the line you're casting, the longer your arc needs to be, say, 9 o'clock and 3 o'clock. Shorter lines requires less arc.

Loop control is simply being able to adjust the width of your casting loop to fit specific situations. You may need to cast your fly underneath an overhanging bush; a tight loop will get you there with the least chance of hanging up the fly. You determine the size of the loop by rod movement and the length of your power stroke. A tight loop gives you better control over accuracy and distance. You encounter less resistance and more line speed in the air. Learning to create shallow loops on your casts will give you the edge on that pesky wind.

Another way to ensure your casts are successful is to keep your rod tip in a straight plane. You don't want to arc your rod like it's a windshield wiper. It's not. Another way to ensure a good back cast (which makes for a good forward cast) starts with picking the line up off the water. Do so evenly, smoothly, yet with steady acceleration. Both of these techniques will help prevent tailing loops that can double back and create knots in your leader. Tailing loops are also caused by stopping the forward cast too abruptly, which can cause the tippet to tie itself into a knot. Two easy solutions: one, open the 11- and-1 o'clock arcs on your back and forward casts to 10-and-2 o'clock. (How much depends on how much fly line you're casting.) Two, let the rod tip follow the fly to the water. There, easy! Well, maybe not easy, but simple. It's really not complicated, especially with practice and as you learn the feel of your rod. Remember, it's worth spending the time to learn. If you can't cast, fly-fishing isn't fun.

Once you've learned basic casting, you can move to false casting. False casting is a continuous forward and backward movement without the line touching the ground (or water). This type of casting is necessary for getting more line out, accurately presenting your fly and drying a water-logged fly. If you want to change directions on the water, the false cast is an excellent way to, slowly, by degrees, rotate yourself so you can cast to a rising fish.

Here's how to false cast: cast your line forward and backward without letting the line fall lower than your head. Until you do it by feel, watch behind you to make sure the line falls at the right height. Another way is to say your name—"My name is Jeff"—as the rod reloads the line on the back cast. Then you're ready to begin the forward movement. Eventually you'll know what your back cast looks like just by the feel of the rod.

The forward cast doesn't require any more energy than the back cast. Many men tend to throw too much power into the forward cast, creating an uneven, loopy result as well as a jarring presentation that can easily spook the fish in clear water. You're working for what's called delicate presentation.

Presentation refers both to the completion of a well-executed cast and to the gentle deposit of the fly on the surface of the water. When the fly and the line land on the water, they should create the least possible disturbance to avoid spooking wary fish. A dry fly must land very softly or it will break the surface and begin sinking. A nymph can hit the water with a little more force, providing it doesn't scare the fish.

After a while of false casting, pull out line (3 feet for starters) with your left hand and let it dangle below the reel. Holding the line firmly on the back cast, let go and let it run through the snake guides on the forward cast. This is how you make longer and longer casts, but don't worry about distance casts: most fish you'll catch will be within 30 feet of you and accuracy is much more important than distance. Then practice, practice, practice until you can direct the fly to nearly any point forward on the grass.

Practice false casting while you slowly turn—90 degrees one way, then 90 degrees the other way. Being able to face all sections of the water, fly in the air, will enable you to navigate the water and present to rising trout.

But what if you're out fishing one day and the spot you desire is crowded with brush? If you can't reach the hole from the other side of the stream or river, you can still cast without having to bring the line behind you. What you need is a roll cast.

This type of cast must be practiced on the water because the water's surface tension makes the roll cast work. Start by false casting about 20 feet of line out and removing any slack in the line.

Then slowly but with steady acceleration pull the line toward you by raising the rod tip until it is behind you at 1 o'clock. Stop the backward movement, hold it for a second, then briskly bring down the rod tip to move the line back out to the water. Let the rod drop to a horizontal position.

One fly caster at LL Bean noted that the most common enemy of the roll cast was in not stopping long enough after raising the rod tip to 1 o'clock. For the roll cast to work, a belly of line must form—and form completely—*behind* the rod before the rod is brought forward. The easiest way to ensure this will happen is to stop the rod completely at 1 o'clock and wait, keeping the rod completely still. The rod must be *completely still* for at least half a heartbeat—or long enough to allow the line to catch up to the rod, pass it, and then form a belly behind it. Trying to execute a roll cast in one complete, seamless motion often has the novice bringing the rod forward too soon, before the belly of line has formed behind it. The result is a pileup of line at the caster's feet. Once the caster is adept, the pause between stopping on the back cast and then applying the forward stroke can be minimized to the point where the cast appears to be made in one smooth motion, but that only comes with time and practice. Bottom line: *Slow* down on the roll cast.

Another time to use the roll cast is when you're float tubing. Then you don't have to "strip in" (that is, take up) all the line before your next cast. These types of casting are essential to learn, and best under the tutelage of a seasoned instructor. Otherwise, you'll end up watching others fish. That's no fun. Finally, after your cast is done, extend your forefinger and bring in the line under it. This ensures that anytime a fish hits, you can control the line and won't have any unwanted slack in it. Your other hand is free to pull in line (stripping).

A few techniques will help assure that your casting and presentation land you fish. Accuracy is probably the most fundamental component of good fly presentation. During times of heavy hatching activity and insect swarming, when the fish seem to be feeding almost recklessly, it's easy to begin firing cast after cast almost at random. But untargeted casting usually doesn't work.

When huge amounts of food are available on the surface, most of the fish are unlikely to move any distance to feed—they don't have to. Remember, fish are efficient and will expend the least energy for the greatest gain. Some fish will focus all their rises to an area about the size of your coffee cup. Such a restricted feeding zone requires an angler to deliver his fly with precision.

Bigger fish, especially, have a habit of setting up to feed in a small, specific spot. This will usually be a place where a seam in the current or some object funnels an above average amount of food items over their position.

Once a fish has targeted a steady flow of nourishment, it will rarely deviate from that optimum feeding line. To catch fish in heavy hatches, then, the fly must be presented accurately. Learning better casting accuracy should be a priority for those wishing to hone their presentation skills.

To practice, set up a target on your lawn and practice hitting within 3 feet of it. Then set up several targets at various distances. Make a single cast to any one of them and then cast to the next. When you can rotate through the whole batch, hitting all or most of the targets in turn on the first cast, you should be amply prepared for most on-stream situations.

Of course, delivering the fly to the target is only the first step of dry fly presentation. In most cases, the fly must float naturally and drag-free over the fish's position to have any chance of being taken. Insects caught in the surface tension drift naturally with the currents. Fish are suspicious of anything that doesn't float or move naturally.

117

Artificial flies tend to drag or move unnaturally across the surface because they are attached to a leader and heavy fly line. Even on a short cast, the fly, leader, and line are likely to be affected by several bands of current traveling at different velocities and angles. Sooner or later one or more of these current tongues will begin to dominate the drift of the whole process and cause the fly to drag or move at a different speed than the current.

The easiest method of overcoming unwanted drag is to ensure there's slack in the leader or line. This slack should take the form of a series of gentle S curves. Because it takes longer for the current to straighten out an amount of slack, you are buying a few more precious seconds for the fly to pass over the fish in a natural manner.

The simplest way to throw slack is to keep the rod tip high or pull back slightly on the forward casting stroke, then quickly lower the rod tip. This causes the line and leader to spring back slightly and settle gently on the water.

There are many other casts and casting tricks that can be an asset to presentation for those willing to master them. The value of good presentation can be summed up like this: it's better to cast the "wrong" fly and fish it properly than to have the "right" fly and fish it wrong.

Remember, casting is one of the most important ingredients in successful fly-fishing. Continue to practice as much as possible both on the water and on the grass. You won't regret time spent perfecting your timing and training your casting muscles. Now it's time to be a part of the action! You're ready for the water. C'mon, the fish are waiting!

Controlling Your Rod

Fly-fishing can be an elegant and effective way to catch fish, or it can be a frustrating bumble. Whether you're a beginner just out of the gate, or an experienced hand who still believes there's more to learn, give the following tips a try. They can help boost both the level and the pleasure of your game.

Go the Distance

Want to add a quick 10 to 20 feet to your casts? And suffer far fewer tangles and knots? Then make a habit of this simple discipline: stretch the fly line before you start fishing. Fly line's memory causes it to retain the coil-shape of the spool. The longer it stays on the spool unused, the more severe the coiling. Coils create tangles and knots; they stick in the rod guides during the cast and make it difficult to shoot line smoothly. So, before the first cast, pull all the line from the reel, a yard or so at a time, stretching it across your chest. Then stretch it again, bottom to top. Even better, while reeling the line back onto the spool, run it through a cleaning pad or rag dampened with commercial line cleaner or an Armorall-type product. A clean line handles better, floats higher, and shoots through the guides with minimal friction.

Under Control

Never let your fly line hang free and loose during casting, presentation, or when fighting a fish. While false casting, slack line is controlled by the free, or "line," hand; but most anglers then simply let go when they shoot out a cast. Don't. Instead, shoot the line through an "O" made with the index finger and thumb-tip of the line hand. This not only lets you stop or shorten the cast at will by closing the O; it also gives you constant control. When the cast lands, there is no groping for the loose line; nor can the line wrap around the handle or rod butt. Next move: slip the line under the index finger of the rod hand before stripping in the retrieve. If a fish strikes, simply clamp down to lock the line against the grip. Then lift the rod as needed to set the hook efficiently.

Out Cast

Cast out, not down. Most fly casters impair their delivery (and distance potential) by dropping the rod tip too much on the forward cast, in effect casting down instead of out. This is understandable because we generally focus our eyes on the water or the fish. Far

better, though, to stop the forward cast while the tip is moving only marginally "down" (just enough to get out of the way of the forward-moving fly line). An abrupt stop of the rod tip during the forward cast, before the tip drops more than slightly, will send your fly line zinging out over the water, giving the line and leader a chance to turn over fully, dropping the fly on target.

Slow Down

Cast less, think more. Watching most fly rodders, you'd think they were getting paid by the false cast. Line whips back and forth, spending more time in the air than on the water. Anglers are in too much of a rush, making too much commotion, fishing on apparent autopilot, catching nothing but dubious exercise. Hot tip: Slow down. Observe the water carefully before rushing in. Apply a little angling theory to the scene. Example: there's no hatch on, but trout are rising occasionally; wind is flagging the branches—a logically good time to think about terrestrials. Choose an appropriate fly pattern. Now reason out your approach: start from here, casting to there; move up a few yards to there. . . . All of this can be done in relatively few minutes, but it's an exercise that adds depth, calm, and effectiveness to a day's fishing.

Well-Timed

To cast elegantly and well, think timing, not power. If you are muscling the rod or relying on power to make the rod work, your timing's probably haywire. Go back to fundamentals: a very short line—30 feet, say; just enough to load the rod—where muscle isn't necessary. Pick up, back cast, transition to a forward cast, light forward snap (mostly wrist), abrupt stop of rod tip, line shooting out. Timing. Stay with the short line until the sense of proper timing is ingrained.

Are the ferrules on your two- or three-piece rod a little loose? Don't risk the rod coming apart during a cast, or when a good fish is on. Rub the male sections on all sides with any kind of wax (even a tube of lip balm will do in a pinch) to tighten the connec-

tion. With a graphite rod, be sure to twist the pieces together as you line up the guides.

Mark your fly lines below the leader connection for quick and easy identification, thereby avoiding unintentional mismatches when changing spools or moving reels to different rods. Use a black indelible pen. A wide bar signifies 5; a narrow slash, 1. So: bar, slash, slash is a 7-weight. Three slashes equals a 3-weight, and so on.

Don't string up your rod the usual way: by poking the thin leader through each guide, then grasping to pull it through. If you lose your grip, the line slips back down through all the guides and you must start over. Instead, double the fly line below the leader and push it through the guides. Not only is the thick line easier to handle; if accidentally released it will spring open and catch itself in the nearest guide, preventing a good deal of irritation and nasty language.

Types of Casts

Roll cast: an on-the-water cast in which there is no back cast and the line forms a loop that rolls forward away from the caster. It is made by slowly lifting the rod to 90 degrees and dragging the line toward you. When the line has stopped moving, make the forward portion of a regular cast to form the loop, followed by a quick speed up and stop of the rod.

Pick-up-and-lay-down cast: pick the line up from the water, make a single back cast and a single forward cast, then lay the line back down on the water.

False casting: keeping the line up in the air (aerializing) by making continuous forward and back casts.

Reach mend: a cast in which the rod is "reached" or extended to one side, either a right reach or left reach, so the line falls to the tip of the rod away from the caster. It is used when casting across different current speeds to correct for line drift.

Mending Your Line

It's important that the fly drift downstream as naturally as possible. However, a current carries floating line downstream faster than the fly trailing behind it. This interrupts the fly's natural drift and fish will refuse it. The simple but effective technique of mending solves this problem. Before the current has straightened out your line and before the fly starts to curve unnaturally, you can mend the line by partly raising your rod and moving it abruptly in a semicircle upstream. This throws the butt section of the line (closest to you) upstream and keeps the line from out-running the fly and preserving its natural drift. Some fly fishers give the line a slight tug as they arc the rod upstream during a mend.

Mending line: throwing the line which is already on the water upstream or downstream to correct again for differences in water currents between the rod tip and the fly.

Mend cast or in-the-air mend: a cast in which the mend is introduced during the cast so the line falls on the water with a curve that will correct for the current drift. The cast is made by moving the rod tip to the side after the forward power stroke. The longer the delay in time between the end of the power stroke and the sideward movement places the curve closer to the caster. The longer the length of time the rod is deflected, the longer the curve. The greater the amount of deflection, the deeper the curve.

"S" or wiggle cast: a cast performed by wiggling the rod rapidly side to side after the power stroke. It is a series of rapid left and right, in-the-air mends. This cast is useful when currents are irregular so a single mend cannot compensate for them.

Puddle cast: a cast made by shooting the fly line high over the target then dropping the rod tip rapidly down so the leader falls in a big puddle of line on the target. The leader does not lay out in the usual sense, so there is plenty of slack leader to compensate for drag. This cast is useful for casting into an area of quiet water surrounded by moving water, for example, the water in back of a log or around a boulder in the middle of a river.

Parachute cast: a cast made to trout feeding downstream. The rod is kept high after the cast so the line looks like a parachute cord hanging from the rod tip. The rod tip is then gradually lowered at the speed of the drifting fly to put it in the feeding lane of the trout. If the cast is not in the feeding lane, it can be skittered across the water into the feeding lane before feeding the trout the fly.

Curve cast: a cast made by whipping the rod tip to the right or left during the end of the power stroke (during the speed-up and stop). This causes the leader to curve to the right or left respectively. This cast is different from the mend cast in which the curve is introduced after the power stroke.

Tuck cast: a nymphing cast in which the rod tip is abruptly stopped at the end of the power cast and more energy than is

necessary is put into the cast so the nymph and leader bounce back underneath the fly line and the nymph enters the water closer to the caster than the end of the fly line. It allows the nymph to go deeper, faster, and with minimal drag.

Pendulum cast: a cast in which the loop in the fly line is reversed so it is under the line and the fly travels up at the end of the cast like a pendulum. It is made with the rod to the side and it is really an upward curve cast at the end of each power stroke. It is also called a figure 8 cast since it looks like the rod tip is writing a figure 8 lying on its side. It is a cast useful for getting the fly under low-lying branches. When exaggerated the pendulum cast can lay the line down like a puddle cast since the fly and leader are traveling up at the end of the cast.

Steeple cast: a cast in which you turn your wrist upside down, allowing you to make a back cast straight up into the air (like a steeple), then turn your wrist and body forward to make the usual forward cast. This cast is used when your back is to a high bank of brush or trees and there is rapidly flowing water in front of you so you can't make a roll cast.

The Art of the Landing

When a fish strikes, it's vital to know how to control the line, set the hook, fight the fish, and land him. While you're fishing, a good habit is to hold the line against the handle of the rod with your index finger. This way you can set the hook quickly and with authority simply by using your finger to tighten down on the line. If you are righthanded, you will retrieve your fly by pulling on the line with your left hand, allowing it to slip under the index finger of your right hand. The line will coil by your feet in large, loose loops.

Novices are usually not prepared for a strike on the first cast, but they need to be. It happens all too often. It helps to take stock of your surroundings before your first cast. If you hook a fish from the bank, will you be able to step down into

All Hung Up

I think one of fly-fishing's most infuriating frustrations is getting snagged on a tree or bush. Just when you think you're becoming proficient at false casting and you spot a couple of hungry trout, oops! Your line gets snagged behind you.

If you are fishing with barbless hooks, most snags are easily removed. However, sometimes you can't get to a tree or bush to remove the snag. That's when you may need to employ an oft-used technique. First, point the rod at the snag and take up all the slack. Wind up a little more line and pull on the snag, then immediately release the line so it bounces back toward the snag. Sometimes this bounce is enough to free your hang-up, other times you have to repeat it several times.

the water and follow the fish if you have to? Often that first step off the bank is into water that's deeper than you thought, or you may sink into soft mud.

If the current is swift, set each foot firmly before moving to your other one. It's difficult to wade deeper than waste-high, so if you enter the water, be sure you know its depth ahead of time. If you get into a tricky area, be sure you can get out. Your waders may create a lot of water resistance, and moving about in fast water is not easy. A wading staff will come in handy.

The clearer the water, the more gently you need to wade. Sloppy wading kicks up rocks and sediment and can ruin your fishing prospects for many yards around you. Use stealth to get yourself into position to approach rising and feeding fish.

If you're a beginner, don't become so absorbed by techniques in casting and knot tying that you forget about fishing. Many do. They put all their energy in the cast but forget how to fish! Don't omit readying yourself for the obvious—a fish on the line. Depending on what you are fishing, whether dry flies, nymphs, streamers, or "bugs," always be prepared for the strike.

If you're fishing dries, keep your eye on the fly. A trout will often hook itself. If you're fishing the subsurface nymphs, keep your eye on the strike indicator if you're using one. Subsurface strikes require setting the hook because in an instant a fish will inhale and expel your nymph.

When you feel the first tug on your line, you'll need to set the hook yet not strike too hard. *Pull the hook home smoothly by simply stripping in line.* Don't rip the rod back.

The pull of the line is what frightens the fish and panics him into seeking cover. The harder you pull, the harder he pulls. If the fish runs, let him go, unless he is obviously tearing off to a tangle of weeds, underbrush, or rocks. In that case, increase tension to turn the fish before it runs into snags that will break you off. Turn your rod horizontally and parallel to the water for a few seconds so the fish has to turn its head, first to one side, then the other. Keep it fighting line, rod, and current as you begin to retrieve line and work it into a calm stretch of water for landing.

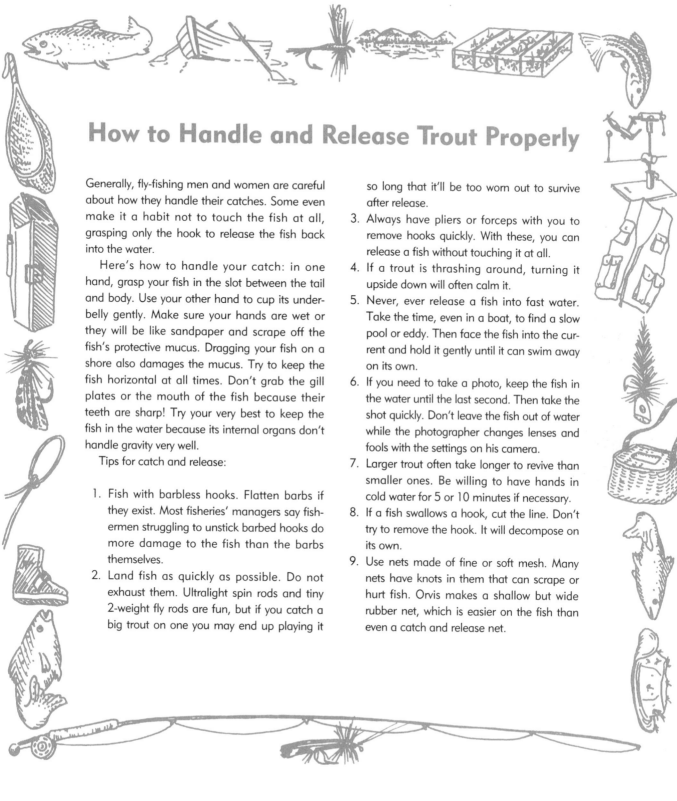

How to Handle and Release Trout Properly

Generally, fly-fishing men and women are careful about how they handle their catches. Some even make it a habit not to touch the fish at all, grasping only the hook to release the fish back into the water.

Here's how to handle your catch: in one hand, grasp your fish in the slot between the tail and body. Use your other hand to cup its underbelly gently. Make sure your hands are wet or they will be like sandpaper and scrape off the fish's protective mucus. Dragging your fish on a shore also damages the mucus. Try to keep the fish horizontal at all times. Don't grab the gill plates or the mouth of the fish because their teeth are sharp! Try your very best to keep the fish in the water because its internal organs don't handle gravity very well.

Tips for catch and release:

1. Fish with barbless hooks. Flatten barbs if they exist. Most fisheries' managers say fishermen struggling to unstick barbed hooks do more damage to the fish than the barbs themselves.
2. Land fish as quickly as possible. Do not exhaust them. Ultralight spin rods and tiny 2-weight fly rods are fun, but if you catch a big trout on one you may end up playing it so long that it'll be too worn out to survive after release.
3. Always have pliers or forceps with you to remove hooks quickly. With these, you can release a fish without touching it at all.
4. If a trout is thrashing around, turning it upside down will often calm it.
5. Never, ever release a fish into fast water. Take the time, even in a boat, to find a slow pool or eddy. Then face the fish into the current and hold it gently until it can swim away on its own.
6. If you need to take a photo, keep the fish in the water until the last second. Then take the shot quickly. Don't leave the fish out of water while the photographer changes lenses and fools with the settings on his camera.
7. Larger trout often take longer to revive than smaller ones. Be willing to have hands in cold water for 5 or 10 minutes if necessary.
8. If a fish swallows a hook, cut the line. Don't try to remove the hook. It will decompose on its own.
9. Use nets made of fine or soft mesh. Many nets have knots in them that can scrape or hurt fish. Orvis makes a shallow but wide rubber net, which is easier on the fish than even a catch and release net.

Watch out: if the fish gets below you, heading downstream, you have to decide if you can turn it or follow it downstream, either by wading or following along the shoreline. Renowned salmon angler Bill Hunger explained his technique of stripping line off his reel, allowing the slack to land in the water. Eventually, a belly of line formed in the current below the fish. This put tension on the line downstream of the fish, which naturally reacted by running back upstream toward the angler. With a few turns of the reel, the line was back under control, and the fish was soon in the net. It may sound crazy, but it can work, providing the fish is well hooked in the first place.

Playing the fish is a give-and-take affair. If the fish is small, you can usually line it in, meaning stripping the line in by hand without the reel. But you may find landing a fish more enjoyable if you play it from the reel the whole way through. That way you can play the fish against the combined action and cushioning effect of the reel's drag, the rod's springiness, friction of the guides, and stretch of the leader.

When your catch stops, gently reel him back. Keep your line taut at all times, no slack, to keep him on the shortest line possible. This will give you more control as you help him wend his way to the net. The constant, steady exertion you put on the fish is what tires him out. Keep him working at all times, but gently. Don't overstress yourself or your equipment. When the fish shows obvious signs of tiring, such as rolling on to his side, gently bring him in to the net.

If you prematurely try to bring in your catch before he tires, you run the risk of snapping your tippet off. The more the fish runs, jumps, and fights the current, the more quickly he will tire. But use balance. Tiring a fish excessively or overexhausting him is hazardous to the fish and threatens his very survival after you release him. Also, the longer you fight the fish the greater the possibility for the hook to enlarge the initial point of penetration, then fall out of the fish's mouth.

Use a net only if you intend to keep your catch. Despite what your instincts tell you, it is not proper technique to chase the fish with the net. Place the net about halfway down in the water and draw the fish toward it headfirst. Try to keep the fish's head close to the surface. Handled properly, a hooked fish will actually swim into a net.

You can often unhook your fish while he is still in the net. A fish usually doesn't have to be lifted from the water, particularly with a barbless hook. A quick twist and shake of the hook will usually free it. If not, use a pair of forceps or needlenose pliers to grab the hook's shank and twist it loose. Fly-fishing usually hooks the fish in the lip or jaw, but occasionally, particularly when fishing nymphs, a fish may be hooked in the tongue. Or the hook may penetrate through its mouth and into the eye area. Use your judgment. If a legal fish is bleeding freely or is mortally injured, keep it, because it will only die downstream.

If, after being caught, your fish is tired but in good condition, take some time to gently cradle the fish in calm water. Slowly move the fish backward and forward so its gills are forced to open and close. This delivers oxygen to an oxygen-depleted fish. Wait until the gill plates are moving again before releasing the fish back into the water. The worst thing you can do to a fish is to quickly release him into fast-moving current. Hold the fish underwater for as long as it takes until he regains his strength and equilibrium. It will dart from your hands when ready. That's all there is to it, but what a thrill!

Tips on Landing a Big One

Too many anglers give little thought to the importance of hooking, playing, and landing fish until they find themselves attached to a really good one. And then it's usually too late, because things have a way of happening so quickly that the fish can decide the matter in its favor in an instant.

When you have a fish on the line, it's not really important whether you work the fish with your reel or with your hand

When the Fish Aren't Biting

- Sneak up on the fish, crouch, or hide behind bushes.
- Change to a finer tippet.
- Your dry fly or nymph may be creating drag; let it go into a dead drift.
- Learn to fish like a heron: simply watch, study fish movements, and enter the water more cautiously.
- Change from a dry fly to a wet fly or nymph.
- Switch to a smaller fly.
- Rest the water by leaving and coming back in a few minutes after the trout return.

directly on the line. Some feel they have more line control if they tire the fish with line in hand instead of using the reel to take up line. Whichever you prefer, there are reasons why some fishermen land far more good fish than they lose. They take care of details and eliminate as many possibilities for failure before the first cast is made.

The hook is a huge item to inspect. If hooks are not needle sharp, they won't penetrate deeply and cleanly. Dull hooks find a way to pull or tear loose during a lengthy battle. When a fish strikes, a sharp hook sets firmly and doesn't stress (or possibly break) a light tippet. Use a whetstone or file to put a sharp point on a new hook or to recondition a hook dulled by thumping along the river bottom.

Another important item is the leader tippet. Check them frequently for nicks, kinks, abrasion, or anything else that could possibly weaken this last link between angler and fish. With time, stress can compromise the strength of knots. If you have caught several fish on the same fly, it's a good idea to snip it off and re-tie the knot attaching it.

As you inspect your fly-fishing rig, ask yourself, If I knew this was going to hook the biggest fish of my life, would I be satisfied with this setup? If your answer is anything but a confident yes, make some adjustments.

A point about big fish: if he is hooked well, he will almost always wind up in the net. If the fish is not hooked well, he will almost always get away, no matter how gently you play him. So experienced anglers play every fish with confidence that the hook will hold long enough to wear him out. You'll need to tire most game fish (bass, trout, salmon, pike, tarpon, etc.) before bringing them to the net. When first hooked, most game fish will either jump, make a long, powerful run, or use their size and strength to hold their ground.

In the case of a fish that runs, your reactions in those first critical seconds can make all the difference. If there are no obstructions where the fish can tangle or cut the leader, the best strategy is to let the fish do what he wants and expend as much energy as possible. After an initial flurry, the fish begins to tire.

If the fish has gotten downstream any distance, try to make it swim back toward you by applying steady pressure. Get this fish on the reel and reel in your line instead of stripping it. If the current is too strong or the fish refuses to budge, your best bet is to walk toward it, reeling in line as you go. When you have moved into position, either across from or slightly below the fish, you can resume the battle of wearing him down with steady pressure.

Never let a big fish get below you and wallow or thrash about on the surface. It seems like more fish are lost this way than any other. Lower the rod tip and surrender a few feet of slack to make the fish submerge once again. The idea is to keep the fish under control and bring it ever closer, yet be prepared for twists, turns, or surges the fish might happen to make.

Let the rod's bending capacity tire the fish. But what makes the job more complicated is the reality that big fish rarely live in open water. Logs, sharp groups of rocks, ledges, undercut banks, tree roots, and weeds are a few types of cover that Big'uns like to call home.

If you hook a big fish under or near some obstruction, try to force it away from the cover immediately by applying every ounce of pressure you think your tippet can withstand. Once you have it away from the cover, try to position yourself between the fish and the obstruction. Then, in the later stages of the battle, if the fish does make a run back to cover, you'll have a better chance of stopping him.

If the fish wants to bolt for another run after you've got him into position for netting, let him go. Then you still have a chance of getting the fish in again. If you try to prevent the fish from taking that last desperate run if he wants to, you'll lose it every time.

One way to lose a big fish is while netting him. Many times your net is too small for the job. Carrying a good-sized landing net around is certainly no fun, but if you're fishing waters containing trophy fish, you'll be glad you took a trophy net.

Strike!

As beginner's luck would have it, you'll probably have no problem landing your first fish. Those to follow will probably take more work and concentration.

Dry Flies

Watch your fly carefully and don't leave slack in the line. The more slack you take up, the more sensitive you will be to the slightest twitch. If you're using a strike indicator, be sure to set the hook before the fish spits out the fly.

All in all, however, reacting too quickly is probably the main reason novices lose fish taking dry flies. Relax. Let the fish strike first, then strip in the line so it tightens. Once you've got him on the line, be careful to keep the line taut at all times.

Wet Flies

It's more difficult to discern a striking fish using sinking flies or nymphs. If you're using a strike indicator, react the moment the indicator bobs. Lift the rod and take up the line with your other hand.

As you're bringing the fish in, don't chase the fish with the net—a mistake often made by novices. Even a tired fish can swim faster than you can swipe at it with a net in the water. Hold the net under the water and lead the fish over it, headfirst if possible. Then firmly bring the net up out of the water with the fish inside.

It's disappointing to lose fish, and I was recently downcast on the Owens River. After a nice brown took my caddis nymph midstream, the line stopped. I set the hook and, applying constant pressure, spent time properly tiring him. I steered him back and forth across the currents, letting him run a bit if he wanted to. Then, within a blink of an eye, he darted to a position directly below me and used the full force of the current to struggle against the hook. I should never have let him get directly downstream because within a few seconds I lost him.

Next time, I'll go in after him and chase him downstream if I have to! If not, at least I'll make sure to keep the fish out in front of me.

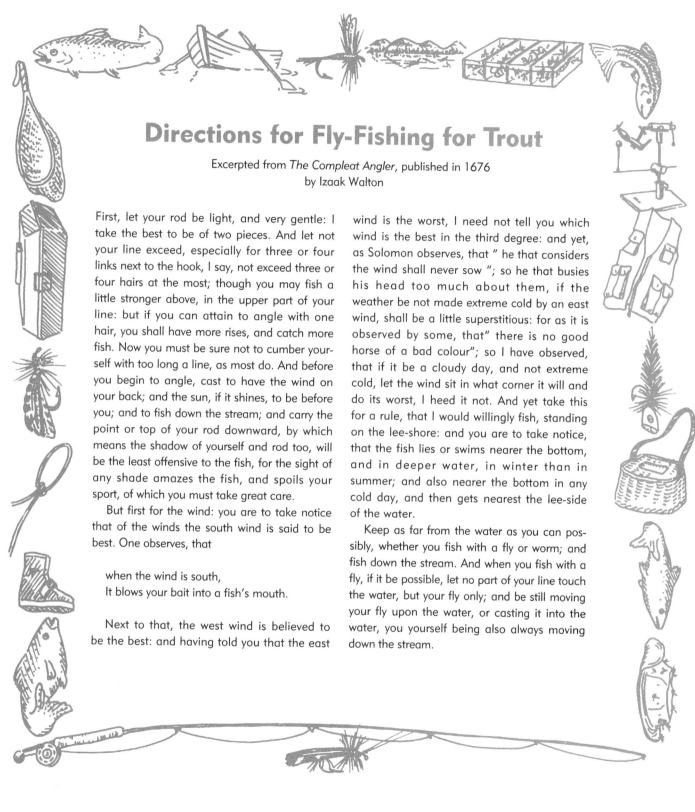

Directions for Fly-Fishing for Trout

Excerpted from *The Compleat Angler*, published in 1676
by Izaak Walton

First, let your rod be light, and very gentle: I take the best to be of two pieces. And let not your line exceed, especially for three or four links next to the hook, I say, not exceed three or four hairs at the most; though you may fish a little stronger above, in the upper part of your line: but if you can attain to angle with one hair, you shall have more rises, and catch more fish. Now you must be sure not to cumber yourself with too long a line, as most do. And before you begin to angle, cast to have the wind on your back; and the sun, if it shines, to be before you; and to fish down the stream; and carry the point or top of your rod downward, by which means the shadow of yourself and rod too, will be the least offensive to the fish, for the sight of any shade amazes the fish, and spoils your sport, of which you must take great care.

But first for the wind: you are to take notice that of the winds the south wind is said to be best. One observes, that

when the wind is south,
It blows your bait into a fish's mouth.

Next to that, the west wind is believed to be the best: and having told you that the east wind is the worst, I need not tell you which wind is the best in the third degree: and yet, as Solomon observes, that " he that considers the wind shall never sow "; so he that busies his head too much about them, if the weather be not made extreme cold by an east wind, shall be a little superstitious: for as it is observed by some, that" there is no good horse of a bad colour"; so I have observed, that if it be a cloudy day, and not extreme cold, let the wind sit in what corner it will and do its worst, I heed it not. And yet take this for a rule, that I would willingly fish, standing on the lee-shore: and you are to take notice, that the fish lies or swims nearer the bottom, and in deeper water, in winter than in summer; and also nearer the bottom in any cold day, and then gets nearest the lee-side of the water.

Keep as far from the water as you can possibly, whether you fish with a fly or worm; and fish down the stream. And when you fish with a fly, if it be possible, let no part of your line touch the water, but your fly only; and be still moving your fly upon the water, or casting it into the water, you yourself being also always moving down the stream.

FISHING LICENSE

CHAPTER 7

Saltwater and Freshwater Trophies

Saltwater: Fishing in a Marine Wonderland

Nothing can match the excitement of saltwater fly-fishing, and no book would be complete without mentioning it. From baitfish to big game, the ocean variety is mind boggling and the challenges worthy of the most ardent saltwater fly rodder. Action is fast and furious, providing the angler is properly equipped, observant, and has a spirit of adventure.

There are more than 10,000 miles of coastline in the continental United States. Many of these areas, which comprise bays, inlets, lagoons, river mouths, and so forth, are accessible by the boatless fly fisherman. There are many tiny saltwater creeks that hold surprisingly large fish, as well as bays, inlets, and brackish to salty ponds. Your quarry will most likely be sailfish, bonefish, rainbow runners, crevalle, barracuda, tarpon, sea bass, amberjack, cobia, king mackerel, albacore, bonito, yellowtail, the tunas, sharks, and a few other species such as the Bermuda chub.

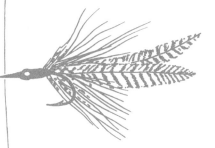

Saltwater fly

Fly-fishing down in saltwater structures is not that different from negotiating the rocks and submerged ledges of a large river. The ocean can be a dizzying myriad of currents, upwellings, surging waves, and undertows, which endlessly tug on your fly line. Arming yourself with the proper equipment and knowing how to use it will determine the degree of your success.

One of the most important pieces of that equipment will be your fly line—most often a super-fast-sinking shooting head. These extremely fast-sinking, lead-core lines make it possible to seek saltwater fish that were once considered targets only for those slinging hardware or bait. Shooting heads have done more to broaden the horizons of saltwater fly anglers than any other tackle development in the past two decades by allowing them to overcome adverse conditions with regard to distance, depth, and current.

You can get by with a fairly light fly rod like a 9-foot with a #9 weight-forward line instead of a shooting line, if you choose. Both types of line will get your fly submerged. With a 9-weight rod and line, the average caster can deliver a saltwater fly to a spot 40 to 50 feet away with a 15 mile-per-hour wind blowing.

Another piece of essential equipment is a sturdy, stainless steel or anodized aluminum fly reel to withstand corrosion. Line capacity is more important in saltwater. You'll need plenty of line to play your larger ocean-going catches. Most experienced anglers agree that minimum capacity is 200 yards of Dacron backing plus the full fly line.

A 9-foot fly rod with fast or stiff action will have enough muscle to handle the heftiest creatures, yet they're light enough not to unduly tire the caster's arm during a day of fishing. High-speed graphite also provides greater sensitivity, an important asset when considering how many fish inhale a fly on the sink or while it's drifting along in deep, swift currents.

Many reef dwellers respond well to the basic "Joe Brooks–style" popper or skipping bug, sizes 1/0 to 3/0. These are usually smaller fish that live in the upper layers of the water column. The "Big Moes" of the reef world, however, the trophy-sized snappers, roosterfish, and others, will require a popper the size of a small bird to entice them up.

Sometimes a way to entice a fish is to have a fishing buddy cast a noisy hookless teaser over the reef or near the rocks, working it quickly back to the boat. The teasing partner draws the fish into range and the fly fisher casts the popper. When the teaser reaches the popper, it is yanked from the area and the fly fisherman takes over.

In taking on the marine environment, the fly angler can expect to encounter several types of structure: protruding rocks, grottos and fast-breaking shoreline reefs, subsurface structure (shallow reefs and wrecks), and raging rips that form around points, through cuts, and over shoals.

Grottos and rocky coves, particularly those found in tropical regions, are absolutely beautiful, fishy-looking places, and are my favorite beats. Generally these areas are easier for the fly rodder to explore, since currents and swells are markedly reduced. Deeper, submerged reefs and wrecks are usually more difficult to work, offering a greater challenge but with satisfying rewards.

Leaders and Flies

When using fast-sinking shooting heads, overall leader length should rarely exceed 3 feet. Long leaders must be tapered to cast properly, which is especially critical when you're sightcasting to fish in clear, shallow water.

Short leaders don't have to be tapered because, during the cast, energy has to be transmitted only a few feet beyond the tip of the fly line. These leaders are frequently used with sinking lines because with a long leader the line will often sink faster than the leader and fly.

For shallow water and calm air, you'll need a long leader. A good starting point for using leaders with floating, intermediate, or wet-tip line is 9 feet. For spooky fish in clear water, you may need as much as 16 feet of leader. (See *Practical Fishing Knots* by Mark Sosin and Lefty Kreh for more detailed information on leader systems for saltwater fly-fishing.)

The most universal fly pattern in all saltwater fishing is the white streamer because it's the most common color for baitfish. Most species have at least some white or white/silver. White also has high visibility under a wide range of water conditions, making it an easy target for predator fish.

An assortment of small, 1- to 2-inch bucktails with a little flash will do for smaller-reef species, like jacks, pompano, mackerel, and bonito. There are dozens of other great saltwater flies that will work marvelously for this kind of angling. Check out books like *Salt Water Fly Patterns* by Lefty Kreh; *Flies for Saltwater* by Dick Stewart and Farrow Allen; *A Fly-Fisher's Guide to Saltwater Naturals and Their Imitation* by George V. Roberts, Jr.; and *Streamers & Bucktails, the Big Fish Flies* by Joseph D. Bates, Jr.

Lessons from a Bass Master

Successful fly-fishing for bass requires special techniques and methods. Expert Dave Whitlock has patented the Whitlock Straight-Line System, which is the result of years of field research and bass fishing. It has proven to be an efficient way to fish for bass. Basically, a fly fisher must present, control, animate, and retrieve the fly with a tight line, then strike, hook, and control the bass with aggressive authority. These steps, taken together, make up a precise system for most effectively fly-fishing for bass.

Presentation and Control

This technique begins with a direct-to-the-water presentation. The forward and down part of the cast must be in a casting plane that causes the fly to hit the target immediately after the leader turns over. This gives you the best opportunity to hit the target perfectly. Study the illustration to get a strong mental picture. An overhead or sidearm straight-to-the-water cast accomplishes this best, depending on obstructions, wind, and the direction from which you must cast.

By the time the fly strikes the target you should have the rod tip at the correct angle and your two-point control system started. Establish two-point fly-line control by grasping the line in your line hand and pinching it between your rod-hand index finger and the rod grip. Do this as the fly begins to drop to the water but before it actually hits the water. You must establish control so quickly because bass often strike the fly as it falls or immediately as it hits the water. You must be ready for a strike at any time.

As the fly hits the water, and before all the fly line settles on it, point the fly rod straight at the fly and drop the rod tip to the water's surface. This eliminates fly-line slack and premature fly movement caused by the high rod-tip angle common to trout fly-fishing. Because the fly line is heavy, it sags to a perpendicular angle from the fly rod tip if the rod tip is held high. The sag pulls the fly line toward you. Three to 5 feet of slack line can tug a fly an equal distance away from the target. Both results are counterproductive and wrong. So keep the tip low—right at water level.

When the fly, leader, and line come down on the water, usually there are some slack curves in the leader and the line. Keeping the tip low, pull in this slack with your line hand without moving the fly. This makes a straight, tight line path from your hand to the fly. Practice this delivery so you can consistently put

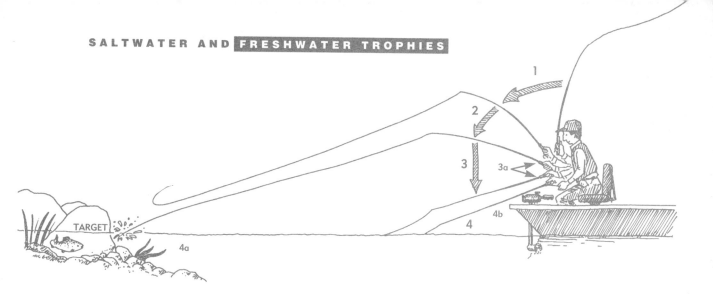

The Whitlock Method for Straight-Line Presentation

1. Always make your forward casting stroke on a downward plane, and aim the fly directly at the target.
2. Stop the stroke at a high rod-tip angle to allow a loop to unroll high and directly toward the target.
3. Lower the rod tip to the water as the fly, leader, and line land.
3a. As the fly falls to the water, establish two-point control.
4. Establish a tight straight line by using your line hand to remove any slack between the fly (4a) and rod (4b).

the fly on the water and remove the small amount of slack in your line without moving the fly. You don't want the fly to move until you initiate the retrieve.

These steps in the Straight-Line System give you precise control of the fly, allowing you to keep it in place, move it, feel a strike, and set the hook in the most effective way possible.

The Basic Retrieve

When the fly lands, you may allow it to rest motionless, let it sink, or begin to animate and retrieve it. To do the latter, maintain the low rod tip and straight line you established during your presentation, and use your line hand to make a series of fly line strips that will move the fly with whatever animation you want it to have. If you keep a tight fly line and low rod tip, the fly will move with the exact rhythm and pattern you create by stripping the fly line with your line hand.

Maintain your second point of line control by squeezing the line against the rod handle with the index finger of your rod hand. Relax your grip slightly as you pull in the fly line with your line hand. After making a strip of about 18 to 24 inches, coil the line in your palm or grip it and then grasp the fly line at the rod again to begin a new retrieve. Using your line hand in this manner is the most efficient way to maintain control of fly line tension for retrieving and hook setting.

Do not use the rod tip to move the fly. This causes immediate slack line and loss of fly control. Do not use the rod to pull or jerk the fly over or through land- or water-based obstacles. For best results, continue to use straight-line hand pulls.

Animation—The Key Ingredient

Animating and retrieving a bass fly provide pleasure on every cast. No matter how cleverly or cunningly these flies are tied, they're only as effective as you make them with your ability to place the fly where you want and animate it on or in the water. You are the key to the effectiveness of the flies. The tackle control system should provide you with the best method to make these flies do exactly what the real creatures do—attract and entice a bass to seize them.

To animate and retrieve bass flies most successfully, follow the straight-line method. Don't twitch your rod. Twitching the rod causes many feet of slack line to form so you cannot feel a strike. And when you don't feel the take, you lose strikes, particularly from larger fish.

Before you fish any bass fly, observe its action in or on the water: floating or sinking or sitting still and under various moves. A well-designed bass fly looks good when it is both dormant and in action. Most bass, especially large ones, are efficient and crafty; they prefer to ambush a helpless or careless creature than engage in a tiring high-speed chase. On the contrary, most fishermen like to move lures quickly and almost constantly, which may be more entertaining to us than to the fish.

Practically every big bass I've caught took the fly when I accidentally or purposefully let it sit a long period (10 seconds or more) or when I moved it very little after it hit the water. Some of my better catches came when I was precisely inching the fly in, over or around structure, as if I were trying to sneak the fly out of danger.

There are times, however, when bass will chase and strike rapidly moving flies. Some bass experts believe that fast-moving flies do a better job of fooling larger fish because the fish don't get a chance to scrutinize the fly, or because the fisherman can cover more water with fast retrieves. If a big bass is in a rare aggressive mood, the fast retrieve works better. If this reckless attitude were common among big bass, there would be few of them swimming around.

No one retrieve is always the best. Foods, temperature, water conditions, and individual fish habits vary. That's why fishing flies and catching bass never gets boring. Don't hesitate to experiment with all types of actions and action speeds.

Mending

Drag is caused (1) by the current or wind pulling on the fly line. Use the rod to lift the dragging line off the water. Then without pause, place the line straight across the current (2), and lower the rod tip to regain straight-line control (3). If your retrieve is slow or long, mending may have to be repeated.

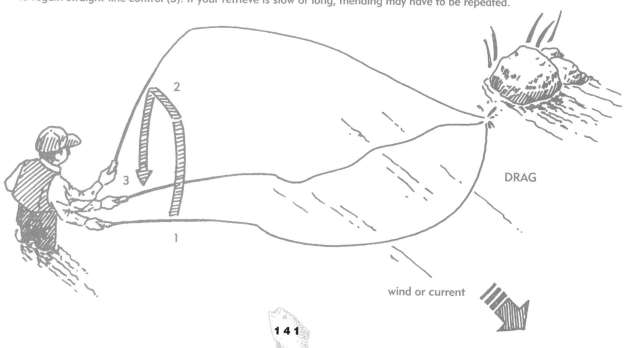

DRAG

wind or current

Before discussing action-retrieve routines, let me emphasize that to have true control of the fly's movement in still, windy, or flowing water, you must use the low-rod-tip, straight-line, two-point control system; understand how to mend your fly line to keep it and the fly from developing excessive drag caused by wind or current; and fish from a stable, stationary position. Any time you cast across water currents or a windy surface, the water movement causes drag, which affects your control of the fly. Study the illustration of how to control drag by mending the line with your rod.

Basic Fly Actions

A number of basic fly actions work well for bass flies. The following sections cover four of the more important actions.

No Retrieve

The fly is cast to an exact spot that you feel has fish nearby. Establish straight-line control, let the fly float or sink, and remain there a good while. This is a particularly effective method where the water is clear or where the fish are pressured or selective.

Use this method when you suspect a bass is under a structure. Put the fly as close to the log, stump, or boulder as you can and keep it there. This method is also ideal if there is just a small open space of water in lily pads, milfoil, or cypress stumps. In these areas the bass will not or cannot move far for prey, and it will usually respond well to the sitting fly. With this method, usually the longer you keep the fly sitting, the bigger the bass you can expect to catch.

Twitch and Pause

Cast the fly to a spot you feel has a bass nearby. Let the fly sit in place about 3 to 5 seconds, then twitch it an inch or so. Pause and repeat the twitch several times, then make another cast. You want the action of a more or less helpless creature or one that's relaxed and moving slightly. If you're using a surface or diving fly, vary the twitch from a silent move to an audible pop or bubble. More noise works best on rough surfaces, and in dark, murky, or densely structured water. This effective method can be used in combination with the no-retrieve method by twitching and pausing after you let the fly sit a while in the same restricted structure or pocket areas. It's also excellent for moving the fly off of, up to, and just past ambush points, such as brush, stumps, boat docks, log ends, or drop-offs.

When using both methods, watch the water around the fly carefully for telltale signs of fish movement, such as a small wake, bubbles, a nervous minnow or minnows, or movement in grass or lily pads. Often if you fail to see these telltale movements, the strike comes at the spot which the fly just vacated as you lift it off the water for another cast. If this happens, immediately cast back or wait 5 to 10 minutes, then cast. Often when a bass misses its prey, it becomes nervous and hides, but eventually relaxes and returns to its original ambush position.

Strip and Pause

Cast the fly well past where you suspect the bass is waiting. Let the fly settle a second or two or until it sinks to the level at which you want to fish it. Then begin a series of fly line strips, from an inch to a foot long, pausing between them. Vary the strips and pauses—that is, one strip, pause; three strips, pause; one long strip; and so on. Retrieve the fly up to, through, and past the area you think holds the bass. The more irregular the stripping rhythm, the more effective this method is. Such a method duplicates the natural movements of a handicapped creature. Use this method to fish over and past more extensive structures, such as a series of logs, rocks, stream pockets, and moss beds, as well as across points and along creek channels.

Panic Strip

Cast the fly hard against, past, or over the area or structure you want to fish. When the fly lands, begin an immediate series of rapid fly line strips from inches long up to a couple of feet in length. This fast retrieve usually imitates a panicky prey fish such as a minnow.

Repeating this retrieve over a particular area often excites a single bass or groups of fish into a frenzy. This method is excellent for covering large areas of open, still, and flowing water where bass are apt to be intercepting and chasing schools of fast-moving minnow. It is also a good tactic to use to "pound" a spot like a reef or flooded timber area with lots of casts to bring deep-water fish to the surface.

These are the four basic methods. Obviously, they are only guidelines to animating bass flies, but if you practice them and incorporate your knowledge of what the natural food does, where the fish are, and how conditions affect the fish's behavior, you'll have good results. Be certain that you cover each area correctly and thoroughly. Don't hesitate to change flies or action if you know fish are there. Bass can be psyched into striking if you are clever about retrieving. They often respond to repeated casts to the same areas.

Fly-fishing uniquely allows the bass fisherman to fish the fly just in the water area where he thinks the bass are holding, wasting no time reeling in over unproductive water. In other words, you can fish your fly over productive spots two or three times for every one cast and presentation made by a lure fisherman.

Some days bass will hit any fly retrieved any way; other days they'll be terribly selective. You must never become rigid in your thinking about which flies to fish and how to fish them. Always look for a pattern of behavior on a particular day.

Hints on Fishing Bass Flies

Probably the greatest problem faced by bass fishermen is getting the fly constantly snagged or hooked on trees, logs, lily pads, cattails, moss, stumps, and rocks. The monofilament snag-guard is a must for bass flies, but it isn't effective if you retrieve your fly improperly in close cover. Jerking or pulling quickly on the line can compress or deflect the hook guard, exposing the point of the hook to the snag. Always pull the fly over, around, and through these obstructions slowly and with the rod tip pointed down toward the water. Pulled slowly, a fly escapes the snag because the fly can avoid or crawl over the object without its snag-guard bending down.

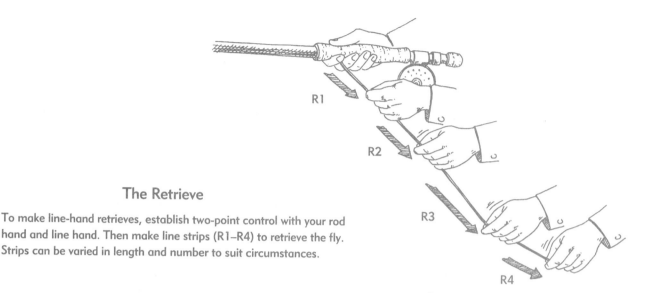

The Retrieve

To make line-hand retrieves, establish two-point control with your rod hand and line hand. Then make line strips (R1–R4) to retrieve the fly. Strips can be varied in length and number to suit circumstances.

A fly snags because the head, not the hook, engages the obstacle first, stopping the fly. Then if you pull hard, the head comes free, but the snag-guard deflects or compresses and the hook slams into the object. If you jerk or move the fly quickly with your fly rod, the fly snags in the obstruction.

If you do get snagged, do not pull hard on the fly; that simply snags it more. Either wiggle the rod and fly line to shake the hook loose or make a roll cast so the fly line loop rolls behind the snagged fly (away from you), then pull sharply on the line. That should pull it free of the snag.

If that doesn't work and you cannot reach the fly by foot or boat, point the fly rod at the snagged fly, tighten the line, then quickly release it. This sometimes causes a reverse spring action that frees the fly. If that fails, again pull the fly line taut with the rod pointed straight at the snagged fly and continue to increase pressure until the fly tears out or the leader breaks. Many fly fishers use their fly rods as a derrick and yank the fly, hoping it will come free. Violent jerking is seldom successful and may damage your rod or line. If yanking on the fly makes it come free, the recoil may send the fly rocketing at you or a companion.

Strike Detection

If your fly remains visible as you retrieve it, you'll see the bass strike it. But if the fly is out of sight—underwater or at night—you must sense or feel the strike. Usually bass strike hard enough for you to feel the take if your fly line is slack-free and your attention is riveted on it. You can also watch your visible fly line, especially at the point where it is closest to the fly; the line usually makes some movement other than what you are imparting when the fish grabs the fly. This unusual movement can indicate a strike. The fly line may get tight, feel heavy, twitch forward, become slack, or suddenly or slowly move to one side or the other.

When fishing subsurface flies, develop the habit of watching the water for abnormal movement or faint flash. Sometimes you will see the water bulge in a swirling eddy near your fly's position. This indicates that the bass has rushed the fly, though you do not actually feel a take.

React quickly if you want to hook most bass that take your fly. Your fly may look, act, feel, sound, and smell real, but most bass quickly become suspicious once they take the fly into their mouths. They usually hold the fly for only a second before they spit it out. Set the hook as soon as you suspect a strike. Unless you develop this reflex reaction to any unusual line movement or feel, you will lose many fish.

Striking and Hooking

When you see, sense, or feel the take, react quickly with a line-hand pull, with your rod tip still low and pointing at the fly. This tightens the fly line and leader against the hook and fish. The instant you feel the fly's resistance, increase the line-hand pull power and begin to strike with your rod hand by pulling back and lifting with the butt section of the rod.

Study the illustration carefully. Do not raise or rotate the rod tip as you do when striking a trout. The fly-rod tip is an efficient shock absorber, so it is not a good hook-setter. The butt is the shock transmitter and hook-setter that can drive the hook deep into the jaw tissue of a bass. Don't stop with just one hook-setting combination. Continue a series of short pulling jabs with your line hand on the line and the rod's butt section. Why? Because bass and other large predator fish use their jaws, teeth, and tongue to hold, bite, and crush any active and sizable food item so it cannot escape.

Bass, pike, stripers, and snook, even large trout, have tough-skinned, bony mouths. For a hook to penetrate these tough mouths you must use a sharp hook with a small barb or, preferably, one with no barb. Larger bass-fly hooks in sizes 6 to 5/0 with high barbs don't penetrate a bass's mouth deep enough or fast enough, because the high barb actually obstructs full penetration. You will lose fewer fish if you use sharp, barbless hooks.

Some fish, especially really big ones that have grabbed a large, bulky bass fly, are not easily intimidated and continue to bite and hold the fly for a minute or two before opening up and spitting out the fly, never being hooked. This happens with large bass, pike, muskies, pickerel, brown trout, and snook. If your rod tip is not low and if slack line exists, you'll find it difficult to hook these larger fish.

To test this method, stick the hook or your bass fly into a 4- or 5-pound object—a cardboard box with sand in it is a good prop. Place it on a floor, sidewalk, or other smooth surface. Put 30 to 40 feet of fly line and leader between the fly rod and the hooked box or object. Tighten the fly line and try to pull and move the object toward you with the low rod tip, butt, and line-pull strike described above; it will move. Now try to move it with the traditional high-rod trout-fly strike. It will be nearly impossible to move the box; the rod and fly line absorb most of the strike energy.

Fighting the Fish

Once the bass is hooked, you must exert enough rod and line pressure to gain the initial upper hand. Force the fish to come toward you with fly line pulls and your fly rod's leverage. When you're sure you have the fish hooked and under control, begin with your line hand to take up any slack fly line between your rod finger's grip and the fly reel by reeling excess slack onto the spool.

If you have several yards of slack, it must be put on the reel evenly, with enough tension to avoid tangling problems. Using your line hand, quickly place the fly line under your rod hand's little finger and use that finger to keep the fly line under control and under tension as you reel up the slack.

The sooner you reel up slack, the fewer problems you'll have with line tangles. This is called "getting the fish on the reel." If you cast from a float tube or boat to the shoreline, bass will often come straight at you when hooked, seeking the safety of deeper water, and you will have lots of slack to recover. Sometimes, however, they run in the opposite direction and pull out all the slack line. In this case, with the slack gone, switch immediately to control with the reel. Then fight the fish by reeling in or giving line from the reel.

Keep the fish away from the various underwater structures they like so much. The strength of your leader and the stiffness of your fly rod, especially in the butt section, is important in handling this situation. Keep your rod angled up no farther than 10 or 11 o'clock for best leverage and shock-absorbing control on the fish. Control of slack is the key to maintaining this optimum angle. If the rod gets to 12 or 1 o'clock or farther, you'll lose leverage and line control, and usually the fish.

Landing the Fish

Because bass have large, tough mouths and the flies and leaders you use are strong, you can fight hard with a fly rod. As soon as the bass begins to surface and weaken near you, it's probably ready to land. Reel the fly line–leader junction to a point just outside the tip-top guide and, using the rod's leverage, slide the bass toward you.

You can now seize the fish in several ways. A landing net is the safest and surest if you use it properly. Place it under the water a few inches, pull the bass over it, then loosen the rod's pull and the bass's head will drop into the net; as it does so, lift the net. Never try to capture or scoop up a bass, as you would an insect in a butterfly net, or you'll lose the fish.

You can also hand-lip the bass. Most fly fishers prefer this landing technique. Simply grasp the bass by its lower lip and jaw with your line hand's thumb and index finger and lift up on the jaw. This method immobilizes the bass, allowing you to unhook it.

Special Methods

The following methods work especially well for specific situations or flies:

Floating fly line with jigging fly: to jig a fly, use a floating fly line and an 8- to 10-foot leader. Allow the jig fly to sink to the bottom or as deep as you want to fish it. Make a fly line strip, then pause. This causes the fly to hop up and down abruptly, or "jig." Bass go crazy over a jig fly that sits on the bottom for 2 or 3 seconds, then suddenly jigs once or twice.

Sinking-tip fly line with floating fly: to obtain a unique floating/diving/subsurface swimming-floating retrieve, use a sinking-tip line and a 6-foot leader with any surface or surface-diving fly. Cast the fly and allow the sinking tip to sink. When you make short strips of the line, the fly will work on the surface. An abrupt or longer pull causes it to splash or pop and dive following the sunken line tip. Keep pulling and the fly swims to the depth of the fly line tip. Stop pulling and the fly turns head up and returns to the surface as long as the line tip does not sink deeper than the length of the leader. Bass foods such as frogs, salamanders, turtles, snakes, and minnows have this type of surface-to-surface action.

Full-sinking fly line with floating fly: to swim a fly deep over the bottom structure, use a floating fly and 2 to 4 feet of leader on a fast-sinking, full-sinking line. The heavy fly line sinks to the bottom, pulling the buoyant fly with it. But the floating fly suspends off the bottom in relationship to its buoyancy and the leader's length. Each time you pull or quickly strip in fly line, the fly dives toward bottom and then rises when you stop pulling. If you pull the suspended fly slowly along, it swims without encountering or hanging up on structure obstacles such as moss beds, sunken logs, brush, and rocks. This deadly method is excellent for fishing deep for big bass in heavy brush or weed cover.

Want a Braggin'-Sized Trophy Trout?

If you're in hot pursuit of a Big'un—the kind mounted on the walls of fishing lodges and tackle shops—you need to think big. If you were a big fish, where would you hang out? What would you eat? Big fish don't get that way by being careless. Big trout are cautious trout. They're very cover-oriented and don't often show themselves by splashing around the surface as smaller trout often do.

A big trout wants cover, shade or low light, and good food availability, and he doesn't want to work too hard, so he'll want a fast current carrying food next to a slower current that he can rest in. The classic spot is a deep-plunge pool in the shade of a cliff or a stand of trees, but many good spots aren't nearly that obvious. Cover can be almost anything: a fallen tree, a logjam, deep water, deep shade, cloudy skies, or broken water. Look for the most difficult places to fish—something like a deep, shady slot overhung with alders way over on the far side of a ripping fast current.

Trophy trout won't come to you—you must go to them. While smaller fish may be found in the shallows, on the surface, or just about anywhere in the lake, the trophy fish will be more selective of their hangouts. It helps to guess where he's hiding and to use tactics and gear specifically suited to him.

During the day try fishing deep along the bottom of a fairly shallow lake, along the deep side of a drop-off in a larger reservoir, or down among the deeper aquatic vegetation. Big fish require cover and plenty of food. You won't find one if either is missing. Large trout often take up a comfortable position during the day and actively feed only on foods that swim right in front of them. Remember, they will expend the least energy possible.

Rivers and creek inlets and natural springs are like magnets to large fish. Cool, oxygenated water is important, especially during the heat of summer, and you should work such areas over well. If you can locate an underwater spring, trophy fish are likely to be close by. This is especially important in shallow, desert lakes. Summer sunshine warms the water, bringing fish to congregate around the cool springs.

Finding underwater springs can be a job. Often, it is only a matter of trolling a fly until you encounter fish. A water thermometer periodically lowered to the bottom can be a big help in locating these springs. Pay attention to sudden, dramatic drops in water temperature. If you find such an area, fish it over well. Make a plan of attack, then go after your trophy.

You will need several fly lines to effectively fish all types of water. Full-floating lines for the shallows, sinking-tip lines for working over weed beds, and full-sinking lines for dredging the bottom. When using sinking lines, use whatever density of line it takes to get down fast.

It may be easier to pick up and lay down line with a sinking tip because much of the line floats. However, it's difficult to fish deep with sinking-tip lines because your fly can't work the bottom if the water is very deep. Even if you can get your line down, when you start your retrieve the sinking tip will tend to float up and soon be out of the big-fish zone.

Lake fishermen often use sinking lines that require shorter leaders. Deep-swimming trout aren't leader shy, so 3 or 4 feet of leader is all you need. If you use a much longer leader, your fly will tend to drift up, defeating the whole purpose of using a sinking line in the first place. If your fly isn't hitting and you're not occasionally removing gunk from your fly, you're not deep enough.

Large trout require plenty of food to maintain their size. They didn't get big by eating only midges and tiny mayflies. Your odds of catching a trophy trout are best if you use a large fly—throw some meat and potatoes at them. Give them large food items that they are used to seeing, like the leech. The leech is one of the most consistent fly patterns for large trout and available in most water. Since leeches swim slowly, the trout expends very little energy to get it. This is important to know when it comes to catching big fish.

Novices tend to fish leeches too fast. Either they strip them in too fast, or troll them from a boat or float tube too fast to be effective. If you just make your fly inch along the bottom, you'll get more strikes from larger trout. Remember, the larger fish is a smarter fish, so it's even more critical that your leech swim like the real thing. Where a smaller, reckless trout will hit nearly anything, use a slow retrieve on a tight line for hunting trophy trout.

Large trout will eat nearly anything they can fit in their mouths. If you're really after size, not numbers of fish, try terrestrial patterns that imitate foods like mice, frogs, and smaller fish. Big brown trout are especially fond of smaller fish, and you'd be amazed at just how large a fish they'll tackle. Don't be afraid to use minnow imitations that are a few inches long, especially in the large reservoirs where some trout take on mammoth proportions.

In many cases larger trout feed more actively at night, especially during summer, and especially big brown trout. Many states allow night fishing, and the results can be rewarding. On several occasions, 5- and 6-pound trout are caught at night from waters that yield much smaller fish during the daylight hours. If a trophy is what you're really after, night fishing might be for you.

Hunting Salmon in Kodiak Island

Every summer fly fishers flock to Alaska's Kenai Peninsula, undoubtedly the easiest place in Alaska to float a fly in front of a salmon. Streams abound between Anchorage and Homer at the southern terminus of the Sterling Highway. But the highway gets crowded with lumbering motorhomes and everything from stream banks to campgrounds teeming with anglers of all types intent on filling their coolers with salmon fillets.

But there are ways around the crowds. You can hike and put as much distance as possible between you and the road, or fish the midnight sun's extended daylight hours when force of habit drives most anglers into bed.

Another strategy is to look beyond Homer where the road ends. The average road-bound angler doesn't have the finances to strike out into the hinterlands of Alaska, and that's exactly why you should look south of Homer to Kodiak Island.

Kodiak Island is, of course, perhaps best known for brown bears rather than salmon fishing. It's also not thought of as a place where you can drive around and fish because, after all, it is an island and you can't drive there. You can, however, get to Kodiak rather inexpensively. Once there you can drive to its dynamite fish locations.

The Alaska Marine Highway ferry service runs between Homer and Kodiak on a regular basis. These ferries are equipped so you can drive your car and other vehicle aboard for the passage, or you can simply don your pack and board as a foot passenger. Ferrying your car is pricier than going without, but it saves on renting a car once in Kodiak.

A one-way trip from Homer to Kodiak takes just under ten hours. You can make arrangements with the Alaska Marine Highway by calling 800-642-0066. Alternatively, you can fly to Kodiak, then rent a car. The daily jet service between Anchorage and Kodiak, about an hour's flight, is the quickest and easiest way to get to the island. Alaska Airlines (800-426-0333) serves Kodiak Island. And, lastly, the Kodiak Island Convention and Visitor's Bureau at 907-486-4782 can give you the lowdown on places to stay.

The Day the Big Bass Struck

Whether you hear the tale from Dallas, Texas's Lake Fork guide Dan Lynch or the two anglers he was guiding that day, the account of the fight with the big bass is equally harrowing. Fishing the spring spawn, the trio of anglers had eased their bass boat into one of the many small coves filled with fallen timber and stickups when they spotted a huge female largemouth lurking around a bed with a smaller male bass.

After landing the male—a respectable 5-pounder—Houston angler Mark Kalish began casting at a "big dark shadow" that moved up on the bed. "I knew it was big," Kalish recalls. "I just didn't know how big."

If you find yourself at Lake Fork, one of the state's most heavily fished lakes, you might find yourself at a great advantage. Among some 300 pro guides on Fork, Dan Lynch is the only one who specializes in fly-fishing. He operates B'wana's Guide Service.

For deep-water fish, it's best to go with shooting tapers or uniform density fly lines. In the past two years, Lynch and his clients have reportedly caught thirty-five bass weighing 10 pounds or more on fly. Lynch's custom fly patterns are bigger and bulkier than most bass flies you see in fly shops.

It took some persistent casting, but Kalish finally hooked the big female. The trio watched open-mouthed as the wide-bodied bass boiled up and then jumped right in front of the boat. With his friend Dan Edwards yelling for him to set the hook harder, Kalish held on as the fish twice wrapped line around a stump, somehow came free each time, and then ran under the boat. At that point, with the butt of Kalish's rod jammed against the side of the boat, Lynch stepped in.

"I knew we were in trouble and we had to do something quick," Lynch says. "So when the fish came by, I made a grab at her, the line wrapped around my thumb and the hook pulled out." After the bass got off, Lynch says Kalish "just sat there looking at me. You could tell it was a mega-disappointment."

Estimates on the size of the fish vary from 12 to 15 pounds, depending on which of the eyewitnesses you talk to. Everyone agreed, though, that it was the bass of a lifetime. "You could have put your hand around a baseball, stuck it in her mouth and you wouldn't have touched the sides," Lynch says.

Bass of this size and bigger are not that unusual at Fork where thirty-six of the state's top fifty bass have been caught and all have weighed 15 pounds or more. The difference was that this fish was hooked on fly tackle and would easily have qualified for an International Game Fish Association (IGFA) fly rod world record in the 20-pound line class. The fly rod world record on 20-pound tippet, the size leader that Kalish was using that day, currently stands at 9 pounds, 5 ounces.

Bucktail

This bass got away, but other big largemouth are being taken on fly tackle at Lake Fork these days, and not just during the spring spawn. For the last several years, Lynch has developed techniques for taking big bass at Lake Fork on fly tackle year-round. In addition to the more traditional fly-fishing approach of using poppers and deer hair bugs to entice bass when they are up shallow along the shorelines, he and his clients have hooked hefty largemouths at Fork when they are schooling on top in open water or down at depths of 20 feet or more.

In the last three years, Lynch has attracted a loyal following of fly fishers. A fly fisherman for forty years who is also adept with level-wind gear, Lynch drives a Champion bass boat equipped with the latest in fish-finding electronics and a 175 hp Mercury outboard. He has proven he can hold his own with the other guides on the lake when it comes to catching quality fish.

Dallas fly fisher Dwayne Rowe fished with Lynch this past spring and caught a 7-pound bass on a Whitlock softshell crayfish fly pattern. It was his biggest fish ever on fly. Despite high winds on the lake's open water, Rowe said the coves were holding large numbers of fish from 3 to 10 pounds.

Also last spring, Waxahachie angler Jim Simpson, a fly fisher also experienced at throwing spinner baits with conventional tackle at other big Texas reservoirs like Toledo Bend, caught seven bass on fly tackle fishing with Lynch at Fork. All of them weighed more than 4 pounds; the biggest was 7½ pounds.

In some cases fly fishers have an edge at Fork, one of the state's most heavily fished lakes, especially when the fish are up shallow during the spawn and post-spawn periods. "On Fork, the bass will tell you what date your spinner bait was built," Simpson says. "They are starting to see flies that are a lot more lifelike."

Steve Poarch, who is in charge of management of Lake Fork for the Texas Parks and Wildlife Department (TPWD), says there is so much fishing pressure on the lake that the fish, on occasion, turn off to the usual plugs and spinner baits they see all the time. He says anglers willing to use float tubes or small watercraft and smaller lures and flies can get back in coves behind road bridges and find fish that haven't seen many artificials.

With Fork's reputation for big fish growing every year, it was inevitable that fly fishers would be among the bass anglers attracted to the 27,000-acre lake. Up until two years ago, when Lynch arrived on the scene at Fork, fly rodders would have to do it on their own or book a conventional guide who may or may not be comfortable taking out a fly fisher.

In addition to the bed fishing in the spring and top-water action in the fall, Lynch has experimented with techniques to take deep-water fish and school fish on flies, offering his clients virtually year-round opportunities.

For deep-water fishing, he uses his fish finder to track movements of bass suspended over submerged roadbeds and other underwater structure. He recommends shooting tapers or uniform-density fly lines for the deep-water fishing. Although it is more tedious than casting a deer hair popper along a grassy shoreline, Lynch says the fly fisher who can patiently work a fly at deeper depths or make cast after cast to entice a big bass to finally crush a fly on a bed has the best chance to land a double-digit fish at Lake Fork.

Lynch admits that the deep-water fishing is the toughest sell to fly fishers, but a big bass down 20 feet suddenly bending a fly rod double has made believers of some skeptics. "There are some [fly fishers] who just will not swing over and even look at deep-water fly fishing," Lynch says. "But bass are on to about six or seven months out of the year. Why wait until they get on top or move up on the beds?"

Veteran Dallas fly fisher Mike Huffman, another Lynch client, says the Lake Fork guide has not found a magic formula for hooking bass on a fly in deep water, one of the most difficult challenges for a fly fisher. "If you are talking about the real slow, touchy-feely plastic worm stuff, there is no way with a fly rod," he says. But Huffman says Lynch has learned to capitalize on the deep-water schooling behavior of big bass at Lake Fork, a phenomenon that doesn't occur at every reservoir and farm pond. "You think of the bigger bass as generally being homebodies and occupying their lair and cruising only in a certain area, while at Fork you have this massive behavior," Huffman says. "And if you drag your fly through a school of twenty or thirty of those big fish, there will be one or two that will hammer it hard enough that you will feel it."

If you haven't fished with Lynch at Fork, seen his on-the-water videos, or talked to his clients, it might be difficult to buy some of his accounts of Lake Fork fly-fishing. In the last two years he claims he and his clients have caught thirty-five bass weighing 10 pounds or more on fly, all of which would have surpassed the existing IGFA world record on 20-pound tippet. Lynch's biggest bass from Fork is a 12-pounder.

While Lynch uses a fly rod as light as a 7-weight for sight-casting to smaller fish around the beds, he has used up to 12-weight fly rods to stop some of the larger fish. "We break rods, we have had lines snap, we have 25-pound leaders break," Lynch says. "A lot of different things happen out there."

Instead of running all over the lake, Lynch finds a variety of bass habitat within close proximity of his launch point. He targets fish in neighboring coves and occasionally slips out in the middle of the lake to chart activity on his fishfinder. During the course of the day he rarely travels more than 2 or 3 miles from the put-in point. Depending on the time of year and lake conditions, he will make a short run out to open water to fish over submerged structure.

Frequently, Lynch spots bass from the faintest outline or movement of a tail or fin. On two trips with Lynch last spring we saw dozens of spawning largemouth in coves and along open shorelines in front of summer homes that other boaters seemed to be passing by.

One of Lynch's goals is to have one of his client's catch and donate a bass on fly tackle large enough to qualify for the Lone Star Lunker program.

Lynch has developed a number of techniques that work for him on Lake Fork. Some of his approaches are borrowed, like the crawfish and jiglike epoxy head fly patterns he ties. Some are new, like the braided Kevlar line he likes to use for a leader when fishing around heavy moss. When a big bass gets on, the thin, strong line cuts through the moss, he says, preventing the kind of break-offs that usually happen when monofilament collects a pile of debris.

Lynch's custom fly patterns, including his jiglike "B'wana's Mop Fly," tied with the thick hackle feathers from a dust mop, are bigger and bulkier than most bass flies you see in fly shops. He says he designed them that way after he saw how a big female largemouth could move traditional bass flies out of a bed with one flick of the tail. These large flies are also needed to get the attention of large bass feeding in schools down at depths of 20 or 25 feet, Lynch says.

A few days after Kalish tangled with the big bass, I was fishing the same cove with Lynch in the hopes of a repeat performance. Lynch made sure we entered the cove the same way, positioned the boat the same way, and threw flies at the same bed surrounded by the same stickups.

When a husky bass came charging out of the bed with crawfish pattern firmly attached to its jaw, the fish made a run for the nearest sunken timber and then ran under the boat. The fact that it was a male fish weighing in at 5½ pounds didn't diminish the excitement. Taking a fish of this size on a fly rod at most lakes is a major accomplishment. At Lake Fork it is just practice for the real thing.

The fly caster who can patiently work a fly at deeper depths or make cast after cast to entice bass on the beds has a realistic chance at a double-digit Lake Fork largemouth. Brightly colored fly patterns designed by Lynch are for throwing to schooling bass on Lake Fork.

Lake Fork's flooded timber, submerged stumps, and stickups provide ideal habitat for bass and ideal targets for fly casters. Float tubes or small watercraft allow fly casters to approach secluded coves that haven't yet seen conventional lures, much less specialty bass flies.

On Flies, Natural and Artificial: To Catch a Trout

Excerpted from *The Compleat Angler*, published in 1676
by Izaak Walton

Now for Flies; which is the third bait wherewith Trouts are usually taken. You are to know, that there are so many sorts of flies as there be of fruits: I will name you but some of them; as the dun-fly, the stone-fly, the red-fly, the moor-fly, the tawny-fly, the shell-fly, the cloudy or blackish-fly, the flag-fly, the vine-fly; there be of flies, caterpillars, and canker-flies, and bear-flies; and indeed too many either for me to name, or for you to remember. And their breeding is so various and wonderful, that I might easily amaze myself, and tire you in a relation of them.

There are twelve kinds of artificial made Flies, to angle with upon the top of the water. Note, by the way, that the fittest season of using these is in a blustering windy day, when the waters are so troubled that the natural fly cannot be seen, or rest upon them.

The first is the dun-fly, in March: the body is made of dun wool; the wings, of the partridge's feathers.

The second is another dun-fly: the body, of black wool; and the wings made of the black drake's feathers, and of the feathers under his tail.

The third is the stone-fly, in April: the body is made of black wool; made yellow under the wings and under the tail, and so made with wings of the drake.

The fourth is the ruddy-fly, in the beginning of May: the body made of red wool, wrapped about with black silk; and the feathers are the wings of the drake; with the feathers of a red capon also, which hang dangling on his sides next to the tail.

The fifth is the yellow or greenish fly, in May likewise: the body made of yellow wool; and the wings made of the red cock's hackle or tail.

The sixth is the black-fly, in May also: the body made of black wool, and wrapped about with a peacock's tail: the wings are made of the wings of a brown capon, with his blue feathers in his head.

The seventh is the sad yellow-fly in June: the body is made of black wool, with a yellow list on either side; and the wings taken off the wings of a buzzard, bound with black braked hemp.

The eighth is the moorish-fly; made, with the body, of duskish wool; and the wings made of the blackish mail of the drake.

The ninth is the t-fly-fly, good until the middle of June: the body made of tawny wool; the wings made contrary one against the other, made of the whitish mail of the wild drake.

The tenth is the wasp-fly in July; the body made of black wool, lapt about with yellow silk; the wings made of the feathers of the drake, or of the buzzard.

The eleventh is the shell-fly, good in mid-July: the body made of greenish wool, lapt about with the herle of a peacock's tail: and the wings made of the wings of the buzzard.

The twelfth is the dark drake-fly, good in August: the body made with black wool, lapt about with black silk; his wings are made with the mail of the black drake, with a black head. Thus have you a jury of flies, likely to betray and condemn all the Trouts in the river.

FISHING LICENSE

CHAPTER 8

Beyond the Basics

Fishing from a Drift Boat

You can cover many miles of great fly-fishing in a drift boat, stout raft such as an Avon, or small aluminum john boat. It is a good idea to explore your areas before floating, and to check put-in and take-out areas for vehicle access. Be sure to take along food, fresh water, a first-aid kit, flashlight, and other incidentals you may need. It may be a long walk out to the road should a mishap occur.

Be prepared to walk your craft. Rivers can narrow in spots. Shallows and turns may not be navigable from the boat. Check with a fly shop or guide before engaging a river or stream by boat.

The history of the McKenzie-style drift boat is interwoven with the rich historical fabric of the rough, whitewater rivers in southern Oregon. The heavy rapids in the McKenzie and Rogue rivers made boat fishing almost a necessity. The quest to build a boat that could be controlled in such turbulent water, while still providing a stable fishing platform, began about 1900. Early, turn-of-the-century river dories were built entirely of cedar planking. They had a wider, squared stern but with much less freeboard than today's drift boat.

The true drift boat design was the result of two Eugene-area boat builders: Woody Hindman and Tom Kaarhus during the 1930s. These two were prolific boat builders for many years. They developed good reputations for the boats they produced, and their boats were sought after by many of the best guides of that era. A few of the boats they built thirty or forty years ago are still in use. Hull designs were named for rivers on which they were used, primarily the Rogue and McKenzie. Eventually the differentiation between the two became blurred, resulting in two major styles of drift boats: the McKenzie, or Rogue, depending on who is doing the calling, and the Rapid Robert.

Today there are only a handful of Rapid Robert–style boats left. They are characterized by the broad stern with the bow at the oarsman's back. While the bows of both style boats are to the oarsman's back, which would be upstream, the "bow" of the McKenzie/Rogue has been sheared off to accept a small motor. Only the "stern" of the McKenzie/Rogue now remains pointed.

How to Use a Drift Boat

Just as in fly-fishing, you need to read the stream with an eye toward working with the currents, rather than against them. Although rowing is not difficult, the novice oarsman will often react by moving the drift boat in the desired direction down river, which is the exact opposite of the correct response. With practice, rowing will become second nature.

The first rule in rowing a drift boat is to do everything with backstrokes. As you and the bow of the boat face downstream, develop the habit of backstroking to maneuver and avoid obstacles. The backstroke is much stronger than the forward stroke because it combines the energy of the arms, back, and legs. When a boulder or a log needs to be avoided, you can depend on the backstroke. The problem with using the forward stroke is that with the current, it speeds up the boat, driving it even harder into the hazards you are trying to avoid.

While rowing, you will be dodging low casts, spotting fish, tying on flies, or getting something from the cooler. To avoid surprises, map your course to allow ample time to set up properly. Beginners tend to over-row, using more strokes than are necessary, and end up zigzagging all over the river. With practice it will become second nature. Observe experienced boatmen. They maneuver efficiently, without wasting a stroke, missing rocks by inches. A minimal amount of rowing helps maintain a steady casting distance from the bank or target water.

On swift, rocky rivers, you seldom have a moment's rest between slowing the boat and maneuvering. Wearing light gloves can help to avoid blisters. The faster the water, the sooner the setup must be to avoid obstacles. In boatman's parlance, "setup" means to know what's coming up, to maneuver the boat to the appropriate angle for backing away, and to begin to row early enough to avoid the danger. It is very easy to underestimate the power of rapidly flowing water, which can be dangerous.

On really windy days, you're better off wade fishing along the banks. Early morning and late evening are often the least windy times, which conveniently coincide with many hatches.

Try to keep the drift boat straight or parallel to the banks or target water whenever possible. This keeps each fisher on board from tangling each other. Keep the floor of your boat as uncluttered as possible.

Sooner or later, you're bound to broadside a rock in your boat and be pinned there by the current. The beginner's usual reaction is exactly the opposite of what it should be. When you broadside something, lean into it, not away from it! The rushing water will tend to climb the upstream side of your boat and push it under water. Your natural reaction, leaning away from the object that you are going to slam into, only facilitates flipping your boat or wrapping it around the rock. If you know that you're going to broadside an obstacle, get ready to lean into it and push or spin off of it with your hands, feet, or oars.

If you are floating water that you wouldn't feel safe swimming in, don't be ashamed to wear a life jacket, a supply of which the U.S. Coast Guard says must be in every boat.

Be sure to leave prepared for the day's float. Have rain gear, jackets, life preservers, a spare oar, first-aid kit, waterproof containers, the proper amount of food and drink, sunscreen, toilet paper, flashlight, keys, and anything else you may need for a long day on the stream. Keep a sharp knife within arm's reach. It may be necessary to cut the anchor line if the anchor becomes snagged. (A badly snagged anchor in fast water can pull the transom of the boat down, sinking the boat.)

Float Tubing in an Easy Chair

Whereas a drift boat helps you in fast-moving water, float tubing is primarily for lakes and slow-moving currents. Personal watercraft such as a float tube or kick boat offer access to limited areas, freedom from the confines and restrictions of a boat, versatility, comfort, and plain old fun. If you use swim fins to propel your float tube, your hands will be free for fishing. You don't have to worry about anchoring your boat, clanking oars, noisy feet in the bottom of the boat, or even wind. You can steal your 8-foot rod into tight places preferred by trout.

There are three basic techniques: (1) dry fly stalk—locate rising fish, hold a position, and cast to the rings; (2) half-asleep troll—paddle around with the line trailing behind; (3) prospecting—maneuver to likely looking holding water and blind-cast with floating or subsurface patterns. These methods will often reward you with a bend in the rod and a fish on the line.

But in case you're striking out, don't fall asleep in your floating easy chair. Here's a tip: hungry fish respond aggressively to flies or streamers moving through the water at a constant speed, and trolling in a float tube mimics this action better than conventional hand-stripping of the line. So after casting, let your fly sink to the depth you feel the fish are feeding, then use your fins to turn the tube in a circular motion to most naturally mimic a smoothly

Got a Bamboo Rod?

Question: *I am new to fishing with a bamboo fly rod. Can you provide information on the care and upkeep of a bamboo rod?*

Answer: *The following are a few points regarding the care and use of a split-bamboo rod reproduced from the 1927 catalog of the Shakespeare Rod Co. It is still valid advice.*

Jointing a rod. Join the tip to the middle joint, putting tile butt on last in order to avoid undue strain on the delicate tip. Never lubricate the joints with anything other than dry soap or parafine wax. Be sure that the guides are in line and that the reel is fastened securely on the reel scat underneath the rod. Reeve the line through the guides and pull enough line through the top so that you can work without unnecessary strain on the rod.

Taking down the rod. Grasp the rod sections firmly in both hands, holding the butt away from you and the tip underneath the arm. Pull apart, separating first the butt from the middle joint and then the middle joint from the tip, just the reverse of the order in which the rod was set up. If the rod joints stick tightly, try this method: In a slightly stooping position, hold the rod or rod sections underneath the knees. Press the knees apart against the hands as they grasp the rod. This pressure will be all that is required. Do not pull with the hands; let the knees do all the work. This method will disjoint many an otherwise balky rod and will eliminate all hazard of sudden jerking and breaking.

Never twist a rod either in putting it together or in taking it down, and keep all pressure off the guides. If the rod sections "gum" as they sometimes will under strenuous use and resist all efforts to disjoint them, drop a little kerosene around the rim of the ferrules, and let stand a day or two. Two days at the most should loosen the tightest joint.

To straighten bent sections. Lay the bent section on a board and drive in two nails near each end. Next, bend the rod section a little more than straight and secure the position with a third nail. A week or so of this treatment will take the set out enough so that you can finish the correction by hanging it up with a weight attached to the bottom.

Putting the rod up for the winter. A fine split-bamboo rod should be stored in a moderately cool place, since heat causes shrinkage and loosens the mountings. Hang your rod, all assembled, by the tip to a hook or a brad in the wall. The suspended weight will straighten any tendency to set that may have developed from a season's fishing. It is a good idea, too, to lubricate the ferrules with vaseline before hanging the rod up for the winter.

If you will follow these few simple directions in the care of your rod, it should give you many years of satisfactory service. One does not willingly part with a rod that has grown to be a friend, and like a true friend and fishing pal, a fine split-bamboo rod will repay good treatment with interest.

moving insect or terrestrial. Turn no more than 180 degrees, then reel in the slack as you turn 180 degrees back. Repeat.

Be ready—it's at the point where the fly begins to move upward toward the surface that many strikes occur. Inexperienced anglers may be too quick to get their fly out of the water in preparation for a recast. I've seen raging smallmouth bass shoot up from the murky depths to attack a Woolly Bugger just as it broke water. Why bass or other fish often wait until the last minute to strike is anyone's guess. So don't hurry the last few inches below the surface. This technique works best for deeper water.

Another float tubing technique is skirting the shoreline. Some salmon and trout, leery of becoming bird fodder, hide in the reeds that border lakes. Insects also prefer the reeds. If the fish are not taking flies off the surface, try presenting wet flies (nymphs, streamers, emergers) that dart in and out of the vegetation.

Slowly troll within a foot or two of the reeds, allowing for the ins and outs of the vegetation. You'll have to keep your fly as close to the plants as possible because spooky fish won't risk exposing themselves too far out. To do this, mend your line close to the shoreline because the tendency is for the fly to move away from the bank rather than toward it. Watch the line and continually keep the fly as tight as possible to the bank, reeds, weeds, rocks, or structures as you troll the shoreline. Snags will occur, but be patient.

The U-Boat

Open-ended float tubes are like fishing from a floating lounge chair. They have many advantages: ease of entry, removal of any obstruction across your legs, and no longer being hung in a harness. The U-Boat weighs just over 5 pounds so it's light and easy to pack into a lake, inflated or deflated. The air-valve system uses standard inflation equipment, foot pumps, or high-volume pumps, comes with a patch kit and an unconditional guarantee. Other features include mesh stripping apron/taps measure, removable foam fly patches to dry flies, two side pockets and one top pocket for gear, and accessory straps on side pockets. An adjustable tension strap allows anglers to fit the U-Boat to their size and weight, free pack straps, rod holder, and second rod holding straps, carry handle, and D-rings to hang gear.

Some models have triple-stitched seams so the materials will not pull apart. On other models, the tube material actually expands if it is accidentally punctured, giving you as many as three hours to return to shore. Back storage pockets often include a secondary floatation device.

Other models have the following features:

- Removable insulated drink holder (can be changed with fly patch)
- Large side pockets
- Huge dry storage wraps around back of tube
- Extra-long Velcro holders so your rods or guns don't fall out
- Back rest designed for maximum comfort and secondary flotation
- Padded seat built wider for better leg support, wader protection, and maximum comfort
- Removable fly patch (can be exchanged for drink holder)
- Carry handles and D-rings located around the unit for your accessories

One recommended model for taller people is the Kodiak Model #1000 & 1001, which boast a mesh bib. Optional back pack straps and reed skirt for an abrasion-resistant cover turns the camouflaged tube into a duck- and/or bird-watching blind and may be purchased for these models.

They Only Come Out at Night

Some of the most magical moments in all of fly-fishing are those spent watching a speckled brown rise from the depths of a stream to devour your dry fly floating blithely downstream. But if that magic doesn't occur, night fishing can save the day.

The Endangered Salmon

Within the past fifteen years the North American salmon has dwindled from 800,000 to 200,000. In 1991 Canada began a salmon moratorium and bought out commercial salmon fishermen in Newfoundland, New Brunswick, and Nova Scotia. Catch-and-release regulations were implemented and enforced.

These were steps to protect mature ocean-bound salmon so they would return to freshwater rivers and streams to spawn and reproduce increasing numbers of young fish.

Disaster struck in the summer of 1997, when less than half the expected number of salmon entered the rivers of Newfoundland. With few exceptions, the rivers of Labrador and Nova Scotia fared little better. Governments closed rivers to fishing.

Many feel the Atlantic salmon are a sensitive barometer of change because they depend on the health of oceans and fresh water for survival. Salmon are said to be a first-line indicator of the consequences of overfishing and global warming.

Save the Bull Trout!

In June [1998] Secretary of the Interior Bruce Babbitt signed the bull trout's "threatened status" on the banks of the Blackfoot River. The threat: Canyon Resources planned to open and operate a cyanide heap leach mine on the banks of the Blackfoot River near Lincoln, Montana. This was thought to pollute a world-class native trout fishery and pose an added threat to the bull trout that spawn near the headwaters of the Blackfoot, where Canyon Resources hoped to develop the mine.

The members of this genus (*Salvelinus*) are by far the most active and handsome of the trout. They live in the coldest, cleanest, and most secluded waters. Bull trout are a member of the North American salmon family, which includes salmon, trout, whitefish, char, and grayling. The bull trout got its name from its large head and mouth. It is distinguished by its predatory nature; the adult bull trout's diet consists largely of other fish. But when given an opportunity, it will eat frogs, snakes, mice, and ducklings.

The bull trout is presently listed by the U.S. Fish and Wildlife Service as a Category 1 candidate species for listing under the Endangered Species Act. Lobbyists are hoping to have the Blackfoot bull trout listed immediately since they are in the greatest danger of extinction if the Canyon Resources mine is ever permitted.

Bull trout have historically faced another threat: fishermen who, in the mistaken belief that this species of trout ate the eggs of other trout, placed bounties on the fish. It has since been proven that the bull trout will eat only the eggs of other fish when those eggs have broken loose from the nest.

Native to the Pacific Northwest, including Montana, Idaho, and northern California and Nevada, the bull trout has some of the most demanding habitat requirements of any native trout species—mainly because it requires water that is especially clean and cold (no more than 64 degrees Fahrenheit). Abundant a century ago, dams, siltation from logging and farming, and efforts by state game agencies to poison it have greatly reduced its numbers and range.

In 1992, a Montana Department of Fish, Wildlife and Parks review of the status of the trout in Montana found that bull trout occupied less than half of their historic range. The remaining population was fragmented, meaning many isolated communities of bull trout might not have enough numbers to maintain a viable population.

After this report came out, several Montana-based conservation groups petitioned to have the bull trout listed under the Endangered Species Act. After reviewing the fish's status in 1994, the Fish and Wildlife Service decided that listing was "warranted but precluded" because other species that were more in danger needed listing first. While the bull trout is threatened, as defined by law, its numbers and distribution remain sufficient to ensure that it is not at immediate risk of extinction. Today, the bull trout remains one of 179 candidates for listing.

The metabolism of trout rises as the water temperatures rise, but only to a certain extent. Even though daytime fishing may be slow, the trout are eating more and at a different time. The angler willing to fish "after hours" is often in for a treat. Fishing an oversized leech pattern in the shallows on a floating line is usually all it takes to make a believer out of you.

If permitted in your state, night fishing often produces some hot and heavy action. Of course, night fishing is not for everyone, and there are certain safety issues that need to be considered. But for those of sound mind and not afraid of the bogeyman, night fishing offers plenty of rewards. Watch out, though, for often snakes descend from nearby rocks and desert areas to cool waterside in the evening. So be careful not to tiptoe at night!

Some hunters fish strictly at night and often float tubing on large reservoirs. Night fishing isn't for everyone and there are certain obvious dangers. Common sense goes a long way here, and if you plan on fishing at night you must keep safety your main concern. Fish only waters you know very well at night. Tubing may be the safest way to fish after dark, with the least chance of error if you use common sense. Wear a life jacket and carry a good waterproof light.

During the security of darkness, the edges around many lakes come alive with fish that have moved from the depths to feed. Again, large patterns are called for—the leech being a favorite. At night, all that's needed to fish a leech is a floating line. What I like to do is cast in tight to shore since feeding fish can be found in extremely shallow water at this time. They'll sometimes hit your fly as soon as it touches down, very much like a largemouth bass.

Trout, of course, don't need to see at night; they can sense movement of the leech in the water, then strike. You don't need to cast more than 10 or 20 feet of line at night when fishing a shoreline from a float tube. You won't spook the fish, and the more line you have flying around, the greater your chance of tangles or injury. Back casts should be avoided as much as possible, and use barbless hooks.

Can't Fish till Fall?

Spring is traditionally the best time of the year to fish for trout in western lakes and streams. But fall may actually be better to catch a nice rainbow or two.

By the time fall rolls around, fishing stream waters are normally low and clear. Visibility is good, wading is easier, and more of the water is fishable. Days are shorter and the water is cooler, so instead of rising in the mornings and evenings and moping through midday heat, trout are likely to bite from dawn until dusk.

On a crisp September or October day, the morning hatch blends into the afternoon hatch. Even when conditions are less than ideal, the dead spots between the morning and evening rises will be shorter.

Whether you are working streams or lakes, chances are the cooler temperatures and the shorter days have triggered a more active feeding pattern in the trout living there.

And, while there may not be as many fish in a particular lake or stream during the fall because they have been worked over by anglers since the waters opened in March or April, it's a real good bet they haven't been totally fished out. Since the fish that are still there have been feeding and growing throughout the summer, the fish you do catch should all be nice fat ones.

Spawning browns and brook trout often feed in a frenzy to store up energy before the spawn. Spring spawners like rainbows and cut-throats seem to know winter is coming and are desperate to get as fat as they can.

In early fall you can fish during what can be some of the most beautiful weather of the year, and you'll have the lake or stream to yourself because most people have either traded in their fishing rod for a shotgun or given up on trout fishing for the year.

Selective fishery lakes "turn on" again after the hot days of summer have subsided. Some of the very best trout fishing days come during late September and October. This is also the time of the year that the rivers and streams are in excellent shape for fishing. Autumn rivers offer some excellent trout fishing as the leaves begin to turn colors.

In area lakes, trolling a fly from a small boat or float tube can be extremely effective. If the days are still warm, patterns like dragonfly nymphs in different colors work well, as do the old standbys like the Woolly Worm and Woolly Bugger.

If you aren't into trolling, the lakes can still be fished effectively from the banks with a fly rod. Some of the same flies can be used in the streams for fall trout. There won't be as much top-water activity during the cooler fall days, but there will be some, so dry flies will work. Selected dun patterns, stonefly imitations, and others can catch fish. Bright-colored traditional streamer patterns as well as Muddler minnows and sculpin imitations will also work well.

Tips

Use stealth. While trout are eager to rise, crystalline waters make them spooky. It's risky for a trout to expose himself in clear, slow currents. He will do it to eat, but he'll be nervous about it and will flash for cover at the first sound of wading or a splashy cast, or even at the glimpse of a rod's shadow on the water. That's why the fishing is usually better on cloudy days than on bright, sunny ones. Trout seem to feel safer under the cover of an overcast sky.

So stealth, often the key to any kind of trout fishing, can be even more important in fall. But you can't just dink a fly on top of a rising trout. Plan an approach that lets you stay low and quiet and keeps your shadow off the water. In such situations seasoned fly fishers use their longest casts, or crawl in on hands and knees to cast without spooking the murky inhabitants. These are the kinds of conditions where a good caster will out-fish a poor one.

Another angle to fall fishing is fly selection. In swift, roily currents, a big, bushy dry will usually work just fine. It floats high and so the fish can see it, but because currents carry it downstream quickly they don't have a lot of time to study it. In autumn's low, clear, slow-flowing water, the trout often want more sparsely tied flies. They also may be fussier about size and color. Use small,

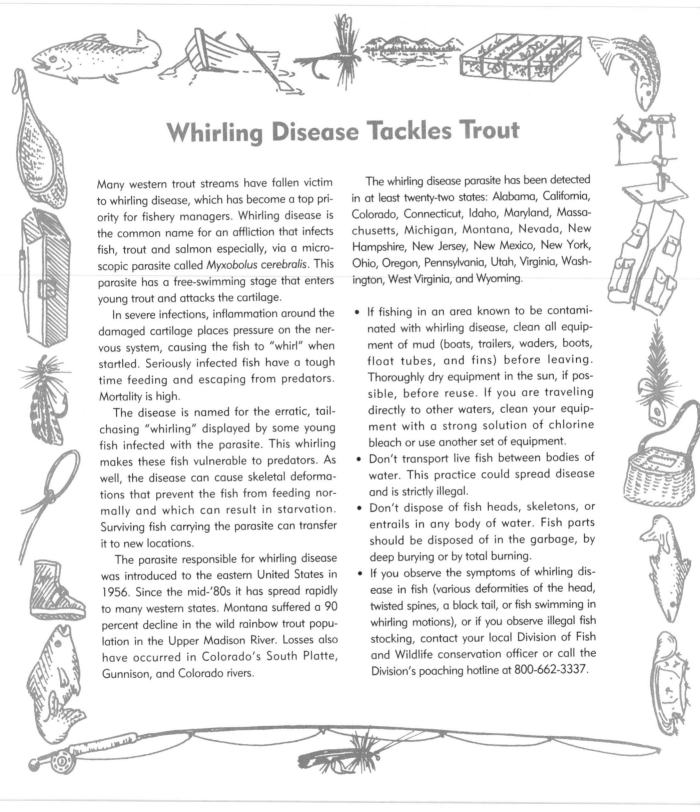

Whirling Disease Tackles Trout

Many western trout streams have fallen victim to whirling disease, which has become a top priority for fishery managers. Whirling disease is the common name for an affliction that infects fish, trout and salmon especially, via a microscopic parasite called *Myxobolus cerebralis*. This parasite has a free-swimming stage that enters young trout and attacks the cartilage.

In severe infections, inflammation around the damaged cartilage places pressure on the nervous system, causing the fish to "whirl" when startled. Seriously infected fish have a tough time feeding and escaping from predators. Mortality is high.

The disease is named for the erratic, tail-chasing "whirling" displayed by some young fish infected with the parasite. This whirling makes these fish vulnerable to predators. As well, the disease can cause skeletal deformations that prevent the fish from feeding normally and which can result in starvation. Surviving fish carrying the parasite can transfer it to new locations.

The parasite responsible for whirling disease was introduced to the eastern United States in 1956. Since the mid-'80s it has spread rapidly to many western states. Montana suffered a 90 percent decline in the wild rainbow trout population in the Upper Madison River. Losses also have occurred in Colorado's South Platte, Gunnison, and Colorado rivers.

The whirling disease parasite has been detected in at least twenty-two states: Alabama, California, Colorado, Connecticut, Idaho, Maryland, Massachusetts, Michigan, Montana, Nevada, New Hampshire, New Jersey, New Mexico, New York, Ohio, Oregon, Pennsylvania, Utah, Virginia, Washington, West Virginia, and Wyoming.

- If fishing in an area known to be contaminated with whirling disease, clean all equipment of mud (boats, trailers, waders, boots, float tubes, and fins) before leaving. Thoroughly dry equipment in the sun, if possible, before reuse. If you are traveling directly to other waters, clean your equipment with a strong solution of chlorine bleach or use another set of equipment.
- Don't transport live fish between bodies of water. This practice could spread disease and is strictly illegal.
- Don't dispose of fish heads, skeletons, or entrails in any body of water. Fish parts should be disposed of in the garbage, by deep burying or by total burning.
- If you observe the symptoms of whirling disease in fish (various deformities of the head, twisted spines, a black tail, or fish swimming in whirling motions), or if you observe illegal fish stocking, contact your local Division of Fish and Wildlife conservation officer or call the Division's poaching hotline at 800-662-3337.

trim flies with little or no hackle. Many fishermen believe that trout can get leader-shy, and so go to lighter leaders and tippets in slow, clear currents.

Most streams and rivers have more or less predictable autumn hatches. Many of them are small mayflies—hooks size 16 and smaller—and even smaller midge flies. Ask for local advice or contact the fly shop or guide service nearest the water.

Fall dry fly fishing is both rewarding and challenging. The trout have seen a lot of flies and lures and are about as smart as they're going to get that season. But then, by September, you've been fishing a few times yourself and you're as smart as you're going to get, too. Most days, it balances out.

Do Fish Feel Pain?

Animal rights groups attack catch-and-release fishing, believing the pain system in fish is the same as in birds and mammals. Zoologist Austin Williams claims that "fish are sentient organisms, so of course they feel pain." Fish experience fear, he says, and react with increased heart and breathing rates.

Others insist angling doesn't hurt fish because of the fundamental difference in the nervous systems between higher and lower vertebrates. For example, a fish will return to the same fly, time after time, to be hooked and released many times within a short interval. Contrast this with the behavior of higher animals, wherein avoidance of a painful stimulus can be learned in a single experience.

Dr. Hilary W. Thompson, professor of ophthalmology, biometry, and neuroscience, relates his account of fishing for largemouth bass in south Florida. The fish was clearly visible in shallow water. "I threw a yellow rabbit strip leech at him and he clobbered it immediately," Dr. Thompson said. "Released, he swam quickly back to his station, and I threw at him again. Once again he took the fly and when released, took up the same stand." On the fourth catch the bass was moving more slowly, so Dr. Thompson terminated his experiment. "As far as I could tell, he took with as much energy the fourth time as the first." That hook hurt, no doubt—all animals try to escape from painful stimuli once perceived and struggle for freedom. "But the little bass never suffered an anticipation of the pain as a human would."

As soon as the pain stops, fish resume the business of feeding and schooling or nesting or ignoring flies or whatever fish work they were engaged in. Says Dr. Thompson: "Their brains are not wired up like ours and don't even have all the same parts that our brains do."

Therefore, the argument that catch-and-release fishing is unethical because it causes fish to suffer as humans do seems illogical.

However, though angling may not hurt fish, many anglers leave behind them a trail of tackle victims. Birds, turtles, and other animals suffer debilitating injuries after swallowing fish hooks or becoming entangled in fishing line. Officials with the Virginia Marine Science Museum Stranding Team say fishing line is one of the top three threats to aquatic animals.

Fish During Winter in Arkansas

Arkansas's Upper White River offers plenty of winter fly-fishing. Anglers consider mid-October to mid-February prime time for quality fly-fishing on the White. Gone are most of the summer Jon boats. This is one time a person can find solitude on the river.

Bigger fish are the rule now. Huge brown trout begin to move up the river to spawn. They are preparing to lay their eggs in gravel areas, and many times they can be found in extremely shallow water. During the brightest part of the day they may retreat to the deep pools, but on an overcast day they may spend all day there, unless they are spooked. During this pre-spawn period heaviest feeding will be in the early morning or late evening hours.

Good choices for flies are sculpin patterns in #6 or #8 or a
black or olive Woolly Bugger in a size #8 or #10. Browns are aggressive at this time and opportunistic feeders. A bait with a lot of bulk
can trigger violent strikes in low-light conditions.

This feeding pattern will continue until about the middle of
December, when the browns move onto their redds (the light-col-
ored circular areas you see out on gravel bars). The browns have
cleaned out these areas with their tails so they can lay their eggs in
them. Once the browns are on the redds, the feeding comes almost

to a standstill. The majority of strikes that occur from browns are due to their attempts to remove your bait from their nest.

The browns have slowed their feeding habits, but rainbows are still going strong. Rainbows are on an egg binge, picking up eggs that have washed loose from the redds. These fish are active from first sunlight until late afternoon. Use a #8 or #10 olive or black Woolly Bugger (black on overcast days or in low light periods). Sowbug patterns in a #14 or #16 are still productive, especially in slow, flat water areas around moss beds. A strike indicator is helpful when fishing sowbugs and other nymphs on flat water stretches.

"The most important thing with a sowbug is to keep it light," recommends one local angler. "I like to fish them with a good cross-stream cast, put a big mend in the line, then let the line flow down past me. I don't like to use them on a strike indicator. A strike indicator casts a big shadow on a clear, sunny day . . . and makes the leader butt sit up high and cast a big shadow."

Weighted nymphs and flies are the rule for most fly-fishing in the winter months. On a good, clear day, however, you might be surprised by a hatch of tiny tan caddis or dun-colored baetis. In this case a #16 or #18 elk hair caddis or a #18 or #20 Adams fly should cover these hatches handily. You should also have a couple of local patterns: a #16 RFSN (red fox squirrel nymph) or a #18 blue meanie should always accompany you.

Give winter a chance . . . it's just like having a second season, only much better! For more information on winter fishing, contact Gaston's White River Resort in Lakeview, Arkansas, at 501-431-5204.

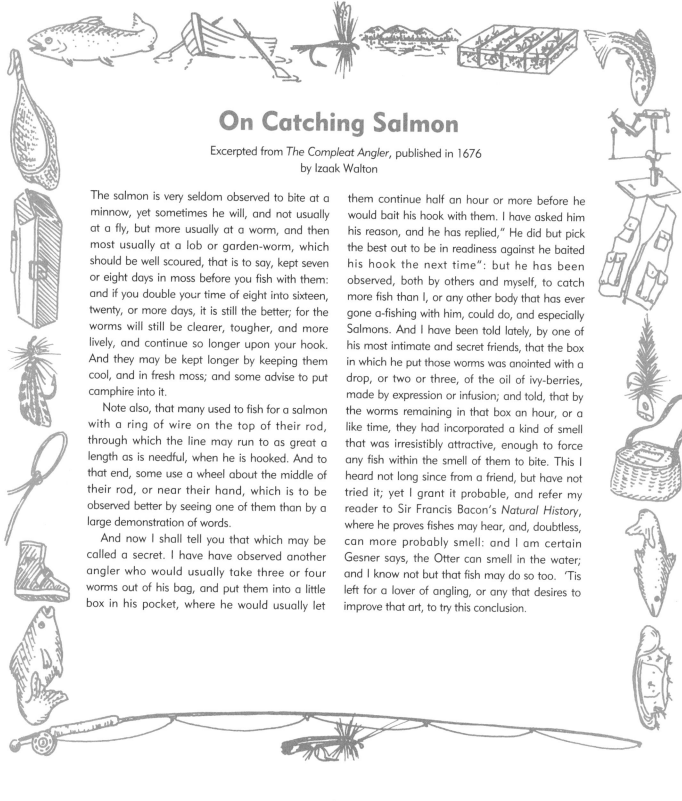

On Catching Salmon

Excerpted from *The Compleat Angler*, published in 1676
by Izaak Walton

The salmon is very seldom observed to bite at a minnow, yet sometimes he will, and not usually at a fly, but more usually at a worm, and then most usually at a lob or garden-worm, which should be well scoured, that is to say, kept seven or eight days in moss before you fish with them: and if you double your time of eight into sixteen, twenty, or more days, it is still the better; for the worms will still be clearer, tougher, and more lively, and continue so longer upon your hook. And they may be kept longer by keeping them cool, and in fresh moss; and some advise to put camphire into it.

Note also, that many used to fish for a salmon with a ring of wire on the top of their rod, through which the line may run to as great a length as is needful, when he is hooked. And to that end, some use a wheel about the middle of their rod, or near their hand, which is to be observed better by seeing one of them than by a large demonstration of words.

And now I shall tell you that which may be called a secret. I have have observed another angler who would usually take three or four worms out of his bag, and put them into a little box in his pocket, where he would usually let them continue half an hour or more before he would bait his hook with them. I have asked him his reason, and he has replied," He did but pick the best out to be in readiness against he baited his hook the next time": but he has been observed, both by others and myself, to catch more fish than I, or any other body that has ever gone a-fishing with him, could do, and especially Salmons. And I have been told lately, by one of his most intimate and secret friends, that the box in which he put those worms was anointed with a drop, or two or three, of the oil of ivy-berries, made by expression or infusion; and told, that by the worms remaining in that box an hour, or a like time, they had incorporated a kind of smell that was irresistibly attractive, enough to force any fish within the smell of them to bite. This I heard not long since from a friend, but have not tried it; yet I grant it probable, and refer my reader to Sir Francis Bacon's *Natural History*, where he proves fishes may hear, and, doubtless, can more probably smell: and I am certain Gesner says, the Otter can smell in the water; and I know not but that fish may do so too. 'Tis left for a lover of angling, or any that desires to improve that art, to try this conclusion.

FISHING LICENSE

CHAPTER 9

Knots and Necessities

Knot's Landing

If a chain is as strong as its weakest link, then the knot is the weakest part of the fly fisher's rig. With practice, you can learn to tie knots that hold, but it takes time. A perfectly tied knot compromises the line by only 5 to 15 percent, meaning that the best knots when tied correctly should reduce line strength by no more than 85 percent.

Practice tying knots with heavy cord or light rope rather than fine, nylon monofilament, which is hard to handle and can slice your fingers almost as easily as a razor.

It's much better to learn to tie two or three knots correctly so they hold fish, rather than seven or eight knots less than perfectly. The fly angler who doesn't take time to learn to tie correctly at least a few knots might as well hang up his or her rod because fishing will be only one frustrating defeat after another. That, or have someone else tie the knots for you.

The most critical area of knot tying is the leader—both ends. Skillfully knotting the leader butt to the fly line and the leader point to the fly means the difference between simply hooking fish and *landing* them. More fish are lost because of a bad knot than for all other reasons combined.

The first step is making sure the knot is shaped correctly before tightening it. Take your time and form each knot slowly, being sure each turn is as it should be, each loop in its proper place. When the knot has been formed correctly, moisten it before drawing it up. This helps to seat the knot. Then draw the knot up slowly and evenly. Never yank. You can't overtighten a knot, so go ahead and test it but without yanking. A sudden yank can pop the line, leader, or backing. No part of the fly line or leader is made to withstand sudden yanks—that's why your fly rod bends!

Trim a knot as close as possible. Don't worry: if the knot is tied correctly, you won't pull the ends out. One of the best tools for trimming knots closely is a pair of nail clippers. One expert uses pliers to flatten the trimmed end so it won't pull through the knot.

Nail knot step #1

Nail knot
step #2

Nail knot step #3

Nail knot step #4

Among the many knots that fly fishers prefer, a handful are most essential: the Nail knot for attaching fly line to the backing, a Loop knot for attaching leader to the fly line and fly line to the tippet, and the Clinch knot (also called Fisherman's knot) for attaching tippet to fly hook.

First, if you decide to use backing on your reel, it must be attached first. Use a simple reel-spool knot (also called Arbor knot) to secure the backing to the reel. Make one overhand knot in the line and another at the very end of the line (see diagram 1). If you do not use backing, you can attach the fly line directly to the reel.

Once your backing is secured on to your reel, you're ready to tie on the fly line. A good knot for tying together two lines of different thicknesses is the Nail knot. It is a small knot that won't catch on the rod's snake guides. Place the two ends of line to be joined alongside a small nail or air-pump needle. Wind the finer line around the thicker line and the nail while holding all three together. Make five turns, then feed the end of the finer line back through the center of the loops. Pull out the line through the coils. Gradually tighten by simultaneously pulling on the two ends of the finer line.

A Nail knot is often simpler if you use a heavy gauge sewing needle with an oversize eye. Start by filing down the point or clipping it off (save your finger pricks for the Red Cross). When tying the Nail knot, lay your fly line against the needle and wrap the butt end of your leader or backing around the needle. Once you have finished with the wraps, bring the tag end of the backing or leader up through the eye of the needle, and keeping your fingers tight around the wraps to keep them in place, pull the tag end through by pulling the needle through.

Next comes the leader. Since you may be switching among floating and sinking leaders or leaders of various lengths, it's often easiest to use loop-to-loop joints. The Loop knot begins by forming a loop with the end of the line, leaving about 4 inches loose at the end. (See diagrams, p. 185.) Repeat the action by creating another smaller loop around the first loop. Pinch both

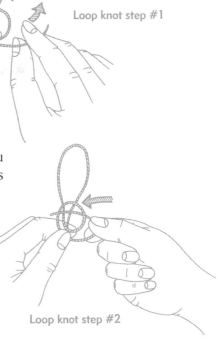

Loop knot step #1

loops between your thumb and forefinger. Run the end between the two loops and continue to pinch together. Pull the second, small loop through the first loop and start to tighten the knot slowly until snug.

You now have a loop in the end of your fly line. Now tie the same type of loop in the end of the leader you want to attach to your fly line. (See diagrams, p. 186.) After you have two loops, you can easily attach the two, then detach if necessary. Lay the two loops down facing each other. Insert the first loop into the second. Fold back part of the line with the second loop, feed it through the first loop, then pull the entire length of the line through it. The two loops lie against each other.

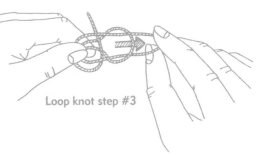

Loop knot step #2

To undo the loop-to-loop joint, simply push one end against the other, and pull the shorter section through the first loop. Loop-to-loop connectors also work for attaching the tippet to the leader so the tippet section doesn't shorten each time a new one is tied on.

Finally comes attaching the tippet material to the fly with the basic Fisherman's knot (also called clinch knot, see diagrams, p. 187). Thread the end of your line through the eye of the hook and pull about 10 inches of line through. Wind the end around the main line five times. Bring the end back through the loop of line at the eye of the hook. Use some saliva to wet the loops for extra hold. Then tighten and clip the end so only one-sixteenth of an inch sticks out.

Loop knot step #3

Ethics, Etiquette, and On-Stream Courtesies

Every year more people take to the streams and rivers. Some believe that stricter regulations are needed to limit access to the best fisheries, to preserve them as natural resources. Instead of overregulation, perhaps the best solution is to adhere to the long-standing sportsman's code of etiquette, ethics, and responsibility.

Loop knot step #4

Loop-to-loop
joint step #1

Loop-to-loop
joint step #2

Loop-to-loop
joint step #3

Loop-to-loop
joint step #4

The fly fisher's creed is best summed up this way: Treat other anglers, your surroundings, and your fish with respect.

Courtesy Toward Others

First, if people are near the water, you will want to take stock. Let's say someone is sitting on the bank next to a pool. They may be "reading" the water, waiting for the fish there to resume feeding after being disturbed. Before casting, ask the other angler if you may fish there. Cross streams downstream or upstream away from other anglers so you will not disturb them. When two anglers meet on a stream, the one casting upstream has the right of way. When another angler gives you a fly, open your box and invite him to take one of yours.

If you're boat fishing on a lake or on the ocean, don't cut between another boat and a school of fish or flat that the other boat is working. Keep your distance from another angler whose boat is trailing a hooked fish.

Never cross private property without asking permission first. Close all gates behind you. Try not to stir up the bottom as you wade. Slogging through a stretch of muddy streambed unearths clouds of silt and can destroy the fishing of those downstream. When you need to cross a stream, do so well above or below another angler.

Respect the privacy of other anglers. If you see a stranger catching fish, it is considered bad taste to ask what fly pattern he or she is using. On a crowded river, this "rule" is often overlooked. An experienced angler is more willing to share information if you have shown him or her respect. Trudging through their water will not earn their respect. Let the other person offer information before you ask. If you are having problems on the river, think about getting a guide or at least asking someone at the local fly shop for a few tips.

Courtesy Toward the Environment

Fly fishers traditionally have great respect for their surroundings. Pick up trash, even when someone else left it. Aldo

Leopold, wildlife ecologist, once said, "Take only pictures, leave only footprints."

When you clip off any kind of fishing line, put the waste in your pocket and dispose of it at home. When crossing streams, cross gently, so you don't disrupt the stream bottom, which is the heart of the trout's ecosystem. If you remove stones to inspect for insects, replace them to preserve stream habitats.

Use paths rather than blaze trails along banks of rivers and streams. Bank erosion deposits silt in the stream that can interfere with aquatic insect life and fish reproduction. Be aware of your impact on stream-side vegetation.

Join a conservation organization dedicated to protecting natural resources. For more than thirty-five years Trout Unlimited has been the leading trout and salmon conservation organization in the United States. The address is Trout Unlimited, 1500 Wilson Blvd., Arlington, VA 22209 (703-522-0200). The largest nonprofit fly-fishing association in the world is Federation of Fly Fishers, founded in 1965 to help conserve, restore, and educate through fly-fishing. Their address is P. O. Box 1595, Bozeman, MT 59771 (406-585-7592).

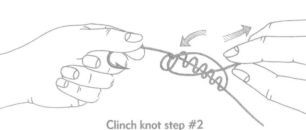
Clinch knot step #1

Clinch knot step #2

Courtesy Toward the Fish

Use the heaviest possible leader so you can subdue a fish quickly, without exhausting it. Always use barbless hooks. If you can, release a fish without touching it. If you plan to keep your fish, kill it quickly with a sharp blow to the head with a rock or blunt object. (Don't let it gasp for air in a creel.) Gut it and bleed it as soon as possible, then store it in ice. It will taste better if cleaned as quickly as possible after being caught and cooked while fresh.

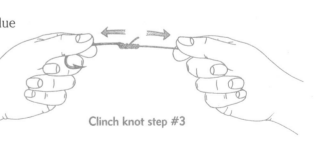
Clinch knot step #3

A Woman's Watery World

So, here it is, guys, a few simple rules to follow when you see a woman, any woman, afield. Tear it out, fold it up, and put it in your wallet. Next time, you'll know what to do.

1. If she is catching fish, and you are not, think about it. She may know something you don't. Beginner's luck really doesn't help much during difficult conditions.
2. Don't let the coy smile fool you. If she has a bunch of wind knots in her line, she could pluck them out just as easily as you, but will use all her charms to make sure it isn't she who's working instead of fishing.
3. When it comes to landing a big fish, she does like a little help . . . with tailing and netting. Indiscriminate streamside advice will be ignored.
4. If it is cold and she didn't bring a jacket, she will be happy to wear yours.
5. She can, and will, impale her own bait on her hooks; worms, maggots, minnows . . . whatever.
6. If the fishing is slow, really slow, she does not feel the need to stay unless the ambiance of the day demands.
7. She does not like to be ignored. If she is fishing to blank water on an unfamiliar stream, tell her. If she tells you that you are fishing to blank water, listen.
8. If she's catching fish and you're not, treat her like one of the guys; ask for help.
9. If you're catching fish and she's not, offer a pair of those special flies, but never in a condescending way.
10. Go ahead and take her picture when she catches a "big one." Enjoy her success.
11. If this is her first time out, be patient, encourage her. Remember, this is fishing, not war.
12. Be kind and courteous. If you play it right, she may just share her bottle of Dr. Pepper and bag of Jolly Ranchers with you.

Buying Kids Their First Fly Rod

Giving your child her first fly rod is like giving her the keys to the family car for the first time: you're pleased that she has reached this state of readiness but are more than a little apprehensive about what comes next. Perhaps the easiest way to get her a rod is to give her one of yours. Unfortunately, this can turn out to be an expensive proposition. The sequence goes like this: she gets the rod and is delighted. You smile. Soon the smile fades. You are looking at your rod rack and notice the vacancy. Initially, you are vaguely aware of a notion in your mind that the vacancy should be filled. The notion turns to desire and the desire grows to obsession. Suddenly, you're not sleeping at night, you're tired during the day, and your grouchiness hits stratospheric limits.

The pressure builds until you feel as if you will burst. With abandon you rush out and plunk down the next two months' rent on a sweet piece of Tonkin fitted with nickel silver. There is momentary solace, a reprieve. Then, surely as winter follows autumn, you are swept away by buyer's remorse, coupled with an eroding sense of guilt that you did not really give your daughter your rod for her sake; it was purely a rationalization to justify your own gross consumerism and self-indulgence. You cad.

Take it from a cad who knows and save yourself from this shameful series of events. Be happy with your existing tackle. It has served you well and with the proper care you're giving it, will continue to do so. Besides, if you give her your rod and she breaks it, then despite your verbal protestations you will always be upset that she broke your rod. So go out and get her one that is truly her own, one that comes as straight from your heart as from your wallet.

And what should that something be? First of all, resist fiberglass. The low cost of a glass rod will hit your brain like the sweet perfume of an evil temptress. You've seen such rods hanging by the hundreds in plastic blister packs at your local

On-the-Water Child Safety

I will always wear my cap and glasses when I am casting and when I am near anyone who is casting.

I will only wade with adult supervision, and I will obey the rules of safe wading.

I will use only barbless hooks.

For all fish not meant to be eaten, I will practice catch-and-release.

I will not litter.

I will not be profane, and I will respect the rights of other anglers.

I will be familiar with my local fishing regulations.

I will not engage in risky behavior whether on or near the water.

I will work hard in my life to preserve and restore our natural resources.

I will not be a fly-fishing snob. This is our earth, and we're all in this together.

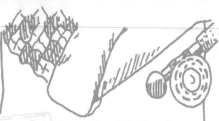

Getting the Kinks Out

Here's a tip from fishing expert Joe Petralia: kinky or twisted nylon leaders mean trouble for fly fishermen. A kinked leader makes accurate casting difficult, ruins the fly presentation, and makes the correct drift or float of a fly unlikely.

There are several ways to get the kinks and twists out of a leader, but one quick and easy method is to draw the leader repeatedly through a folded leather wallet so the leather rubs the leader on all sides. A few quick swipes should straighten the leader perfectly.

Other ways to get the kinks out: draw the leader across the rubber sole of a hip-boot, wader, or sneaker, or use a small square of rubber from a tackle shop or cut from a discarded automobile innertube.

department store. Although such rods were state of the art when we were kids, they just can't compare with graphite. The cost of graphite has come down since its introduction in the 1970s. Now the price differential between a glass rod and a low-end graphite model is almost negligible. When you buy one, insist on at least 96 percent graphite, not those composite jobs that contain mostly glass with a smidgen of graphite thrown in just so the manufacturer can put the word graphite on the label. If the salesperson cannot tell you the percent of graphite composition by checking the manufacturer's specifications, walk away.

Another thing you should resist is a short rod. By short I mean anything less than 8 feet. Many reputable manufacturers of fine tackle sell youth outfits that contain short rods. Maybe they think small hands need small rods. I think this is crazy. With the advent of ultralight graphite materials, the weight difference between a long and short rod designed for a given line size is not worth losing any sleep over. A large rod will do a better job of enabling the child to lift the line off the water, and, more important, the longer length will keep the fly farther away from the child's head and body. I've not found the cork grips on longer rods to be too large for my children's hands, but Christopher and Amy are big for their ages. If your child's hands are small, a local rod maker should be able to sand down the grip for a nominal fee. Unless you are an experienced craftsman, do not take on this job yourself.

Every expert says never buy a rod that you haven't personally casted. Now this may make sense if you've had fly-fishing experience, but if the rod is for your daughter and she's never casted before, telling the salesman to rig up the rod so she can try it right there can lead to interesting results, one of which might be that your daughter never speaks to you again. However, don't think that just because you're genetically related to her, the rod will feel as right in her hands as it feels in yours.

In this situation, the best solution is to test the rod's action. This is a simple maneuver and nobody gets embarrassed. Grip the rod in the usual manner and extend it horizontally in front of you. Now briskly wag it back and forth. Fast-action rods flex mainly at the tip, medium-action rods bend down to the midsection, and slow-action rods flex all the way down to the butt. For children, I strongly recommend a slow-action rod. There are a number of reasons for this. The first is that when casting they are, well, slow. Using a slow-action rod means that the child's reactions do not have to be as quick or as refined as when casting a stiffer model. It also means that there is more time to recognize casting errors and to correct them while the line and fly are still in the air. Slow rods enable the caster to feel the rod load and unload during the back and forward casts; fast-action rods inhibit this. Slow rods are especially suited for turning over wind-resistant flies such as the poppers and hair bugs designed for the child's most likely quarry, panfish. When it comes time to cast smaller flies to more selective fish like trout, the slow rod permits a more delicate presentation. Finally, casting a slow-action rod is so much more graceful and pleasing than wielding a stiffer stick. Watch your child casting and see what I mean. You can imagine Robert Redford at your side, filming your child in slow motion for his next magnum opus.

Given these attributes, you might ask why every fly fisher is not using a slow-action rod. What a slow-action rod lacks is the rigidity to propel the line great distances, and this is why it has fallen out of favor with many adult anglers, especially the macho types. By and large, children won't care a hoot about this factor, nor should adults. The majority of fish in fresh water will be caught within 20 feet of where you're standing, anyway. For the average caster, a slow-action rod can perform nicely at twice this distance.

If these reasons still don't convince you that a slow-action, graphite rod is right for your child, consider this: for years, bamboo aficionados have been saying that graphite lovers are missing out on something incredible. If you've ever had the opportunity to cast a well-made cane rod, you'll know exactly what they mean. What is the

Rules and Regs

Every year before fishing, you must first buy a state fishing license. Every state has a pamphlet that details specific fishing regulations. These "regs," as veterans call them, may require you to buy certain stamps, depending on the species of fish or body of water you plan to fish. For instance, state regulations require that "anyone fishing from a boat or other floating device on the Colorado River or adjacent waters forming the California-Arizona border must have a special use stamp in addition to either a California or Arizona fishing license. The holder of a California license must have an Arizona use stamp, and the holder of an Arizona license must have a California use stamp."

(continued)

major casting difference between bamboo and most graphite rods? The former are almost all slow action! It therefore follows that getting a well-made, slow-action graphite rod is the closest anyone can come to the feel of casting a fine piece of Tonkin—without paying a king's ransom.

The soft-action approach has its limits. You don't want your child wielding a wet noodle that puts excessive vibrations in the line and sends it nowhere. To avoid purchasing a rod like this, go back to the action test described above. As you are wagging the rod back and forth and it is flexing from tip to butt, suddenly stop. The rod should oscillate once or twice and then come to rest. If it doesn't, you've got a noodle in your hands, so pass it up.

The rod should be designed for a 6-weight line. This is perfect for young hands. Rods built for lighter line weights are more difficult to control and rods for heavier line weights are more likely to tire the child. The 6-weight will also handle the largest number of species your child is likely to encounter, from bluegill through trout to small bass.

When you buy a rod, be sure to pick up a rod bag and tube at the same time. There is an unwritten rule in fly-fishing that the longer the interval between buying the rod and purchasing the tube, the more likely the rod is going to be broken by the time it's first put in the tube. Although aluminum tubes are traditional, the Orvis Green Mountain tube is made of high-impact plastic, is cheaper, and has a D-shaped circumference so it won't roll around in the trunk of your car. Be sure to show your kids the proper way of inserting the rod in the tube (keep the ferrules down and encircle the opening of the tube with your fingers to avoid tearing off a guide on the edge of the tube).

Reel, Backing, Line, and Leader

There are no startling revelations here. The single-action reel with adjustable drag is standard. While we're on this subject, let me air one of my biggest gripes. Have you noticed that spinning reels are a whole lot cheaper than fly reels but the spinning

reels have so many more parts? I guess this is because the tackle manufacturers believe all fly fishers are affluent and naive, which most are not. So I have made it my personal mission to try to find a low-priced fly reel that performs as well as the top-of-the-line models. My search always comes back to the same item—the Pfluger Model 1594. Unlike the better-known 1494, the 1594 has the advantages of rim control and a counterweighted spool for only a modest difference in price.

This reel is a terrific buy. Like Timex watches and membership in the American Automobile Association, it's too good to pass up. It is sturdy as a tank, which is good if kids are going to use it, and it has an irresistible feature: when you crank it, it makes a delightful "put-put" sound, kind of like a finely tuned sports car.

If your child is a right-handed caster, he should reel with his left hand and vice versa. Then, following a strike, he will not have to transfer the rod to the opposite hand if he wishes to play the fish from the reel. Switching hands causes slack to develop in the line and hence the fish gets away.

Two admonitions about the 1594 are in order. Changing from right- to lefthand retrieve requires a degree in mechanical engineering and the patience to chase little parts that have fallen off the table and onto the floor. Have the tackle dealer do this for you. Second, buy a small screwdriver so you can keep the screws on the reel posts nice and snug.

Since most children begin fly-fishing in stillwaters where fish often lie deep, a slow-sinking line would seem a logical choice. I don't buy this. I believe it is better for a child to know where the line is at all times, so a weight-forward floating line is my preference. It's easier to pick up off the water, shoots better, and can always be used with a weighted leader or fly if there is a need to go deeper. Also, to aid visibility, select a bright color. I've never seen a fly line color stand out as much as does fluorescent orange. Some anglers make a big deal about using neutral or darker colors to avoid spooking fish. This is the purpose of the leader, not the line, so don't let their opinions sway you.

Rules and Regs

(continued)

The pamphlet will also notify you about fish limits, restrictions, and catch-and-release-only areas. You'll also learn about proposed changes. For example, the State of California is considering establishing (1) a two-bag fish limit in a 2.3-mile area of the Upper Sacramento River, and (2) an 8-inch size limit, barbless hooks, and no more than one trout over 22 inches on all anadromous fish waters of the Klamath River system. *Anadromous* refers to a type of fish that normally lives in the sea but returns to freshwater rivers and streams to spawn. Salmon, steelhead, and shad are examples.

As an angler, you are required to know the regulations on the river or lake you are fishing. This is important. You don't want to go home with a citation for $500! So be sure you know the rules.

Commonsense Tips

We fish to reduce stress, not to pile on more stress. A little common sense goes a long way.

If you take up fly-fishing, eventually you *will* hook yourself. To cut down on such incidents, always wear your polarized sunglasses while fishing. Not only do they reveal the fish but they protect your eyes from ultraviolet rays and hooks! Wear clear glasses when night fishing.

Your hat is another protection from getting hooked in your head.

If you get hooked in the skin, you can usually take it out (especially if it's barbless). Sometimes you may have to push the point through to expose the barb. Then crush the barb or clip the hook near the end. Back the hook out of the skin.

If you get hooked in an eye, do not try to remove the hook. Cut the leader off, bandage the eye, and find a doctor immediately.

Use wisdom when wading or crossing streams. Moving quickly can result in a topple and can also disturb the fish. The sediment stirred up can put the fish downstream off for the rest of the day. And lots of insects are scrunched in the process. Never wade for any distance in the water. Get out of the water and attempt to walk near the stream. Avoid using the stream as a path.

For extra support, many fishermen use a wading staff with a metal tip.

Felt-soled shoes can prevent spills, but you should still proceed cautiously.

If you fall in a river, try to position your feet so they are down-current, and use your arms to maneuver yourself into shallow water.

If someone is fishing in "your" favorite spot, don't jump in. You might say something like, "Hi, how's it going?" If the person replies (and conversation is optional), you might ask if anyone is fishing upstream. If there is no response, keep going. How far? As far as you could fish in half an hour. Or a minimum of 100 yards.

Do not offer suggestions on what kind of fly to use unless asked. It is downright amazing what fish will hit on. If you are having good luck and a fellow angler isn't, you might say, "This Magicfly Special really seems to be working. I have an extra if you would like to try it." Mean it, or don't say it.

When a thunderstorm is approaching, leave the water and find shelter away from tall trees.

Before you set off on a wilderness trip, make sure your tetanus shot is up to date and carry a snakebite kit.

One way to save some cash when buying your child's first fly line is to select a shorter one. He's not going to start out by casting 80 feet anyway—and remember that most of the fish he'll catch will be within 20 to 30 feet of where he's standing. Scientific Anglers' Concept fly line is 57 feet long (most standard lines run 80 to 100 feet) and offers high quality at modest cost.

Do not expect your child to attach his leader to the fly line with a Nail knot. You've heard about braided line-leader connectors? Well, you may curse as you try to get the thing on the end of the line, but once it's in place he'll thank you for it—and you'll be relieved he won't need your assistance every time he wants to change a leader.

A word about backing. Everyone will tell you to put on enough backing so that the fly line comes to within one-fourth inch of the outside rim of the spool. This will keep your line from forming tight coils and will aid the speed of retrieval. For kids, I recommend you ignore this rule. Put on enough backing so that the line comes to within one-half inch of the outside rim. This way, there is less chance of loops of line falling astray when spools are changed, and there is less chance of line catching between the spool and the reel housing. Kids tend to go for flashy colors and now you can get fluorescent backing. Having fluorescent green backing attached to a fluorescent orange fly line in a black reel is, in my son's words, "truly maximum."

Leaders will be of the knotless tapered kind. If you think your child is going to sit there connecting lengths of different-sized monofilament with Blood knots, you're dreaming. For now, tie a perfection loop at the butt end of his leader so he can make a loop-to-loop connection with the braided loop on his fly line. Assuming your child will begin with bluegill, the only leader size you need is 3X. This will handle flies in size 8 through 12, which are just right for the little critters. Add a spool of 3X tippet material to keep the leader from disappearing and you're all set.

Flies

Fly selection is determined by type of quarry. From my earlier comments you know I'm partial to kids beginning with panfish in general and bluegill in particular. This may seem self-evident, given that the bluegill's tendency to strike hard and often is perfectly matched to the child's relatively short attention span. But I have known purist parents who do not want their child to catch anything but a trout, believing that panfish are beneath the dignity of a fly fisher. Given the difficulty in taking trout versus the child's inherent need for immediate gratification, this is a poor match. I'd rather spend an afternoon on a farm pond with my kids catching a mess of bluegills than fishing with them for a weekend on some storied trout water and catching nothing. Not that I can't tolerate being skunked. On the contrary, I'm an expert at it. But at this stage in their development, my children aren't.

If you carry the elitist attitude that panfish are trash fish, so will your children. The attitude is an entirely unnecessary one. I must admit that at one time I harbored a senseless guilt over enjoying these fish, but my subsequent readings told me that if some of the world's most accomplished anglers can wax poetic about them, so can I.

Selecting flies for panfish may seem like a contradiction in terms, since panfish by nature are not very selective. Nonetheless, they are not easy to take on every outing, and there are patterns that are consistently more productive than others. Like most other species, panfish do most of their feeding under the surface, so we are partial to wet flies, particularly those that are yellow (like the McGinty) or white (such as the White Miller).

Panfishing has several close parallels to fly rodding for trout, not the least of which is that taking them on the surface is the most challenging as well as the most fun. Although dry flies will occasionally work, the Adams of panfishing is the small (size 8 to 12) popper. If you really want to hear your kids scream with delight, have them experience a bluegill smashing onto a popper which they are chugging along the surface of the water. It will be one of their most memorable angling experiences, as well as one of yours. (Adapted from *Fly Fishing with Children*, by Philip Brunquell, M.D., 1995.)

A Poem on Fly Fishing

Excerpted from *The Compleat Angler*, published in 1676
by Isaak Walton

Let me live harmlessly, and near the brink
Of Trent or Avon have a dwelling-place
Where I may see my quill, or cork, down sink
With eager bite of Perch, or Bleak, or Dace;
And on the world and my Creator think:
Whilst some men strive ill-gotten goods t'
  embrace;
And others spend their time in base excess
Of wine. or worse. in war and wantonness

Let them that list, these pastimes still pursue,
And on such pleasing fancies feed their fill;
So I the fields and meadows green may view,
And daily by fresh rivers walk at will
Among the daisies and the violets blue,
Red hyacinth, and yellow daffodil,
Purple Narcissus like the morning rays,
Pale gander-grass, and azure culver-keys.

I count it higher pleasure to behold
The stately compass of the lofty sky;
And in the midst thereof, like burning gold,
The flaming chariot of the world's great eye:

The watery clouds that in the air up-roll'd
With sundry kinds of painted colours fly;
And fair Aurora, lifting up her head,
Still blushing, rise from old Tithonus' bed.

The hills and mountains raised from the plains,
The plains extended level with the ground
The grounds divided into sundry veins,
The veins inclos'd with rivers running round;
These rivers making way through nature's chains,
With headlong course, into the sea profound;
The raging sea, beneath the valleys low,
Where lakes, and rills, and rivulets do flow:

The lofty woods, the forests wide and long,
Adorned with leaves and branches fresh and
  green,
In whose cool bowers the birds with many a song,
Do welcome with their quire the summer's Queen;
The meadows fair, where Flora's gifts, among
Are intermix", with verdant grass between;
The silver-scaled fish that softly swim
Within the sweet brook's crystal, watery stream.

All these, and many more of his creation
That made the heavens, the Angler oft doth see;
Taking therein no little delectation,
To think how strange, how wonderful they be:
Framing thereof an inward contemplation
To set his heart from other fancies free;
And whilst he looks on these with joyful eye,
His mind is rapt above the starry sky.

—Jo. Davors, Esq.

FISHING LICENSE

SERIAL NO.

CHAPTER 10

The History of a Unique Sport

As a fitting backdrop to this time-honored pastime, consider those who went before. They share your discoveries, struggles, good days, bad days, triumphs, and disappointments. You can't pick up a fly rod and not take part in history.

Post–Middle Ages

Little is known about fly-fishing before the seventeenth century. We can extrapolate to some extent from our knowledge of the equipment they used: rods 14 feet or more in length with twisted horsehair line fixed to the top of the rod. No reel was used. The limitations of the equipment mean that it is unlikely that fifteenth-century fly fishermen used lines much longer than twice the length of their rod.

If fifteenth-century anglers did cast, it would have been with a simple pick up and lay down, since the false cast wasn't invented until the nineteenth century. We have no details on how a fly was fished; nor do we have a single clue as to whether the fly was fished up or down.

Most fly fishermen were after trout, since salmon easily outclassed the equipment that was available. Salmon were caught on the fly, but it wasn't common.

Field craft advice in early writings differs very little from that in modern books. Anglers are advised to stay out of the sight of the fish as far as possible and are cautioned to avoid even their shadow falling on the water. We might think early fly-fishing was a clumsy affair, but it wasn't. Fifteenth-century practitioners were skilled men and women who caught trout with equipment we would regard as totally inadequate, and caught them in numbers large enough to sustain the possibility of professional fishing.

Fifteenth-century fishermen differed from their modern counterparts in their dependency on and vulnerability to the weather. Our forebears prayed for enough wind to disturb the surface of the water and hide their approach from the trout. And when they had enough wind to fish, they prayed that it blew in the right direction. The day when a fly line could be cast into the wind was centuries away.

In fact, the first mention of casting a fly wasn't until 1620, and then it was by Lawson in one of his more economical moments. To be fair, every word on fly-fishing left to us by Lawson is in the form of footnotes to a poem by John Dennys, a circumstance that must have been fairly limiting for him, and it is a pity that he didn't write more. Even the tone of Lawson's writing suggests that he was an expert fisherman. He advised fishing with "a line twice your rod's length of three hairs' thickness, in open water free from trees on a dark windy afternoon, and if you have learned the cast of the fly."

Fly-Fishing in the Eighteenth Century

There was little in the way of startling breakthroughs in the fishing world of the eighteenth century, a time of consolidation and incremental change. The rod is a case in point. Early seventeenth-century rods lacked running rings, although they sometimes had tip rings. Running rings first appeared on rods toward the end of the seventeenth century. The invention gave anglers much more control over the line while a fish was being played, but it didn't have much effect on casting distances, since the nature of the lines in use at the time precluded much more than a minimal shoot. Early rings were extremely unreliable and had a strong tendency to pull out of the rod when under pressure, which no doubt contributed to their slow uptake.

By the latter half of the eighteenth century, an increasing differentiation between types of rods was evident, and there was increasing sophistication in the choice of materials for the sections. Jointed rods were becoming more common, although the joints (often made of wood, sometimes reinforced with brass) were extremely unreliable. Trout fly rods were still much longer than we are used to: as much as 14 to 17 feet, but the majority were shorter.

Typical rods might measure 12 feet long for fishing with lines that terminated in two hairs or more, 9 feet for fishing single hairs "for the small fly," and 17 feet for salmon. Ash or willow were used for butts, and hickory or hazel for tops, with the by-now standard whale-bone extension. "Bambou cane" was just coming into use for the construction of top sections, chiefly of salmon rods. An experienced angler might reckon to throw 12 yards of line with one hand and 17 with both, using a 16-foot rod. Whether anyone would have wanted to cast single-handed with a 16-foot, 6-inch rod is another question.

Traders were in business making tackle as early as 1600. Gervaise Markham suggested to his readers that they buy their rods in haber-dashers' stores, where there was a "great choice." By the eighteenth century the tackle trade was well established and selling every con-ceivable article a fisherman might need as well as many that they didn't. A multitude of dealers sprang up during and after Izaak Walton's time, including the great firm Ustonson, which began trading in the 1760s and which was to supply tackle to King George IV.

Making rods was one thing, but it wasn't long before the com-mercial possibilities of reels were recognized. It was during this second quarter of the eighteenth century that fishing became popular with merchants and shopkeepers, which accounts for why the tackle trade expanded so greatly at the time.

In the last half of the century, there came an awful development: the multiplying reel. The appearance of the multiplier so early in the history of the fly reel is unfortunate because it sentenced anglers to a century of misery. The multiplier probably arrived on the market about 1750 or so and was a natural response to the poor design of the single-action reels of the day. These tended to be wide, with small diameters and very narrow spindles that made retrieving a fish very tricky if it ran out more than a few yards of line. The multiplier gave the angler a much higher rate of retrieve, but most designs had brass gears, which ground to pieces if they were put under any kind of strain.

Anglers had had to twist their own fly lines, generally out of horsehair, but the Industrial Revolution changed all that. The new ease with which machines could be invented and produced had its first consequences for fly-fishing: a variety of tapered lines became available.

The new tapered lines could be cast with greater accuracy than hand-woven horsehair. The mid-eighteenth century marked the beginning of the end of the use of level lines that incorporated both the running line and the fly line. By 1850 tapered reel lines were pretty much standard issue. Fishermen routinely reversed a fly line when one end had worn.

Rapid advances in line manufacture brought a new set of problems in their wake. By the late eighteenth century lines woven from silk and horsehair had appeared, and by the early nineteenth, twisted and plaited silk lines had come on the market. Horsehair lines were very light and couldn't be cast easily. On the other hand, silk lines absorbed water very quickly, wore out quickly, and became too heavy to cast with, a problem that would not be resolved until the 1890s, when finely plaited dressed silk lines became widely available.

Mixed silk and hair lines were an unhappy compromise, the two materials having quite different properties; nonetheless they were widely used. They were expensive, wore out quickly, lacked strength, kinked easily, and—owing to the protrusion of numberless points of hair—did not run well through the rod rings.

By the end of the century, many fishermen were buying their flies from tackle dealers, rather than tying their own. If considerable advances in rods, reels, and lines had occurred, trout and salmon flies saw very little change in the eighteenth century. In 1790, a fisherman could turn up with Cotton's selection in his fly box and few would have remarked upon it. Forty years later he would have been laughed at. It was the calm before the storm.

Fly-Fishing in the Years 1800 to 1850

The first half of the nineteenth century was the period when the winged wet fly emerged, and marked the beginning of the evolution of the fully dressed salmon fly. It was also a time of experimentation with improvements in rod design, plaited silk lines entering into production, and silkworm gut coming into widespread use.

Early nineteenth-century rods weren't much different from their predecessors, the best being made from ash, hickory, and lancewood. Calcutta bamboo sometimes substituted for lancewood. With the exception of lancewood and bamboo, these materials had been the mainstay of rod-building for two centuries and were to remain so for another thirty years.

Jointed rods were still as liable to snap off short as they ever had been. Much ingenuity was applied to finding a solution to this problem, and a variety of joints were in use by the nineteenth century: a female brass socket taking a wood male end, a brass female socket accepting a brass-coated male end, and screw joints. The quest would not end until it became possible to manufacture strong, thin-walled suction joints.

Despite many other advances, whalebone was still in use for rod tops, a length of 4 or 5 inches being regarded as sufficient. By now, few bothered to make their own rods, but the one piece of amateur rod-making knowledge that was essential for the early nineteenth century angler was an ability to make his own tops, which broke with monotonous regularity (sometimes several a day). The length of a salmon rod was unchanged from Izaak Walton's day, but trout rods were beginning to get shorter. (Walton was a seventeenth-century English angler-conservationist, who wrote the literary classic, *The Compleat Angler*.)The common length of trout rods was between 12 and 14 feet. Salmon rods were longer again, perhaps 17 or 18 feet.

By 1800 the reel was in almost universal use by fly fishermen. The clamp-foot reel was still in widespread use; spike-foot reels were only slightly less popular. Spike-foot reels had a threaded spike that was passed through a hole drilled in the butt of the rod, a wingnut fixing the spike where it emerged on the upper side of the handle.

Many disagreed over whether the reel should go above or below the rod, and the experts were evenly divided on the subject. The majority of those who advocated placing the reel on top fished with multipliers—a position that is still favored for that type of reel today.

Meanwhile, a separate line of reel design was beginning to emerge. The majority of American reels were homemade affairs having crude wooden spools with iron seats. In the early nineteenth century many Americans were still importing their reels or making their own. Old-timers often fished with discarded wool spools, bound into frames by the local tinsmith. But the native industry was gearing up, and single-action brass or German silver reels with curved handles soon became common.

George Snyder, a watchmaker and silversmith from Paris, Kentucky, is believed to have made the first quality reels in the United States, sometime between 1805 and 1810. Snyder realized the need for a reliable multiplying reel, and he set out to invent one. Within a few years, other firms had started up, including Meek, Hardman, and Milam, between them responsible for the further perfection of the design of the multiplying reel.

These "Kentucky reels" worked better than the British multipliers, and it wasn't long before designs emerged that were capable of casting a line directly from the spool—something you didn't try twice with a British reel. Several innovations were first seen on American reels, among them the balanced crank handle and the first free-spool mechanism.

By the beginning of the eighteenth century the majority of lines were made of silk and horsehair. The plaited line was an important development because it was the first step on the way to waterproof, rot-resistant fly lines. The best lines were plaited from silk thinner and stronger than their twisted counterparts. Another important development was silkworm gut "casts" (or leaders, as we would call them), which were beginning to displace horsehair.

Casting distances had improved greatly. In the early nineteenth century, fishermen were beginning to take more of an interest in rod action as silk and horsehair lines allowed them to cast farther. Lines were of high enough quality that the average fisherman was able to cast reasonable distances: 18 to 23 yards with a 16-foot rod; and 10 or 12 yards into the wind. But casting got complicated because it became possible to fish several flies on a cast, thanks to the discovery of gut.

And thanks to a book published in 1836 by Ronalds, trout flies had come forward in leaps and bounds. The patterns were recognizably "modern." Salmon flies had come of age, and the dull patterns that had traditionally been used in the eighteenth century were to be swept away by new creations, inspired by Blacker and Bainbridge, the two outstanding fly tiers of the first half of the nineteenth century. The majority of flies were still tied in the hand. The vise had appeared in the last years of the eighteenth century but was still regarded as a dangerous innovation.

The Quiet Revolution—1900 to 1950

At the turn of the century, a state-of-the-art trout fly rod was single-handed, ideally between 9 feet, 6 inches and 11 feet. Most salmon rods remained in the 16- to 18-foot range, built either of split cane or the heavier greenheart. Greenheart had the advantage of being far less expensive than split cane. But it had a disadvantage: it was extremely difficult for the average fisherman to shoot as much line with a greenheart rod as with a split cane rod, and cane cast better and farther. The last greenheart rod made by Hardy Bros. went out of production in 1952, the material having been used for production since 1885.

By 1900 reel seats were beginning to standardize, and Hardy was promoting the Universal reel seat invented by Dr. Emil Weeger. The Universal had two wedge-shaped holders, one fixed for pushing the reel plate into, the other a loose ring that pushed down to secure the reel foot. By 1913 Hardy had released their patent screw winch fitting. The new reel seat hid the one side of the reel mount in a recess in the cork at the bottom of the cork handle, the other end of the reel foot being trapped by screwing a locking ring into place. With minor modifications, this type of reel seat is in wide-spread use today.

Rods were becoming more comfortable, and cork was coming into widespread use as a covering for handles. Prior to the 1880s, butts were made either by machining a swelling into the material, or sometimes by wrapping it with pig skin. By 1900, many quality rods had natural cork handles. Ground cork was used on inferior rods. Snake and bridge rings were the rule on better rods, and tip rings were lined with agate on quality rods.

The consensus on the length of salmon rods that had held for 300 years was soon to be broken. A. H. E. Wood revolutionized salmon fishing by inventing the greased-line technique in the early 1930s. Wood's revolutionary system of salmon fishing allowed summer fishing for salmon and encouraged the use of shorter rods. His friends took to using strong trout rods 9 or 10 feet in length.

A floating line did not require a long, strong rod to lift it, and the days of salmon fishing as a muscular sport were drawing to a close. Nine feet was the target to beat, and it didn't take long to fall. Ten years after Wood's 1930s experiments, Lee Wulff took the issue to its logical extreme. The arguments that Wulff put forward were so persuasive that the long rod vanished from North American fishing within a decade. The short rod became the trademark of the American fly fisherman, and for a time rods shrank in size. Double-handed salmon rods were virtually eliminated from the fishing scene. They have only begun to make a comeback in the last few years, as a Spey-casting craze sweeps America.

Reels

Few reels can be said to have had more influence on subsequent development than the Hardy Perfect. The Perfect marked a decisive break from the old-fashioned, slow-winding, wide-barrel reel, and was in the forefront of a modern generation of well-designed, fast-winding, single-action devices. The other great reel of the day was the Malloch "Sun and Planet" reel, named after the gearing arrangement within the casing.

The early years of the twentieth century were a time of great innovation, and the design of the fly reel was greatly improved. At long last, the technology was up to the job, and designers were free to experiment. Farlow reels of the period illustrate this well. In 1910 Farlow released the patented Still-Handle Reel, which resembled the Patent Lever in all respects except the handle did not revolve when line was stripped from the drum.

In the same year Farlow marketed the Cooper Multiplying Reel, which had a handle extending beyond the frame for winding but tucked in during casting. A few years later they produced the Heyworth, which had a silent check.

But such rapid development was not to last. The Depression and World War II took their toll on the reel as much as it did on society at large. The years from 1930 to 1950 were a low-water mark in modern European reel development. Many of the reels produced during this period were of worse quality than those manufactured fifty years earlier. The 1960s fueled the recovery of the tackle suppliers, but their ranks had been dramatically thinned out. Many of the old British names were gone. From then on American-designed reels began to lead the way.

Nymph Fishing Begins

The period from 1890 to 1930 was the heyday of the dry fly on the English chalk streams, and the time when American fly fishers developed their own distinct identity in a rush of new patterns and techniques. Perhaps the most important development was the discovery of nymph fishing, by one of the angling greats, G. E. M. Skues. We are still being carried forward by the momentum of developments made during this period.

Leader Material

By the end of the nineteenth century, natural, or "undrawn," gut had had its day. In 1910 a material called "Japanese gut," or "gut substitute," came on the scene. There were various brand names for the material, including "Telerana Nova," "Padrona," "Jatgut," and "Subgut." The basis of this material was silk from silkworm cocoons; this was made into a thread of the required thickness and then boiled in a mixture of animal glue and seaweed extract. The end-product was chemically dried and polished, but the results were unpredictable. Nevertheless, Japanese gut became a popular leader material.

Hairwing Flies

The exact origins of the Hairwing Salmon fly are obscure, but it seems to have originated in the late nineteenth century in North America. Bucktail flies were first used for bass fishing as early as the 1890s. As far as is known, the originator of Hairwing flies was an Idaho rancher named A. S. Trude, who first fished his patterns some time between 1886 and 1890. Col. Lewis S. Thompson saw the flies and had them adapted for trout fishing, trying them much later for salmon on the Restigouche (in 1928, or even a few years earlier).

The motive behind this radical departure from tradition is not recorded, but it isn't hard to guess. Many of the materials used for tying "standard" fly patterns were becoming hard to find in Europe, never mind America, and the temptation to experiment with local materials that were abundant and cheap must have been hard to resist. The major development of the Hairwing was undertaken in the 1920s and 1930s on the East Coast.

The fully dressed wet fly was in widespread use in America at the time, and a group of fly tiers began experimenting with simpler conventional patterns. They worked so well that it wasn't long before they abandoned the use of feathers in the wing and started to tie with local materials such as bear, squirrel, woodchuck, and deer. The success of these patterns elbowed out the traditional British Salmon flies, leading to a new and innovative school of North American fly tiers. We still fish with the products of their imagination.

Fly-Fishing from 1951 to Today

The modern period has been dominated by the development of new materials, and there is no doubt that without plastics, fly-fishing as we know it would be unrecognizable as a sport, although the basic principles would be the same.

Glass fiber rods first appeared in the late 1940s, but it took a while for the new material to be adopted. Suppliers' enthusiasm for the material varied. Hardy's built its first glass fiber rod in 1954, and after a period in which glass and cane uneasily coexisted, their first carbon fiber rod followed in 1976. Rod weights plunged, reaching the point where line weight became a consideration in rod handling. A modern 15-foot carbon fiber rod typically weighs around the pound mark, and a 9-foot rod, 3½ ounces.

Ffiberglass did not replace split cane overnight because glass rods weighed much the same as their split cane equivalents and offered the fisherman few advantages other than price. Carbon fiber, on the other hand, approaches half the weight of either split cane or glass. Once the technical problems of using the new material had been solved, carbon fiber rods entered mass production, and neither of the older materials could offer any contest. Cane was swept away by the mid-1980s, although it is making something of a comeback on aesthetic grounds.

The Fly Line

The postwar period was also dominated by the development of new fly line materials. This was just as well, for Japanese gut ceased to be available to the Allied countries as soon as war was declared.

By 1944–45 other gut substitutes had become available from French and Spanish suppliers, but they were swept aside by a new material—nylon.

DuPont patented nylon in 1938. Immediately after the war, two types of nylon line were manufactured: monofilament and braided. Braided nylon gained immediate popularity with spin fishermen. Early monofilament was not as popular and tended to spring or cut through at the knots with excessive elasticity. The tribulations of fishing with nylon, and the fact that gut was more reliable in the finer gauges, meant that gut soldiered on for a few more years, and a few anglers used it well into the 1960s.

In 1949 polyvinyl chloride (PVC) became available, and the first nylon fly line appeared. As a product, it was far from perfect, but it showed the way ahead. The taper was produced by varying the amount of nylon fiber in the core, which was hollow, with all its attendant disadvantages. In 1952, the discovery of a method of altering the thickness of the PVC coat on the new lines allowed nylon lines to be produced relatively cheaply. The taper on these lines could be controlled to a precise amount, and the invention of methods of altering the specific gravity of the PVC coating (and hence its buoyancy) gave the product greater flexibility than anyone had ever dreamed of in a fly line.

Thus fly-fishing has a long, prestigious, if clunky at times, history that will serve the sport well into the future.

American Museum of Fly Fishing

The American Museum of Fly Fishing, a nationally accredited, non-profit, educational institution dedicated to preserving the rich heritage of fly-fishing, was founded in Manchester, Vermont, in 1968. The museum is a repository for the world's largest collection of angling and angling-related objects. Collections and exhibits provide the public with thorough documentation of the evolution of fly-fishing as a sport, art form, craft, and industry from the sixteenth century to

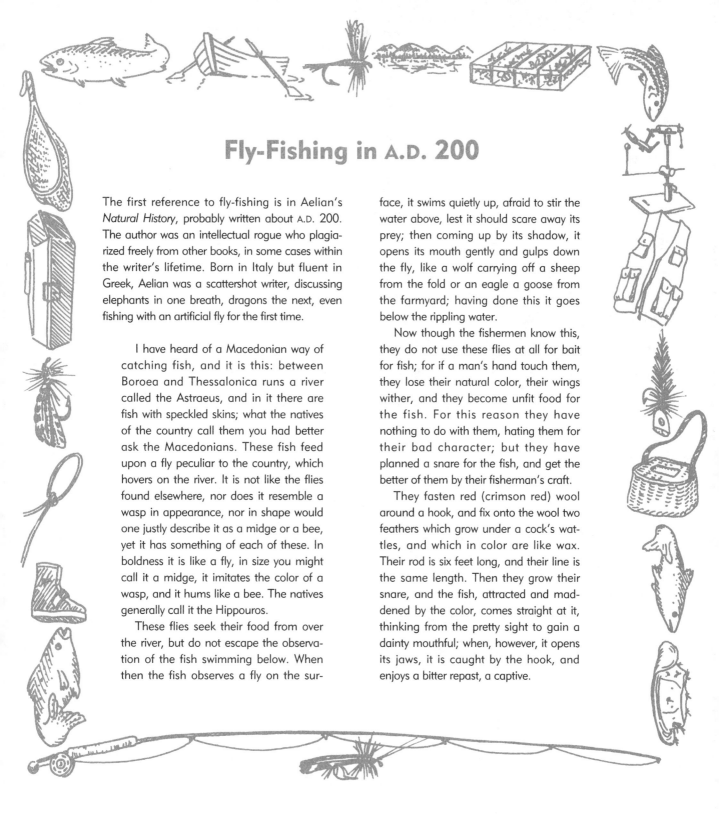

Fly-Fishing in A.D. 200

The first reference to fly-fishing is in Aelian's *Natural History*, probably written about A.D. 200. The author was an intellectual rogue who plagiarized freely from other books, in some cases within the writer's lifetime. Born in Italy but fluent in Greek, Aelian was a scattershot writer, discussing elephants in one breath, dragons the next, even fishing with an artificial fly for the first time.

I have heard of a Macedonian way of catching fish, and it is this: between Boroea and Thessalonica runs a river called the Astraeus, and in it there are fish with speckled skins; what the natives of the country call them you had better ask the Macedonians. These fish feed upon a fly peculiar to the country, which hovers on the river. It is not like the flies found elsewhere, nor does it resemble a wasp in appearance, nor in shape would one justly describe it as a midge or a bee, yet it has something of each of these. In boldness it is like a fly, in size you might call it a midge, it imitates the color of a wasp, and it hums like a bee. The natives generally call it the Hippouros.

These flies seek their food from over the river, but do not escape the observation of the fish swimming below. When then the fish observes a fly on the surface, it swims quietly up, afraid to stir the water above, lest it should scare away its prey; then coming up by its shadow, it opens its mouth gently and gulps down the fly, like a wolf carrying off a sheep from the fold or an eagle a goose from the farmyard; having done this it goes below the rippling water.

Now though the fishermen know this, they do not use these flies at all for bait for fish; for if a man's hand touch them, they lose their natural color, their wings wither, and they become unfit food for the fish. For this reason they have nothing to do with them, hating them for their bad character; but they have planned a snare for the fish, and get the better of them by their fisherman's craft.

They fasten red (crimson red) wool around a hook, and fix onto the wool two feathers which grow under a cock's wattles, and which in color are like wax. Their rod is six feet long, and their line is the same length. Then they grow their snare, and the fish, attracted and maddened by the color, comes straight at it, thinking from the pretty sight to gain a dainty mouthful; when, however, it opens its jaws, it is caught by the hook, and enjoys a bitter repast, a captive.

the present. Rods, reels, and flies as well as tackle, art, books, manuscripts, and photographs form the major components of the museum's collections.

The museum supports a publications program through which its national quarterly journal, *The American Fly Fisher*, and books, art prints, and catalogs are regularly offered to the public. A traveling exhibits program has made it possible for educational exhibits to be viewed across the United States and abroad. The museum also provides in-house exhibits, related interpretive programming, and research services for members, visiting scholars, authors, and students.

Located in historic Manchester Village, the American Museum of Fly Fishing may be visited weekdays between 10 a.m. and 4 p.m. year-round except for national holidays. The museum's research library may be used by students and researchers during working hours. For information contact the American Museum of Fly Fishing, P. O. Box 42, Manchester, VT 05254. Or call them at 802-362-3300. Catch a glimmer of the rich history and tradition of fly-fishing by visiting the following collections in the museum.

The Myron Gregory Collection. Myron Gregory may not be a name many fly fishers know, but his efforts made all angling easier. He founded the International Casting Federation and is responsible for the adoption of a standard line measurement based on weight.

The Rod Crafting Art. Why have these men, so accomplished in other areas of life, dedicated themselves so strongly to splitting and gluing culms of bamboo? Hoagy Carmichael sums up the obsession like this: "I can't stop doing it, I just love doing it. It gets into you. It's a pleasure and it's a challenge."

The Robert Forsyth Livingston Tackle Collection. The collection is truly complete, including tackle boxes, flies, leaders, fly wallets, rods, reels, nets, creels, scales, a leader cutter, and artwork such as cut-out tracings of impressive catches. One is even drawn on birch bark.

The Maxine Atherton Collection. Artist, adventurer, and fly fisher, North Carolina native Maxine Atherton has angled from Pennsylvania to California, from Spain to Labrador, and survived not only the frozen tundra, but a short period in the history of fly-fishing when fly-fishing women were viewed as odd by some and a threat by others.

The Phillipson Rod Company Collection. The Phillipson Rod Company left its mark on the world of fly-fishing, not only because it flourished while other rod companies did not, but also because of its dynamic founder and president, Bill Phillipson.

The William Cushner Fly Collection. Cushner's interest in the fly tier's art was purely aesthetic. For a man who never tied or cast a fly, and didn't fish, his framing work is a remarkable testament to a sport and art form.

Hook History

The hook had its origins in the gorge, a device used by many primitive cultures, and frequently found in prehistoric sites. Gorges were made from slivers of bone, flint, or turtle-shell attached to a line that was knotted through a hole in the center of the gorge.

The fish swallowed the gorge end-first in a bait, and the pull of the line levered the gorge across the fish's throat, trapping it in place. There are many drawbacks to fishing with a gorge. It is hard to conceal, difficult to bait, hard to hook large fish on, and liable to lose its hold while the fish is being played. Despite these problems, in expert hands the gorge can prove highly effective. It is still used today.

We do not know for certain when the hook was discovered, although we do know that Neolithic man used hooks, making them out of bone, shell, or thorn depending on which materials were at hand. By 200 A.D. the Egyptians were fishing with rods, lines, and hooks, a level of sophistication that the Chinese would not match for a thousand years, and which other civilizations, including our own, would wait even longer to attain.

The early Egyptian hooks were simple, copper with no barb. The head was formed by doubling the end of the shank over, opening up the possibility that these hooks may have had eyes. The length of these hooks varied from 2 to 6 centimeters, and the gape was wide in proportion to the length of the shank. By the twelfth dynasty, barbed hooks were beginning to appear, and by the thirteenth dynasty, bronze barbed hooks predominated. These later hooks had the end of the shank flattened to form a wider flange, allowing the line to be attached to the shank below the flange. By Roman times, iron and bronze hooks were in use; bronze of this period was of a harder alloy than it is today.

The first sophisticated instructions on making hooks are found in "A Treatyse on Fishing with an Angle," published in 1496, as part of the Second Book of St. Albans. The author explained how every article of the fly fisher's kit should be made, including hooks, because tackle shops lay two centuries in the future. Most helpfully, the Treatyse includes a woodcut of the hooks, which gives us a general idea of the shape of fifteenth-century hooks. But we shouldn't place too much reliance on the size or gauge of the metal used, due to the limitations of printing methods of the era.

By the early seventeenth century, hooks were commercially available, but many anglers still chose to make their own because commercially produced hooks were unreliable, chiefly due to uncertain temper. There was a prime opportunity for a quality hook-maker to set up shop, and one duly did—the incomparable Charles Kirby. Kirby hooks were of such good quality that the firm dominated the market during the late seventeenth and early eighteenth centuries, losing its advantage only when the crucible process for making steel became widely known. Kirby's great advantage was that he knew how to temper steel reliably, a secret said to have been passed on to him by none other than Prince Rupert, the nephew of Charles I, military commander and inventor extraordinaire.

The problem that the hook-making industry faced was a simple technological one. The exact composition of the iron produced by early processes was difficult to control, and many of the early irons were brittle because they contained too much carbon. With the invention of the blast furnace, which appeared in Europe during the fifteenth century, it became possible to make iron on a large scale.

By the middle of the sixteenth century, demand was such and blast furnaces so common that there was a scarcity of wood for producing charcoal. The shortage became extremely pressing, but it wasn't until the early eighteenth century that it was discovered that coke could be used instead of charcoal. The use of iron declined only when it became possible to generate enough heat in commercial furnaces to produce steel during the mid-nineteenth century. In the interim, steel was made on a small scale, using the crucible process, discovered in 1740. All high-quality steel was made by the crucible process until the electric furnace replaced it in the twentieth century.

Once high-quality steel could be made reliably, needle- and hook-making became a much easier affair, and a large industry sprang up with rival centers in Kendal, Redditch, and Limerick. Kirby had lost his advantage, although the name still had considerable prestige. Hutchinson, a needle-maker, started making hooks in Kendal as early as 1745, being joined by Adlington during the mid- nineteenth century. By 1823, Redditch had seventeen firms of hook-makers established and the Limerick hook industry had been in existence for nearly thirty years.

By the late nineteenth century, hook-making was a routine production process. The quality of hooks remained variable. Hook-making was still in part a cottage industry, with batches of needles being farmed out to families for bending. One major source of complaint was the deep cut which many hook-makers used to turn up a barb. Anglers of the day became resigned to the possibility of hooks breaking off at the barb. Batch tempering wasn't totally reliable, and fishermen became proficient at recognizing soft hooks that were light blue instead of purple-blue.

The Eyed Hook

Until the late nineteenth century, most hooks were "blind" (that is, they lacked an eye). Blind hooks were still being manufactured in the 1930s. Blind hooks are in fact still manufactured and fished today. They are used almost exclusively by Atlantic salmon and steelhead anglers who traditionally tied their flies on such hooks and created the eye from a twisted piece of gut (as you point out). The belief was that a gut eye, being more flexible, allowed for a more subtle and natural drift of the fly. Some ultra-orthodox traditionalists still tie and fish their own gut-eye hooks, but most who actually fish such flies tie their eyes with monofilament or other synthetic materials. Full dress Atlantic salmon flies that are tied for framing and collecting are almost always tied on blind hooks as well—usually with a gut eye, but sometimes not—mostly as a gesture to tradition and authenticity. Reputable mail order fly-tackle houses carry them.

It is a curious fact that the first illustration of an eyed hook was in 1660, in *Les Ruses Innocentes*, by Fortin. The first English illustration of an eyed hook was in Hawker's 1760 edition of *The Compleat Angler*, which has a plate showing a fly dressed on an eyed hook.

It took 150 years for the new invention to catch on, despite the many problems that hooks tied to gut or horsehair presented. The classical method of attaching a fly to gut was, of course, to whip the fly onto the gut. Gut was liable to wear just in front of the end of the hook, rendering the fly useless. After even short periods of storage, gut had a strong tendency to shrink or rot, resulting in the loss of the fly. Both gut and horsehair shared a common problem in that flies tied to them were hard to store because of the "spare" loop of line left to allow the fly to be attached to the cast.

The eyed hook should have recommended itself, but for some reason it was ignored. Instead, tying to straight lengths of gut gave way to tying to a gut loop. The gut loop became popular in the first quarter of the eighteenth century, mostly for large flies. Smaller sizes of hook were still "tied to gut" in the traditional way. It is extraordinary how much suspicion was leveled at the eyed hook, which was denounced by O'Gorman in 1845 as "another Scotch invention." Even the great Kelson distrusted the eyed hook, and all his patterns were tied with gut loops.

There were various attempts to market eyed hooks during the mid-nineteenth century, including Hewett-Wheatley and Warners and

Son, both of whose ventures fell by the wayside. It wasn't until H. S. Hall's eyed trout hook came on the market in 1879 that there was any enthusiasm for a change, and that was fired by the rise in popularity of dry fly fishing, the salmon anglers being quite happy with gut loops. By the end of the century, up- and down-eyed hooks were available in both salmon and trout sizes. A third variety of hook, sometimes called needle-eyed, was also available, with a hole drilled perpendicularly through the end of the hook shank. But the design was flawed and failed to attract a following.

Hook Scales

The large-scale manufacture of hooks in the early nineteenth century brought a new problem for the fisherman; one of comparing different firms' hook sizes. The confusion started in the nineteenth century, when a number of competing scales sprung up. There were various Redditch scales in use. Stoddart quotes one that ran from 1 to 16, with 16 the smallest. 1–7 were salmon sizes, 8–16 were trout sizes.

The unified Redditch "old" scale ran from 1 to 19, with 1 the smallest trout size, and 19 the largest salmon size. Many round bend hooks were sized on a scale that ran from 00 (midge) to 20 (the largest salmon). At one time there were at least five different hook scale systems in operation: Carlisle, Kendal, O'Shaughnessy Limerick, Dublin (or Philips) Limerick, and Sell of Dublin. The confusion can only be imagined! The growing popularity of eyed hooks in the late nineteenth and early twentieth centuries only made matters worse.

If the problem of deriving a common reference scale for hook sizes taxed many good minds in the past, it continues to do so. Various methods of hook measurement can be used: the overall length, the length of the straight part of the shank, and width of the gape, to name but three. All have their problems, which relate to the different proportions each manufacturer gives to their series of hooks. The ratio between width of gape and length of shank varies widely among different lines. Overall length is the easiest to measure, but the different dimensions of the bend of a Limerick and, say, a Sneck bend would result in two hooks with very different lengths of shank being classified as the same size.

Then again, many blind hooks were made intentionally long in the shank so they could be cut to size by the tier. When eyed hooks appeared on the market, the diameter of eyes had to be taken into account, as eye size could make a major difference to the length of a small hook. There were a few brave attempts to produce standard hook scales, notably by Cholmondely-Pennel in the late 1880s and Pryce-Tannatt in 1914. Pennel's scale (running from the smallest, 000, to the largest, 19) was available until at least the beginning of World War II, but Pryce-Tannatt's did not last.

Modern systems concentrate on standardizing the length of the shank, but this is a difficult measurement to make of a hog-backed hook, and differences in bend and eye diameter may conspire to make a small hook appear larger than its official size. No system can take into account hooks that are classified differently by custom, for example, long-shank trout hooks, which take their size from the gape of the hook rather than the length of the shank. Consider the unofficial extension of the current system of measurement to account for sizes below size 16, and we are only marginally in advance of the chaos of the nineteenth century. As long as different makers continue to produce different patterns of hook, we are unlikely to see any improvement.

Doubles and Trebles

The double salmon hook can be thought of as a reasonably mature invention, given that the Bronze Age Swiss used them extensively. As usual, English fishermen treated such an innovation with extreme caution. The first mention of a double salmon hook in the literature was in 1590. Venables discussed flies tied on double hooks for catching grilse and grayling, but the double hook didn't catch on overnight, and it was 1689 before one was illustrated. Doubles didn't become truly popular until much later. Early double hooks were whipped together, but later versions were made by brazing the metal. Cholmondely-Pennell designed and marketed a series of double hooks in the 1880s, by which time the idea was no longer regarded as dangerously novel.

Treble hooks share the checkered history of their cousins. They had little application in fly-fishing until the twentieth century, mainly for live and dead baiting. By the late nineteenth century, trebles, also used for spinning, were a source of much complaint. Hooks frequently broke, the temper having been affected during the brazing procedure. The trouble was caused by the selection of wire that was of too fine a diameter and which became extremely brittle during the manufacturing process. It would not be until after World War II that trebles came into widespread use for fly-fishing, as it was only then that it became possible to manufacture hooks reliably in the small sizes required.

Irish Hooks

If Redditch had a serious rival, it was the Irish hook-makers. The use of Irish products was de rigueur among salmon fishermen in the late eighteenth and early nineteenth centuries. The O'Shaughnessy family were the foremost firm of Limerick hook-makers, establishing their business in 1795. They soon developed a formidable reputation for quality. Their products cost sixpence a dozen and were recommended as a matter of course by eighteenth- and nineteenth-century authors.

The original O'Shaughnessy hooks were hammered out and forged, with the barbs filed out from the metal rather than cut out and bent up as with wire hooks. The founder died about 1820 and by 1834 the business had been taken over by a watchmaker, who had carried on the tackle-making business, turning out Limerick hooks after the original O'Shaughnessy pattern.

By 1845 a dozen cost between 1 and 4 shillings. But anglers got hooks filed from the best German steel, rather than wire hooks which were the rule in Dublin and London firms. By comparison, Sell's hooks cost between 3 shillings and 9 pence a dozen. O'Shaughnessy hooks were so prized that it was common practice to strip the fly from the hook after it had been mauled by fish: not only did the hooks last for ever, they were simply too valuable to

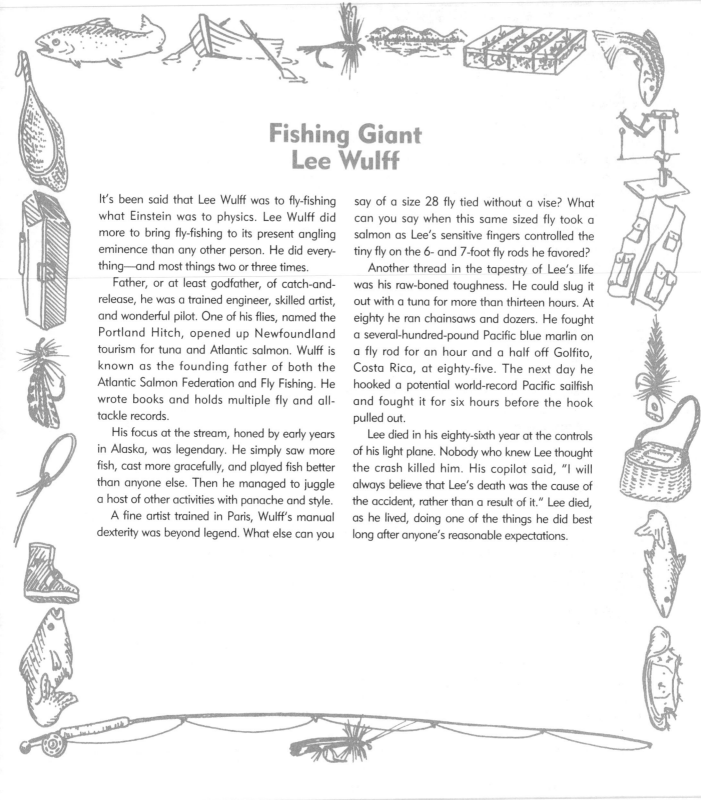

Fishing Giant
Lee Wulff

It's been said that Lee Wulff was to fly-fishing what Einstein was to physics. Lee Wulff did more to bring fly-fishing to its present angling eminence than any other person. He did everything—and most things two or three times.

Father, or at least godfather, of catch-and-release, he was a trained engineer, skilled artist, and wonderful pilot. One of his flies, named the Portland Hitch, opened up Newfoundland tourism for tuna and Atlantic salmon. Wulff is known as the founding father of both the Atlantic Salmon Federation and Fly Fishing. He wrote books and holds multiple fly and all-tackle records.

His focus at the stream, honed by early years in Alaska, was legendary. He simply saw more fish, cast more gracefully, and played fish better than anyone else. Then he managed to juggle a host of other activities with panache and style.

A fine artist trained in Paris, Wulff's manual dexterity was beyond legend. What else can you say of a size 28 fly tied without a vise? What can you say when this same sized fly took a salmon as Lee's sensitive fingers controlled the tiny fly on the 6- and 7-foot fly rods he favored?

Another thread in the tapestry of Lee's life was his raw-boned toughness. He could slug it out with a tuna for more than thirteen hours. At eighty he ran chainsaws and dozers. He fought a several-hundred-pound Pacific blue marlin on a fly rod for an hour and a half off Golfito, Costa Rica, at eighty-five. The next day he hooked a potential world-record Pacific sailfish and fought it for six hours before the hook pulled out.

Lee died in his eighty-sixth year at the controls of his light plane. Nobody who knew Lee thought the crash killed him. His copilot said, "I will always believe that Lee's death was the cause of the accident, rather than a result of it." Lee died, as he lived, doing one of the things he did best long after anyone's reasonable expectations.

throw away! The quality of the Limerick products stood head and shoulders above those of their competitors.

Fishing Gods and Legends

"Fish worship—is it wrong?" My research into fishing legends and people who worship fish brought to mind this slogan printed on a T-shirt hanging in my closet. Seriously, though, people through the centuries have taken quite a liking to fish—even more, fish have long been creatures of awe and inspiration. They are embodied in cultures and religions all over the world.

Images of sharks, porpoises, swordfish, seals, and whales adorn palaces, temples, and homes on every continent. In the Bible, it is written that Jonah was swallowed by a leviathan, or whale, and in his world-famous novel *The Old Man and the Sea*, Ernest Hemingway romanticized the marlin, one of the ocean's giants.

Many fishing families in developing countries still pray to gods of the sea for protection at small private altars before setting out on the water. Often they seek immunity from the shark, which in many societies evokes terror. But for a number of peoples, even those who fear its attack, the shark is respected as a top predator and worshipped as a god. In Hawaii, for example, the shark is known as an *aumakua*, or guardian god of a family, into which it is hoped a child of the shark god will be born. In Hawaiian legend, it is an honor for a dead person to return as a shark, an animal that reportedly helps drowning people safely to shore, goes fishing with humans and shares the catch, kills enemies, and protects families from other sharks.

Similar legends are still told among many fishing peoples in the Pacific to this day. In the Solomon Islands, caves have been carved out for this god of the sea, and in Vietnam, where the whale shark is known as Lord fish, its bones are taken to selected temples and given sacred burials. In the Solomon Islands, elders or shamans engage in "shark calling." After attracting the sharks, they swim with them. In effect, so do avid snorkelers and scuba-divers, often seeking sharks out.

The legends vary, however, and in some cultures the shark is a demon, both worshipped and feared as the ruler of the seas. The constellation of Orion, as it was named by the Greeks, is to the Warran people of South America a cluster of stars depicting a man's leg bitten off by a shark. To the bathers and surfers off the coast of Australia, in what are considered to be some of the most dangerous shark waters in the world, the image of a shark is chilling, especially in areas where they are not held back from shore by a system of nets.

Fish worship is by no means limited to the shark. In Japan, the shark is an important mythological figure, paid homage to as the god of the storms, or the shark-man Same-Hito. The Japanese have also built a Buddhist shrine in honor of the red snapper. Around 700 years ago they created a marine sanctuary that prohibits fishing for this species.

Japanese legend varies. Some say that at the birth of the holy Buddhist monk Nichiren-shonin, schools of red snapper exhibited unusual schooling behavior. The numbers were massive and the waters red with their brightly colored bodies. Some people believe that a huge red snapper saved the life of the monk by carrying him safely to shore. In Japan, the red snapper has been declared a natural monument, and a temple was erected in the monk's honor on the shore near the site of his birth. Upon entering the area, visitors are greeted by a huge sculpture of a red snapper.

Like the villagers of Tainoura in Japan, the Squamish people of the Pacific Northwest welcomed their visitors with the image of a wooden statue in the likeness of the Salmon Chief. Carved in the statue is the legend of "why the salmon came to the waters of the Squamish people." The tale describes how one of four brothers transformed himself into a salmon to entice fellow fish into the waters of the Squamish, how subsequent salmon feasts were shared, and how what is gained from the sea must be returned. It is a parable of generosity and giving.

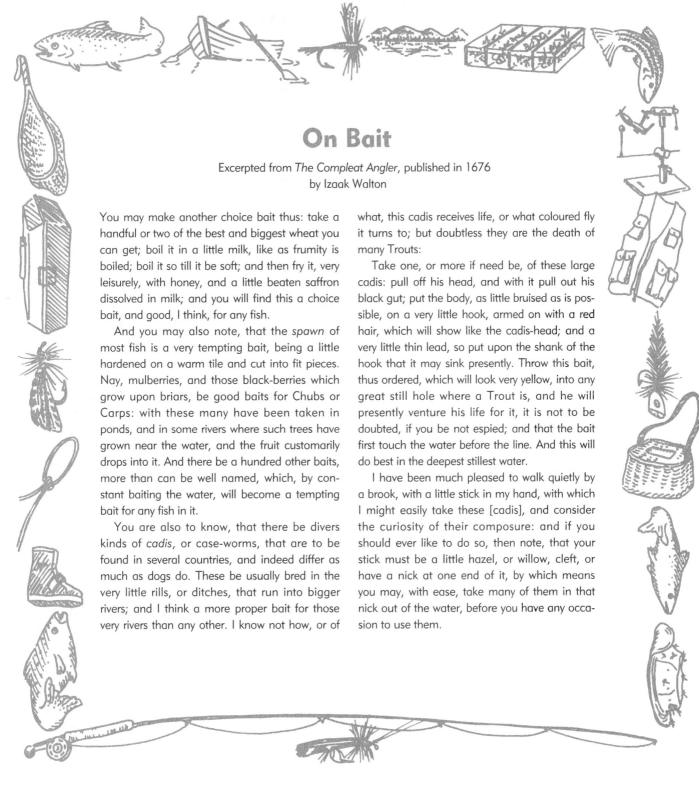

On Bait

Excerpted from *The Compleat Angler*, published in 1676
by Izaak Walton

You may make another choice bait thus: take a handful or two of the best and biggest wheat you can get; boil it in a little milk, like as frumity is boiled; boil it so till it be soft; and then fry it, very leisurely, with honey, and a little beaten saffron dissolved in milk; and you will find this a choice bait, and good, I think, for any fish.

And you may also note, that the *spawn* of most fish is a very tempting bait, being a little hardened on a warm tile and cut into fit pieces. Nay, mulberries, and those black-berries which grow upon briars, be good baits for Chubs or Carps: with these many have been taken in ponds, and in some rivers where such trees have grown near the water, and the fruit customarily drops into it. And there be a hundred other baits, more than can be well named, which, by constant baiting the water, will become a tempting bait for any fish in it.

You are also to know, that there be divers kinds of *cadis*, or case-worms, that are to be found in several countries, and indeed differ as much as dogs do. These be usually bred in the very little rills, or ditches, that run into bigger rivers; and I think a more proper bait for those very rivers than any other. I know not how, or of what, this cadis receives life, or what coloured fly it turns to; but doubtless they are the death of many Trouts:

Take one, or more if need be, of these large cadis: pull off his head, and with it pull out his black gut; put the body, as little bruised as is possible, on a very little hook, armed on with a red hair, which will show like the cadis-head; and a very little thin lead, so put upon the shank of the hook that it may sink presently. Throw this bait, thus ordered, which will look very yellow, into any great still hole where a Trout is, and he will presently venture his life for it, it is not to be doubted, if you be not espied; and that the bait first touch the water before the line. And this will do best in the deepest stillest water.

I have been much pleased to walk quietly by a brook, with a little stick in my hand, with which I might easily take these [cadis], and consider the curiosity of their composure: and if you should ever like to do so, then note, that your stick must be a little hazel, or willow, cleft, or have a nick at one end of it, by which means you may, with ease, take many of them in that nick out of the water, before you have any occasion to use them.

Along a similar line of philosophy, but from a distant part of the globe, one of Germany's best-loved fairy tales describes the wisdom of a fish and the lessons he teaches a fishing couple about the pitfalls of greed. Given the state of the world's fisheries today, humankind seems to have ignored the ancient lessons of its ancestors and has forgotten many stories and beliefs that today are still shared among small-scale fishers.

Early Fishing Peoples

The first semisedentary fishing people known to anthropologists lived along the coast of the Baltic Sea some 10,000 years ago. The main diet of the Maglemosians, who lived during the Mesolithic and then into the Neolithic period, consisted of wild plants and shellfish gathered from the coastal marshes and bogs rimming the Baltic. In addition to fish hooks and serrated harpoon tips fashioned from bone, they also left behind huge shellfish mounds and the remains of the first coastal boardwalks. In warmer climates, fishing societies were well established at the mouth of the Nile some 8,000 years ago and in Japan and Peru some 5,000 years ago.

The first documented fish crisis due to overfishing occurred along the coast of Peru between 3000 and 1000 B.C. Anthropologist James R. McGoodwin suggests that the sequence of events was probably like this: "First, a climatological catastrophe such as the El Nino phenomenon caused a sudden and widespread reduction in marine resource supplies along the coast; second, the large sedentary and concentrated populace that had been accustomed to relying heavily on these resources, probably attempted to exploit them at their usual levels."

This would have prevented recovery of the stocks and led to a collapse of their fishery. The flourishing society had no choice but to find other terrestrial food sources and to stop fishing, or to at least sharply reduce the levels at which they were fishing. This seems logical, and McGoodwin says the Peruvians probably did just that, developing a "passive strategy of fisheries management."

Mexico's Olmec civilization, which began around 800 B.C. in coastal zones along the Gulf, and societies located north of Mexico in California also left behind evidence that they practiced fisheries management. However, other societies, some of which were living along the coast of California, fished themselves into oblivion. Disastrous declines in salmon fisheries caused by aboriginal peoples along the northern coast of California have been confirmed. And overhunting of dolphins for their teeth in the Solomon Islands, and serious depletions of marine resources by indigenous peoples in New Zealand, Hawaii, the Aleutian archipelago, and the Caroline Islands of Micronesia, to name a few, have also been recorded. Like the modern fisheries of today, some premodern peoples managed their fisheries resources and survived, while others depleted them so seriously that they brought about their own cultural extinction.

FISHING LICENSE

CHAPTER 11

Resources

You Have to Be There

My friend and fishing guide Gary Gunsolley tells of fishing for browns and rainbows on the Fryingpan in Colorado. This tailwater flowing out of the Ruedi Dam is "gin-clear." Gary was fishing one day on flat water and catching nice 14- to 16-inch brown trout. He observed an elderly man catching two to his one. "So I pulled my line out of the water and just sat and watched him," Gary recalls. "He was doing the same thing I was—sight fishing, casting to the fish, letting the fly float down to them."

When another man engaged the old-timer in conversation, Gary overheard him say he was using a size 22 Blue-Winged Olive, which is what Gary was casting. The man was also using an 8X tippet while Gary had a 6X.

That could have made a world of difference, but as fate would have it, Gary was out of 8X tippets and had to use a 7X. "I caught more fish, but still the old guy was out-fishing me two to one."

The real reason for his being out-fished became clear when Gary finally overheard the old-timer say, "I've been fishing here every day for twenty years." There is no substitute for experience.

Use a Guide!

My friend Ken tells the story of his unguided tour of Beaver Head River in Montana. The previous year he and some friends had taken a guided tour of the river and pulled out spectacular 5- and 6-pound browns on dry flies. This second trip was to be solo, with no guides.

All winter long Ken, his father, and a friend prepared for the trip. "We tied a gazillion flies and got our own boat for floating," he related. When they arrived at Beaver Head the following June, they found the river was extremely high—so high, in fact, the picnic tables were under water.

"But we had been preparing for this trip all year long and we weren't about not to float down that river," Ken said. So the three-some set the boat in and took off. "We were floating so fast that the flies didn't really have a chance to even hit the water!" No one on

the boat really knew how to work the boat in such conditions, much less cast during such speed.

As the three men barreled downriver, they tried unsuccessfully to negotiate the oars. Later an oar broke, leaving them with only one. "We'd slam into brush," said Ken, who was sitting in the back of the boat. Suddenly they came to a low bridge and, as they all ducked to clear it, the boat caught on a limb. A jagged bolt jutting out of the bridge would have slammed into Ken's head if his friend had not at the last minute grabbed the bolt and shoved the boat free, leaving Ken unscathed.

Barely recovering from the incident, the group soon realized they were approaching a weir dam, or manmade waterfall. The boat was still moving at breakneck speed. "Our plan was, as soon as we got to the next bridge, to hook our feet into the boat and grab on to the bridge to try to stop," Ken explained.

That was the plan—until they got stuck. Ken's father got out and, with water up to his neck and holding his $7 camera aloft, pulled the group to shore. Everyone got out safely, having narrowly escaped serious injury.

"We did not see one fish on that whole float," Ken recalled. "It was the only time we floated the river on our own and I regret it. Guides are definitely worth the money you pay them." That's certainly the moral, but the memories may not be as exciting!

Fishing Holes on the Internet

Want to learn more about fly-fishing but can't pull yourself away from the computer? Try searching for these sites on the World Wide Web.

Flyfish.com
Kaufmann's Streamborn, Inc.
Flyfishing.com
The Virtual Flyshop
Virtual Fly Fishing
Dennis Dickson Fly Fishing Steelhead Guide

Fisherman's Heaven Fish & Humor Page
The Anadromous Page
The Ultimate Fishing Page
Women's Fly Fishing Homepage
Fishfinder Search Engine
FishSculptures
Byte-n-Bass
The Infinite Wildlife Resources Network
Fishing the Northwest
Worldwidefishing.com (lists fishing guides by state)

Top Seven Browns

In recent years fishing for trophy brown trout has surpassed all expectations. The following fisheries represent some of the top destinations for brown trout in North America.

Cumberland River, Kentucky

The 80-mile stretch of the Cumberland below Wolf Creek Dam holds many browns surpassing the 18½-pound state record he caught there in 1988. Catching thirty to forty trout a day from mid-May through November is not uncommon. The browns here average 2 to 3 pounds, but 5- to 10-pound trophies are common.

Guide: Fish Tales Guide Service, 502-426-1839. Information: Jamestown Resort & Marina, 502-343-5253. Accommodations: Jamestown Chamber of Commerce, 502-866-4333.

Fryingpan River, Colorado

Browns in the tailwater below Ruedi Reservoir commonly exceed 10 pounds, and any section of this blue-ribbon stream can produce many 10- to 20-inch fish. Fishing is good year-round, but spring and fall are top trophy times. Anglers can keep two browns under 14 inches on this otherwise catch-and-release-only river.

Contact Fryingpan Anglers, 970-927-3441. Accommodations: Carbondale Chamber of Commerce, 970-963-1890.

Lake Michigan, Wisconsin

The Seeforellen strain of brown trout, aggressive feeders, spring from this amazing river fishery during fall spawning runs. The Manitowoc, Oconto, and Peshtigo rivers host some of the best fishing from October through December. Traditional spring hot spots such as Bailey's Harbor and the Gill's Rock area are expected to be hot again this year. Browns remain near rock humps and bluffs through late May. Nearby Sturgeon Bay is a key spot for postspawn browns beginning in late September.

Lake Guide: Tim Dawidiuk, 414-746-9916. Stream Guides: Mike and Chris Neta, 414-490-7633. Information: Mac's Sport Shop, 414-854-5625. Accommodations: Sturgeon Bay Chamber of Commerce, 414-743-4456.

Little Red River, Arkansas

The 40-pound, 2-ounce world-record brown was caught here in 1992, but guide Bob Brown says bigger fish remain. When browns spawn from October through December, it's common to catch fifty or sixty a day, with a chance to see browns in the 15- to 30-pound class. Fly fishermen favor egg and spawn patterns.

Guide: Duane Hada, 501-452-3559. Information: The Ozark Angler, 501-362-3597. Accommodations: Heber Springs Chamber of Commerce, 501-362-2444.

Madison River, Montana

The lower Madison, from the West Fork to Ennis, produces good numbers of browns in June and July. Best shot at a 30-inch trophy, however, is in September and October, when aggressive prespawn fish migrate upstream to the mouth of the Firehole River in Yellowstone National Park. Sink-tip fly lines and large nymph or sculpin patterns traditionally take the biggest browns.

Guide and information: Bud Lilly's Trout Shop, 800-854-9559. Accommodations: West Yellowstone Motel Reservations, 406-646-9488.

Niagara River, New York

Browns running from 8 to 12 pounds move into the 2-mile stretch of river above Niagara Bay in late February. Fish over 20 pounds aren't uncommon and a 30-pounder is possible. Smaller tributary streams in the area provide excellent postspawn fishing in fall.

Guides: John Delorenzo, 716-297-9424; John Oravec, 800-443-2510.
Information: Wilson Boatyard & Marina, 716-751-9202.
Accommodations: Niagara Falls Chamber of Commerce, 716-285-9141.

San Juan River, New Mexico

Catching trout on some western rivers is a challenge, but the San Juan is an accessible and predictable exception. Browns average about 18 inches, but 25-inch fish are common. From July through December, anglers with a good guide can catch (and release) forty trout a day.

Guide: San Juan Troutfitters, 505-324-8149. Information: Rizuto's San Juan River Lodge, 505-632-3893. Accommodations: Farmington Chamber of Commerce, 505-325-0279.

Best Rivers
The Snake River

The Snake River in Jackson Hole, Wyoming, is one of a few select rivers graced with the honor of having its headwaters in Yellowstone, our nation's oldest and largest national park. About 85 miles of blue-ribbon trout water await the angler who wants to try out his or her skill on the river. The river's predominant species of trout is Wyoming's beautiful native cutthroat.

The river can be broken into eight distinct sections. Due to the size and length of the Snake, it's recommended that the most efficient way to fish the river is to float it either by drift boat or raft. A professional guide is strongly advised. He or she knows the river and can put you where the fish are. Wade fishing is possible but difficult, due to the few access points on the river. The first and upper section from Lewis River to Jackson Lake fishes well from early summer, when it clears, through to the early fall when the large browns make their way upriver from the lake to spawn.

The second section, Jackson Lake to Pacific Creek, is where the river empties out from the lake through Jackson dam. This sec-

tion of the river consists of smooth, slow flat water to almost dead flat water in most areas, meaning the fish have more time to inspect your fly. This section is considered a "match the hatch section" as the trout will most likely be more selective. Attractor patterns such as Royal Trudes, Wulff patterns, and hoppers will still produce, but sometimes the trout in this section are finicky. Here, especially below the dam, the wading is great because the river is accessible from the parking area, and there is a long stretch with easy wading terrain.

The third section, Pacific Creek to Deadman's takeout, has a reputation for producing a good number of fish. Attractors work well throughout this section providing you work the banks and holes thoroughly. Wade fishing is possible at both access points, where Pacific Creek meets the Snake, and at the Deadman's parking area.

The fourth section, Deadman's to Moose, is a great section to fish attractors, Trudes, Adams, Muddler Trudes, and hoppers. Wade fishing is not common on these sections because of inaccessibility to the river. The next section, Moose to Wilson, is one that tends to produce bigger fish. Using an attractor pattern with a beadhead dropper is a great tactic for successful fishing.

The sixth section, now considered the lower part of the river, Wilson to South Park, is probably the most fished stretch of the river. Regardless, the fishing is still productive. Wade fishing is popular by the bridge which crosses over the Snake into Wilson. A road runs along the riverbank for over a mile south of the bridge where you can pull off and fish anywhere on the banks.

The final two sections, South Park to Dog Creek and Dog Creek to West Table, are much slower and deeper sections to fish. Deep nymphing and moving the fly around both produce the best results. Also, big hoppers on the surface can rise some fish. If you float the last section, beware you do not miss the takeout at West Table, because proceeding farther will mean treacherous whitewater.

Prime time to fish these sections is from mid-July (usually when the water clears from spring runoff) through fall. Your fishing arsenal should include a 9-foot, 5- or 6-weight line with leaders tapering down to 4X. The Snake is a great beginners' river. Proper presentation and working your flies thoroughly over lies—not matching the hatch—is what determines your chances on the river. Whether you wade or float, your time on the river will be memorable. The majestic Tetons guard the west bank, creating a magnificent backdrop. The Snake is a rare resource, symbolizing beauty in its most natural form; please respect the river and the wildlife surrounding it when you visit.

South Fork

Beginning its journey from the Palisades Reservoir, the South Fork River, a much larger and heavier flowing river than the upper Snake, has gained popularity as one of the best fly-fishing rivers in the country. Two factors create a superb fishery, big hatches of big flies and large numbers of big fish. The river opens Memorial Day, but the season usually gets under way with the beginning of the famous salmon fly hatch which usually emerges around the beginning of July. Flies hover over the water like convoys of B52s, and it's no wonder the fish are as big as they are. Cutthroats, browns, and rainbows thrive here, making this river a heavenly experience to fish. Because this river is so large, it's almost mandatory that you have either a boat or raft to float. Wading is difficult because the river steeply drops off the banks.

The river can be divided up like the Snake. From the dam to Conant, from Conant to Cottonwood, and from Cottonwood to Poplar are popular and produce outstanding action.

The South Fork is more of a technical river to fish. Matching the hatch becomes necessary in many situations. Dominant hatches are Salmon flies, Golden Stones, Pale Morning Duns, Caddis, and Yellow Sallies. Imitations of these flies will increase your success rate, providing you happen to be on the river when one of these hatches is going off. Attractor patterns, especially hoppers, also produce. They always seems to raise a fish or two when nothing else in your box will work.

Toward the end of August, the river's productivity slumps for a short time, but soon picks up with the emergence of the Baetis flies in early September when the temperature cools down. Getting into the fall months, the browns get into their spawning mode and become aggressive. Your chances for catching a nice 3- to 5-pound brown are best during this time, using large Woolly Buggers and Woolly Worms with rubber legs.

The South Fork is only an hour-and-thirty-minute drive from Jackson. However, you do need an Idaho fishing license. It's a scenic river with a large population of big fish, so it's well worth the short drive for world-class fly-fishing.

Henry's Fork

While other rivers are high and muddy during the spring runoff, meaning unfishable, Henry's Fork runs clear and constant just ninety minutes northwest of Jackson. Considered one of the world's largest spring creeks, it lives up to its reputation as a world-class trout stream. With prolific hatches and an enormous number of rainbows and cutthroats, "the Fork" is a special river with many qualities other rivers don't have.

The sections from Box Canyon to the Ranch and from the Warm River to Ashton open on Memorial Day. This is one of the few rivers in the West that can fish well that early in the season. The section from Island Park to the Riverside Campground opens June 15. The river is recognized as being a technical river to fish. With the abundance of huge hatches, the fish have no obligation whatsoever to take your fly. Matching the hatch is extremely important, aside from having good casting skills and proper presentation. Stalking your fish, especially big fish, is what you should be prepared to do. These fish are not stupid. With so many of them having already been caught and released, catching them demands long hours of patience and a measure of stealth.

Early season brings on massive hatches of Salmon flies, big Stone flies, Green Drakes, and Caddis. Pale Morning Duns are seen on the river around the second to third week of June. Later in the month, the large Green and Brown Drakes make their appearance, raising big trout. When July arrives and the days get hotter, the major hatches begin in the early morning and the late day. Small tippets and long leaders are the standard.

The advantage of Henry's Fork is the variations of water. The section from Box Canyon to the Ranch is primarily a good nymph stretch with faster water and many pockets to work your fly. Beadheads always seem to produce action. From the Ranch area down, the water slows and flows steadily, creating great dry fly action. Because it's completely accessible and easy to wade, the river tends to crowd fast. It's not uncommon to see a line of fifteen anglers working within a 50-yard stretch. On weekends, especially, the crowds are apparent. If possible, fish the river on weekdays, when it is noticeably less congested. One of the best times of the season to be on the river is the fall. Cool days and the absence of tourists create superb opportunities for ambitious anglers to have a truly memorable day.

Henry's Fork captures western fly-fishing in its true essence; beautiful scenery, huge hatches, and the abundance of large trout. When you visit the area, I strongly recommend you visit "the Fork." Purchase an Idaho license and get ready for an unforgettable experience.

The Green River

If the Snake still happens to be running muddy in early July, which it usually is, it would be wise to check out the Green River. Flowing out of the Wind River range, the Green makes its way south through Wyoming into Utah. Although the river is quite smaller than the Snake, its reputation for producing nice-sized browns and rainbows has surpassed that of other rivers twice its size.

The Green slowly winds its way through high desert terrain leaving great areas for wading as well as floating access. Driving an hour south from Jackson, you will encounter a steel bridge, formally known as Warren Bridge, which crosses the Green. Before crossing the bridge, take a dirt road on the left which follows the river for a few miles. There you will find twelve access points for fishermen.

The river gets a lot of attention because it has great hatches all through the summer and into fall. From Golden Stone hatches to

Big Gray Drake hatches in July, a fly fisherman can have a field day if he or she happens to be there when the river "goes off." July is prime time to fish this beautiful river, when the mighty Gray Drake is hatching. Trout can't seem to resist a well-drifted Gray Drake over their nose. Yellow Sallies will do the job also. Some flies that work well are Parachute Adams and Stimulators. The hatches usually get under way in the morning and early evening. The wind picks up heavily in the late morning and blows hard all afternoon. This creates a difficult situation for casting and presentation. Getting to the river early will give you plenty of time to catch numbers of fish.

The rod of choice on the Green is a 5- or 6-weight with a 9-foot setup. The 6-weight comes in extremely handy when the wind picks up, giving you greater power to punch that fly against the wind. There is some pocket water just above the bridge which can produce fish with Yellow Stonefly nymphs. A word to the wise: private property lies below the bridge so possibly angry landowners could spell danger for the unwary angler. It's not possible to wade below the bridge unless permission is given to you by a landowner. Floating can be done, providing there's no contact with the private property. I recommend you fish with a guide on the Green. The river can become technical at times, so hire a professional guide, who has the knowledge to help you out and put you into fish.

The Green is unique, an exciting river to fish. It has all the characteristics of trophy water with a bounty of trout. Crowds congregate on the bigger rivers, so the Green is also a nice river to "get away" to. If you would like to have a chance at a big brown or rainbow, then the Green is the place to wet your fly.

The Tellico River

Wild and stocked trout inhabit 138 miles of one of the Southeast's premier trout fishing destinations, the Tellico River. Shared by Tennessee and North Carolina, the Tellico is just south of the Great Smoky Mountains National Park within easy drive of Atlanta, Birmingham, Charlotte, and Nashville. Tributaries here remain uncrowded and pristine.

Brown trout topping 20 pounds have been taken here, and each year anglers catch trophies of 10 pounds or more. The Tennessee portion of the river, primarily for catch-and-release, contains both stocked and wild trout. All of the Tellico in North Carolina is exclusively wild trout water with rainbows dominating the lower sections. Farther along marks the beginning of the brook trout territory.

With cat-eye markings and a strong red band on each side, rainbows are known for their spectacular coloration, as are brookies. The North River, a tributary to the Tellico, suffers from fishing pressure but has some of the best wild trout fishing in the Southeast.

Anglers wishing to match mayfly hatches will face a challenge in the Tellico area because mayfly hatches are usually scarce. Caddis, Stoneflies, and terrestrials, however, can provide good fishing. Local anglers prefer traditional attractor and searching patterns. For dry flies, they choose various Wulff patterns, a Trude Coachman, or Parachute Adams. For nymphs, they use the Tellico Nymph (so named here), George Nymph, and Zug Bug. But providing year-round dry fly fishing are the yellow and olive Elk-hair Caddis.

Because of rough water, plunge pools, and overgrown vegetation in the Tellico basin, fly-fishing instructor Jeff Cupp suggests small-stream tackle—rods in the 2- to 5-weight range in lengths from 6 to 8 feet and 4X to 6X tippets on leaders as short as 6 or 7 feet.

Tellico Plains has limited accommodations, cabin rentals, campsites, and fly shops. For information call the Green Cove Motel and Trailer Camp (423-253-2069), which sells all the local favorites as well as fishing licenses and permits. Cupp says one of the best southern fly shops is Little River Outfitters in Townsend, Tennessee (423-448-9459).

Guides, Schools, and Services

A fishing guide is an essential part of a successful fishing adventure, whether you are a beginner or a seasoned angler. A good guide will

entertain you, educate you, and share with you a remarkable knowledge of the waters, saving you days of frustration and learning.

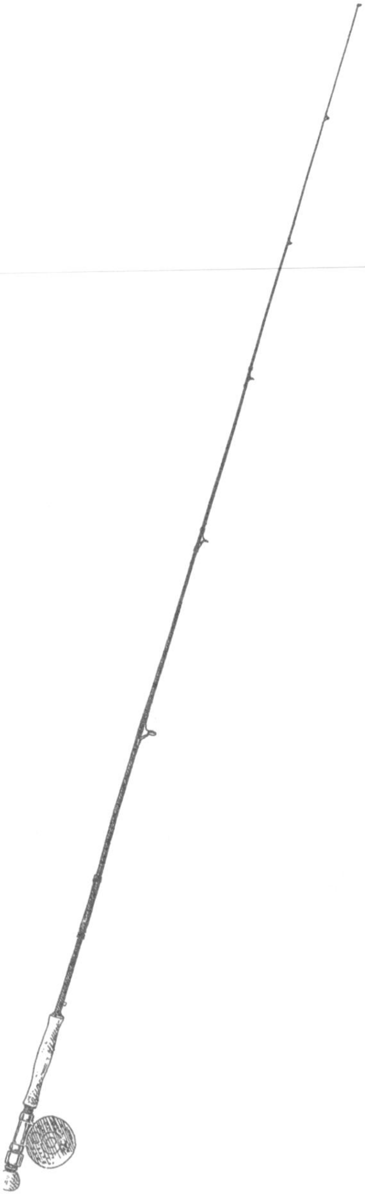

Angler's Academy

The curriculum is an eight-hour course and a lunch break. Lunch is included in the cost. All classes take place right on the stream, so you learn firsthand how to fish a dry fly, a wet fly, or a nymph. The course emphasizes the following:

- Equipment: what is needed to start
- Basic knot tying: nail, blood, slip, surgeons, clinch, etc.
- Entomology: flies and fly selection
- Reading the water
- Fishing strategy
- Catching and releasing fish
- Stream etiquette

Sage rods, reels, lines, leaders, and hip or chest waders are all available at the shop for you to use during this course at no additional cost. All of the above items are fully stocked at our shop.

AA Pro Shop
HC1 Box 1030
Blakeslee, PA 18610
717-643-8000/800-443-8119 (customer orders)
FAX: 717-643-1041
E-mail: aaoutfit@epix.net

Brock's Fly-Fishing Specialists

Located in the heart of the spectacular Eastern Sierra, Brock's is owner operated by Gary and Pat Gunsolley with a full-service fly shop and a fly-fishing school and guide service. Just minutes away is the renowned lower Owens River wild trout section, California's newest blue-ribbon brown trout fishery.

The shop offers an extensive selection of flies; the majority are tied locally. Brock's is Bishop's only Sage dealer and represents

Powell, Reddington, Cortland, Scientific Angler, Rio Products, Wood River, Umpqua, Lamson, Ross, J. Ryall, and other accessories for the fly fisher. Brock's rents waders, fly-fishing outfits, and Wood River V-Boats by the day or in multi-day packages.

The shop offers expert guides familiar with all of the waters that run from high mountain lakes and streams to prime tailwater fisheries. Instructors offer individual and class instruction for the beginner, intermediate, and experienced fly fisher. Brock's offers a four-hour introductory class and in-depth seminars throughout the year. All classes teach the basics of tailwater fisheries, and the lower Owens River is the classroom. All guides are licensed, bonded, and certified Federation of Fly Fisher (FFF) casting instructors. Fly-fishing reports are available at www.fbn-flyfish.com.

Brock's Fly-Fishing Specialists, Ltd.
100 North Main Street
Bishop, CA 93514
760-872-3581/888-619-3581
FAX: 760-873-6003
E-mail: brocksflyfish@telis.org

California School of Fly-Fishing

In operation since 1981, this school has been voted the Best Fly-Fishing School in the Nation. In small groups Ralph and Lisa Cutter will lead you through an intense learning experience in some of the best waters in the state. On-the-water instruction simply can't be duplicated on a city lawn or parking lot. Every year Ralph spends hundreds of hours underwater observing fish behavior. He has combined this perspective with years of guiding experience. Both Ralph and Lisa are fully certified FFF casting instructors.

California School of Fly Fishing
P. O. Box 8212
Truckee, CA 96162
800-58-TROUT
E-mail: cutter@fly line.com

Coastal Georgia Fly-Fishing Guide

Offering fly-fishing guides, deep sea charter, inshore, tarpon, redfish, coastal Georgia's Ducky II is a full-service charter fishing business offering deep sea fishing, inshore fishing, and shark and tarpon fishing in coastal Georgia. Full- and half-day trips are available, and individual, group, and corporate trips are welcome. Package trips are also available (meals not included).

Captain Greg Smith is a native of the coastal Georgia area with more than twenty years of experience in the charter fishing business. Ducky II uses the latest in modern vessels and equipment. All vessels are operated by U.S. Coast Guard–licensed captains and have Coast Guard–approved life-saving equipment. Bait, tackle, and ice are included on all trips. There is a six-person maximum for deep sea trips, and a four to six person maximum for shark and tarpon and for inshore fishing trips.

Inshore Fishing: Trout, spottail bass (redfish), tripletail, flounder, and sheepshead. Year-round but best September through December. Enjoy a full or half day fishing in the rivers and sounds around Saint Simon Island and surrounds. Fish with light or medium tackle. An excellent trip for youngsters and adults alike. Specialty trips such as sight fishing for tripletails (best during May, June, and July), fly-fishing, and fishing backwaters for redfish are available upon request.

A wide range of fly-fishing opportunities await you in the waters of coastal Georgia. Each season brings different species to challenge your angling skills. Sight fish for tripletails in the spring and summer, tarpon, mackerel, jacks, barracuda, and more in the summer, and trout and redfish in the fall and winter. Georgia has a host of fly-fishing possibilities. Fly rods and tackle available upon request.

Deep sea fishing (May through August): king mackerel, Spanish mackerel, cobia, grouper, red snapper, amberjack, and barracuda. Half-day trip is five hours, a good trip for the family or those looking for an enjoyable day on the ocean. Full day trip is eight hours, offers anglers of all skill levels a chance to fish for large ocean species. Snapper-grouper trip is ten to twelve hours. For the hardier or more serious angler, Ducky II offers a trip to the snapper banks, designed with the serious angler in mind.

Shark and tarpon fishing takes place from June through September. Fish medium tackle, 30- to 50-pound test for sharks up to 7 feet (4 feet is average) and tarpon up to 200 pounds (100 pounds average) in the sounds, rivers, and offshore sandbars in the Saint Simon Island area. Extremely exciting fishing on float rigs and on the bottom. Fish are often spotted crashing bait pods. Shark and tarpon fishing peaks in late August or early September. An unforgettable trip for children and adults alike. No one forgets their first shark or tarpon. Full and half days available.

Looking for a fishing vacation? Let Ducky II arrange a trip for you, with accommodations on Saint Simon Island, Jekyll Island, or in Brunswick. Ducky II has a package trip to accommodate your needs. From ocean-front condominiums and villas to quality hotel rooms. Call to plan a memorable fishing vacation. Two weeks' notice normally needed to arrange package trips. Four weeks may be needed during the summer season (May through September).

Ducky II Charter Boat Service, Inc.
402 Kelsall Avenue
Saint Simon Island, GA 31522
912-634-0312
Web site: www.coastalgeorgia.com/ducky

Al Caucci Delaware Fly-Fishing School

The basic three-day course designed for the beginner or novice will prepare the student to fly-fish independently. This is a complete on-the-stream fly-fishing course, not just a casting class. The advanced river guided program was designed for the intermediate (through most expert) angler who wants to bring his or her game to a higher level. Fish and match the hatches for wild browns and bows on our private stretch of the West Branch, the East Branch, and the main stem of the Delaware River. Al personally teaches and guides the programs.

All courses and seminars feature on-the-river instruction where you learn by actually fishing for wild fish with an instructor at your elbow. Some of the tips taught by Al and his staff are available online.

The three-day group school offers classes for both the beginner and advanced fisherman. Students have extended opportunities to fish with instructors on the Delaware system as well as to improve their casting and learn Al Caucci's insect identification and fly selection techniques. The school includes eight meals prepared by gourmet chef Kevin Conroy.

The two-day private schools are available during weekdays and any day in the summer and fall. New one-day Introduction to Fly-Fishing course available weekdays and any day in the summer and fall. New one-day "Advanced River Guided Program" for intermediate to advanced fly fishermen available weekdays and any day in the summer and fall.

Rocky Mountain program features fishing the best of the West with Al and learning the hatch-matching techniques on the great western rivers. Bahamas bonefish program teaches trout fly fishermen how to bonefish plus advanced techniques for catching large bonefish for the advanced angler. Full guide service with both wade guides and drift boats is also available at the Delaware River Club. Guides are knowledgeable about the river and the hatching activity and are expert fly tiers. For more information or reservations, call 717-629-2962 and mention www.mayfly.com.

The Lower Merced River

During mid-fall, the early salmon arrive. The fishing this time of the year is as hot as it gets with 20-pound salmon and striper bass not uncommon. Fishing here above the diversion dam is so good that anglers are offered this guarantee: if you don't catch fish, you don't pay for the services.

Salmon season below Crocker-Huffman closes to all fishing from October 16 to December 31 to protect salmon spawning. Lower Merced River offers year-round fishing and jet/drift boat and wade angling excursions. Rainbow, brook, and brown trout, bass, stripers, and fall salmon are all in one spot.

Also available: one- to five-day fishing excursions for big, wild steelhead on the Smith and Mattole rivers.

Tim Bermingham's
Drift Boat Guide Service

Lower Merced River or Smith River: $250 for two anglers; price includes jet and/or drift boat. All tackle provided. Discounts for multi-day, catch-and-release, or corporate accounts. Special arrangements for accommodations, meals, and transportation.

Mattole River: one person, two days, $500; two people, two days, $500; three people, two days, $700; prices include drift boat and tackle. Due to the remoteness of the area, only three anglers can be accommodated at a time. Special arrangements for accommodations, meals, and transportation.

Tim Bermingham
840070 Melones Road
Jamestown, CA 95327
Phone and FAX: 209-984-4007
E-mail: info@driftfish.com

The Green River

Utah's Green River below Flaming Gorge Reservoir is the stuff of fly-fishing dreams. With some 20,000 trout in the first mile of water, prolific hatches, plenty of sight fishing opportunities, and magnificent scenery, the Green is most definitely on the "A" list of trout super-rivers. In addition, access is relatively simple: float trips, campgrounds, or simply walking the river banks will put you onto good fish.

And while the Green fishes well at basically any time of the year, July can provide some of the most exciting fly-fishing around. Because of the size of the water and the possibilities of truly big fish, a 9-foot rod for a 5-weight line is a good overall choice. When it comes to leaders, cicada fishers can get away with veritable rope: 3X (.007 inch) is a good place to start. For terrestrials, finer and longer leaders are usually the rule of the day (ending in 3–5 feet of 5X or 6X tippet).

Present your fly up or up-and-across current to get the best possible drift on your fly. Be sure to wait long enough on the strike to avoid pulling the fly right out of the fish's mouth.

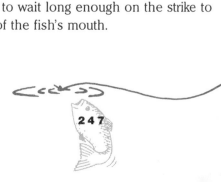

There are a variety of accommodations near the Green River, from basic campgrounds at riverside to the condominium-style cabins of Flaming Gorge Lodge (801-889-3788). Both flies and guides are available locally, and fly shops like the Western Rivers Flyfisher (800-545-4312) can give you the latest on conditions.

Even for those who don't fish, the Green River area provides plenty of entertainment. Mountain biking, hiking, sightseeing, photography, and other outdoor activities await. If you're searching for a great place to spend a few vacation days fishing on the river this summer, the Green deserves a serious look.

The Deschutes River

Imagine yourself on miles of sparkling riffles that are a delight to wade, where native trout prowl for emerging insects. The Deschutes is a year-round fishery, unique in the world. The lower 100 miles of the Deschutes is the most famous trout stream in the western United States. Here wild endemic desert rainbows rise to myriad hatches in riffles and back eddies mirroring green alders and brown basalt cliffs. Rocky Mountain Whitefish add to the spectacular nymph fishing. The canyon is an oasis in the sagebrush-covered Oregon high desert. Bird life is concentrated here, attracted by the hatches that also feed the fish. Game animals come to water. The sun shines an average of 300 days a year. The air is clean.

Get up early after a great night's rest in a comfortable camp and let the sage-laden air fill your nostrils. Drink a steaming cup of coffee, don your waders, and step into the sparkling river as your guide explains the finer points of fishing the morning hatch. Get relaxed as the next acrobatic rainbow bolts through the surface in a shower of spray.

Your fully licensed and insured guide is an avid trout and steelhead fisherman and has many years' experience landing these beautiful fish. He has lived and worked many days (and years) in the area where you will be fishing. You are part of his fishing team. He provides the boat, tow vehicle, camping gear and food, special flies, and expertise. It is his job to row the boat safely, entertain you, cook, set camp, locate fish, teach skills, and help you in any way he can. Deschutes boaters passes and Warm Springs reservation permits may be a necessary extra.

Trout and steelhead day floats: $325, one day, two people; $425, one day, three people. A day of fishing is daylight to dark. Price includes barbecued lunch on the river. Party size can range from two to six people.

River camping trips: $225 per person per day, based on double or triple occupancy per boat. Two days, one night, $450 per person. Three days, two nights, $675 per person. Four days, three nights, $900 per person. All meals and camping gear are provided, except for sleeping bags and personal items. Prices do not include licenses and permits.

You will spend your days fishing and riding in large, stable McKenzie-style drift boats, and you will have to go far to match the evenings in the wild Deschutes River Canyon.

Half-day walking trips: The Sandy River is the best year-round steelhead stream in Oregon. The upper river is best fished by hiking. Combined with two of its tributaries, the Salmon and Zig Zag rivers, it provides the angler with diverse fly-fishing opportunities.

For this reason, the Fly Fishing Shop is proud to offer guided walking trips by the hour. Our guides started fishing here as kids and know every stretch of the river and the methods that take steelhead. These walking trips are available and successful year-round but are best on the upper river June through December. Price: $100 for one or two anglers on the water for four hours. Drift boat trips available by the day.

Much of the lower part of the Sandy River can only be fished by drift boat. This reach of the river offers incredible beauty and is the oldest designated "scenic river" section in the state. Add bright, wild, native steelhead and you can see why this is one of the favorite drifts in Oregon.

Drift boats give access to all parts of the river and fishing is done while wading. A variety of fly-fishing techniques are productive from waking flies to deep dredging. Both single-hand and spey rods are used.

We realize that many anglers don't have a lot of experience fly-fishing for steelhead. Your trip can be a crash course in how to catch steelhead with a fly. All you have to do is ask. Your guide is very experienced in teaching single-hand and two-hand fly rod casting, presentational skills, wading, and fly selection.

Boats are equipped with state-of-the-art fly-fishing rod, reel, and line combos that you can use at no extra charge. Guides are liberal with their newest, hot flies. Clients must provide their own chest-high wading apparel.

To give yourself the best advantage in learning to catch steelhead with a fly, plan to book multiple days. You can make arrangements for room and food accommodations from simple to elegant. Due to water conditions, Sandy River float trips are available November through July only. Summer and winter steelhead are the main target, with spring Chinook and coho available at times. Call for the latest scoop. Price: $295 for one-day float trips (two people). Price includes lunch and snacks.

The Fly Fishing Shop
P. O. Box 368
Welches, Oregon 97067
800-266-3971

Wild Trout Outfitters

Near Big Sky, Montana, this trout outfitter offers you the opportunity to fish spectacular blue-ribbon trout streams in the Yellowstone ecosystem. Cover several miles of prime trout water in walk/wade trips. Gain confidence in casting, knot tying, stream entomology, and wading safety. Streamside topics include western nymph fishing, streamer fishing, reading the drift, and line control. Float tubing for the gulpers of Hebgen and Quake lakes can yield huge rainbow and brown trout. The term *gulpers* originated on Hebgen Lake and refers to the sound made by large trout from mid-June through August as they inhale small mayflies from the surface. In spring and fall, streamer fishing is very productive as trout gather at the inlet before their spawning runs. Call 800-4AFISH2 (423-4742).

Wild Trout University

Even if you are a rank beginner, in just one weekend you'll learn all the basics of fly casting, equipment selection, vest setup, essential knots and splices, line and leader selection, local insect hatches and species identification, correct fly selection, and how to read the water.

Wild Trout University boasts Will Daskal, an avid fly fisher and award-winning professional educator and curriculum writer. Will teaches the fly school. All classes are kept small and personal.

"Our heaviest time is May and June, and I also teach private lessons in summer," Daskal told me. "We have a couple of tailwaters locally, and the east and west branches of the Delaware River, but we also go up into rivers in the Catskill Mountains and Beaverkill." These rivers are about 140 miles (about a three-hour drive) northwest of New York City. After a Friday evening arrival, fly-fishing participants spend all day Saturday and Sunday on the water. For information contact Will Daskal on the Web at willdaskal@aol.com. Or call Wild Trout University at 718-646-0583.

Mangis Guide Service

Professional guide service on Wyoming's Snake, Green, and New Fork rivers. Excellent fly-fishing via scenic float trips. All equipment is provided.

Full-day Snake River trip for two is $275, $195 for a half-day. Full-day Green River trip for two is $300. Full-day New Fork River trip for two is $300. Call for a free brochure and more details on trips.

Klay Mangis
P. O. Box 3165
Jackson Hole, WY 83001
307-733-8553/800-850-1220

West Virginia

Fish for wild trout on the Elk River and its tributaries with Ann McIntosh, the Budget Angler, and Sam Knotts, proprietor of Appalachian Fly-Fishing Guide Service. Fish the least-known, undisturbed waters in the East. Stay at a Victorian inn with hearty, healthy meals. Three-day trips are designed for small groups of anglers. Dates are selected to meet the green drake and/or sulfur hatches on the Elk River. Cost per person for a three-day trip: $575; cost per couple: $960. Prices include guide service, lodging, and meals.

Fish fine streams in West Virginia's Monongahela National Forest and surrounding areas. As an environmentally friendly guide service, a catch-and-release policy is emphasized. You will be furnished flies, a bag lunch and dinner (full-day trip) and transportation to and from streams (when necessary). Three-day out-of-state fishing licenses are available.

Guide service rates are full-day: $125 per person; $175 for two (same party). Half day: $65 per person; $100 for two (same party). Trips and hours can be arranged to fit your schedule. Accommodations are available at local inns and bed-and-breakfasts in and around the area by contacting Randolph County Chamber of Commerce or Cheat Mountain Club.

Fly-fishing instruction on a one-day basis can be arranged for individuals who cannot attend the weekend schools. Prices are the same as the daily guide rates. During the weekend school, several unique aspects of fly-fishing are presented to enhance instruction. You will be instructed on rod-building to see how the principles of casting are dominated by rod construction. Fly tying will be taught so that you will understand the relationship between the artificial fly and the insects fish feed on during the months of the fly-fishing season.

In addition to classroom instruction, you can spend two half-day periods fishing. The first will be at a trout pond to ensure a catch, the second at an area stream to hone your skills. You will receive supervised on-stream instruction. You will have the opportunity to dine on your own catch or have your fish mounted by an area taxidermist. This instruction is for the beginning and intermediate fishing enthusiast.

Cost: $365 per person; $430 to $650 per couple. You will need to purchase a West Virginia license, conservation stamp, and trout stamp locally for approximately $20. Lodging will be arranged with Hutton House Bed and Breakfast.

Visit the fly shop for everything the fisherman needs to make a day on the stream an enjoyable experience, including books and videos. Fly rods repaired, bamboo rods restored, and custom rods made upon request.

Guide Sam Knotts, a lifelong resident of West Virginia and an avid fly fisherman for thirty-five years, ties his own flies and builds his own rods. In addition to the streams of West Virginia, Sam has fished in the East, in the West, and in Alaska. He is a licensed, certified fly-fishing guide with many years of experience. Because of his concern for the environment, he supports the efforts of organizations that preserve the environment for future generations.

Appalachian Fly-Fishing Guide Service
P. O. Box 81
Pickens, WV 26230
304-924-5855

Young's Fishing Service

Columbia River/John Day River:
Walleye—February–April
Sturgeon—May–July
Steelhead—July–December
Salmon—August–October
(Prices are $125 per person for an eight-hour day, with two to six people per boat. Combination trips available on request.)

Deschutes River by jet boat:
Trout—May–July	$135 per person
Steelhead—July–November	$135 per person
Two days and one night camping	$295 per person
	(minimum three people
	for overnight trips)

Deschutes River by drift boat:
Trout—year-round
Steelhead—July–November
Three days and two nights camping $550 per person
(two to three people
for drift boat trips)

Young's Fishing Service is a licensed and insured full-time professional guide service supplying top fishing equipment for most fish species. Lunches are provided for day trips, and all meals for camping trips are included.

Young's Fishing Service
720 East 14th Street
The Dalles, OR 97058
541-296-5371/800-270-7962
E-mail: FishYFS@gorge.net

Alpine Adventures

Want information on Utah fishing? Alpine Adventures has complete information on specific types of flies, fish, and techniques that put you right into the fishing action. They can give you accurate information to help you conquer those hungry trout.

Discount trips to New Zealand, the Bahamas, Florida, Alaska, and many other exotic fishing destinations. Alpine Adventures finds special deals on spectacular destinations, puts together a package, all inclusive, and saves you money. Alpine Adventures will accompany you on these trips (usually four anglers) and will familiarize you with the area, even supply you with equipment, so you have an enjoyable, economical trip. They will keep you constantly updated on these special offers. If you have a special destination, give them a call. Alpine Adventures has many services to offer to the outdoor enthusiast. New products and services are always being added.

Alpine Adventures
7012 South 300 East
Midvale, UT 84047
801-561-1592

Alaska: Wildman Lake Lodge

Gary King of Wildman Lake Lodge offers fly-in-only fishing for salmon, trout, and char in a spring-fed river whose water level and temperature remain constant. "It's a wonderful rearing place for char," says King, whose clients regularly catch large char on dry flies. In addition, this small Alaska Peninsula river, located 450 miles from Anchorage, offers one of the state's heaviest runs of big silver salmon, and these too will attack surface flies in the form of popping bugs. The season at the lodge runs into October, when steelhead enter the river. There's nothing like catching wild Alaska steelhead. For information call 907-522-1164.

Royal Coachman Lodge

If you're looking for the finest in fly-out fishing in the remote Alaskan bush, check out the Royal Coachman Lodge. World-class fishing for all five species of pacific salmon, record breaking rainbow trout, northern pike, sheefish, lake trout, arctic grayling, arctic char, and dolly varden. Call Gary Merrill for more information at 207-474-8691 and leave a message. Fax line is 207-474-3231.

Fly-Fishing in Jackson Hole

You have one day to go fly-fishing in Jackson Hole. Where do you go, and what do you use? For starters, understand that the Snake River, centerpiece of angling in the valley, spends much of the summer sending six months' worth of winter back to the Pacific Ocean in the form of runoff. This means the river is essentially unfishable until runoff has peaked and the water has cleared again, probably sometime in early July this year.

Lake Luck

If you've arrived in June and the Snake isn't fishable, then you might consider float tubing one of the gorgeous lakes at the base of the Tetons. If you don't have a float tube, one can be rented at Leisure Sports at the south end of town. They also rent neoprene waders, which you'll need in order to submerge yourself in these frigid waters just after the ice is out. Fish near the inlets on the west

side of the lakes and use full-sinking or sinking-tip line with a Woolly Bugger or some other large streamer pattern.

Early Rivers

If you're set on fishing a river in June and maybe getting into some dry fly fishing, you can still do it if you're willing to drive a little way. About an hour south of Jackson is the Green River, which generally clears a good two to three weeks before the Snake. A gravel road heads upstream on the north side of the Warren Bridge and offers many public access points. Two other great June options are the Firehole River in Yellowstone National Park and the famous Henry's Fork in Idaho. Both of these streams offer legendary early-season hatches (Pale Morning Duns on the Firehole, Green Drakes on Henry's Fork) and will challenge and excite anglers of all abilities. If you've arrived in July, you'll want to locate some Salmon flies. The South Fork of the Snake, which flows through Idaho's nearby Swan Valley, has one of the West's most prolific hatches of these big, juicy Stoneflies. If the South Fork is still high or off-color during your visit and you happen to be heading north, Montana's Madison River is another great Salmon fly stream.

A Clear Snake

If you're faced with less than a full day to fish and you need to stick close to town, there are two good options: drive south to Hoback Junction and east along the Hoback River, or drive west from town to where Highway 22 crosses the Snake. Park on either side of the Wilson Bridge. The Hoback is stocked during the summer and offers several access points with an abundance of good, fishable water. The dikes along the Snake provide an opportunity to fish from shore for either whitefish or the famous Snake River cutthroat. One of the best ways to find trout, particularly late in the season, is to walk quietly along the banks and look for rising fish. This stalking approach, although it can be difficult, takes much of the guesswork out of locating your quarry and can be very rewarding visually. As for flies, tiny mayfly patterns like Adams and Blue-winged Olives often work, but they are hard to see and they stay on the surface of the water, especially if they aren't tied parachute style. Instead, stick to bigger dry flies like Turck's Tarantula or any variety of hopper patterns.

If you are just starting out, and are only looking to catch something, consider an afternoon chasing whitefish. Though generally thought to be a less noble fish than the native cutthroat, whitefish can provide fun and an exciting challenge, especially for young anglers whose desire outweighs their patience. Also, where you find one, you will usually find many more.

Casting a fly rod with split shot on the line is never easy, but you will need a little weight pinched on a foot or so above your line to get it down where it needs to be. Use a strike indicator and a Beadhead Nymph of some sort, too, if you can cast them without tangling up.

That should be enough to get you started. Hire a guide if you can afford it. If not, then find a fly shop and get as much up-to-date information as you can. Snake River and Yellowstone cutthroat trout are amazing species that face increased pressure every year. Please do everything possible to treat them with respect.

Index

EVERYTHING

The Everything Golf Book

by Rich Mintzer and Peter Grossman

Trade paperback, $12.95
1-55850-814-7, 336 pages

Packed with information about the game of golf, its rich history, the great players and outstanding personalities, tours and tournaments, proper etiquette, as well as anecdotes, trivia, and jokes, *The Everything Golf Book* really does have it all!

From bunker shots to golfing buddy movies, this one volume highlights everything you need to know to thoroughly enjoy the golf game.

The Everything Bicycle Book

by Roni Sarig

Trade paperback, $12.95
1-55850-706-X, 320 pages

The ultimate source book for the bicycle enthusiast! Whether you're thinking about buying your first bike, or considering whether to enter the Tour de France, *The Everything Bicycle Book* has all the information you need to steer you right! You'll learn about the different types of bicycles and how to choose one that's right for you; simple maintenance techniques to keep your bike ship-shape; repair techniques for when it falls apart; the rules of the road to keep you riding safely; as well as the latest in bike lingo.

We Have

EVERYTHING

OVER **ONE MILLION** EVERYTHING BOOKS SOLD

More bestselling Everything titles available from your local bookseller:

Everything **After College Book**
Everything **Astrology Book**
Everything **Baby Names Book**
Everything® **Bartender's Book**
Everything **Bedtime Story Book**
Everything **Beer Book**
Everything **Bicycle Book**
Everything **Bird Book**
Everything **Casino Gambling Book**
Everything **Cat Book**
Everything® **Christmas Book**
Everything **College Survival Book**
Everything **Crossword and Puzzle Book**
Everything **Dating Book**
Everything **Dessert Book**
Everything **Dog Book**
Everything **Dreams Book**
Everything **Etiquette Book**
Everything **Family Tree Book**
Everything **Fly-Fishing Book**
Everything **Games Book**
Everything **Get-a-Job Book**
Everything **Get Ready For Baby Book**
Everything **Golf Book**

Everything **Guide to Walt Disney World®, Universal Studios®, and Greater Orlando**
Everything **Home Buying Book**
Everything **Home Improvement Book**
Everything **Internet Book**
Everything **Investing Book**
Everything **Jewish Wedding Book**
Everything **Low-Fat High-Flavor Cookbook**
Everything **Money Book**
Everything **One-Pot Cookbook**
Everything **Pasta Book**
Everything **Pregnancy Book**
Everything **Sailing Book**
Everything **Study Book**
Everything **Tarot Book**
Everything **Toasts Book**
Everything **Trivia Book**
Everything® **Wedding Book**
Everything® **Wedding Checklist**
Everything® **Wedding Etiquette Book**
Everything® **Wedding Organizer**
Everything® **Wedding Shower Book**
Everything® **Wedding Vows Book**
Everything **Wine Book**

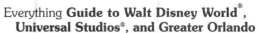